T0132281

The Art of Determination

Isla Stone

BALBOA.PRESS

A DIVISION OF HAY HOUSE

Balboa Press books may be ordered through booksellers or by contacting:

Balboa Press
A Division of Hay House
1663 Liberty Drive
Bloomington, IN 47403
www.balboapress.com
1 (877) 407-4847

Because of the dynamic nature of the Internet, any web addresses or links contained in this book may have changed since publication and may no longer be valid. The views expressed in this work are solely those of the author and do not necessarily reflect the views of the publisher, and the publisher hereby disclaims any responsibility for them.

The author of this book does not dispense medical advice or prescribe the use of any technique as a form of treatment for physical, emotional, or medical problems without the advice of a physician, either directly or indirectly. The intent of the author is only to offer information of a general nature to help you in your quest for emotional and spiritual well-being. In the event you use any of the information in this book for yourself, which is your constitutional right, the author and the publisher assume no responsibility for your actions.

Any people depicted in stock imagery provided by Getty Images are models, and such images are being used for illustrative purposes only. Certain stock imagery © Getty Images.

Print information available on the last page.

ISBN: 978-1-9822-4483-5 (sc)
ISBN: 978-1-9822-4484-2 (e)

Balboa Press rev. date: 03/17/2020

2012/03/10

'Come to the edge.' He said
'No! We are afraid.' They said
'Come to the edge!' He said
They came to the edge
He pushed them over the edge
And they flew

Christopher Logue, 1962

CONTENTS

FOREWORD

This story is honest and straight from my heart. My editor asked me why I wanted to write this book. I said I wanted to help humanity with my story. I do feel I have an ability to relay necessary information to help those who are ready to hear it. But that was only part of it. I wrote it because I love books.

I love reading books and I love stories. I love meaningful words written on a piece of paper, and I love the smell of a well-read book. My favourite place to buy a book is a second-hand bookshop, or even better, a charity book sale. The types of books one finds at these places are the gems. They have been handled; they have been read. Their spines are moulded and folded. Emotions are embedded in them. They have heard the echoes of the touch from the human souls that have handled them.

This is what I love about books: they are timeless. They can be handed down from parents to children, generation to generation, and carry enduring knowledge. They evoke thought, critical thinking and emotion. I could write a whole book about why I love books. As a fearful and lonesome child, books were my only escape. I went on adventures with the friends I didn't have in the real world. I opened books and delved into the mysteries of unsolved crimes, learnt about puberty in fun ways, galloped into sunsets in magical kingdoms, wielded wands, and – most importantly – I escaped.

I started writing this book in mid-2017. Little did I know how much would still change, and how radical that inner revolution would be. I thought I would stop writing at a certain point, but my life became increasingly interesting and multifaceted. I'm planning a new book – the new chapter of my life is a clean slate that deserves a new book. Before that, however, I had to complete this journey of transformation.

During 2018 I experienced a great loss. My mother died. This is the main reason why it took me so long to finish this part of my story in the form of a book. I hope this book gives you something to think about, and perhaps a different perspective on your own life. I hope it gives you hope. I hope it takes you through a colourful rainbow of emotions and allows you to experience a bit of my world, and in the process provide a better understanding of your own. Mainly, I hope that you revel in the enjoyment of reading it.

PREFACE

The Day I Decided

I decided to go to rehab. The day I decided, I woke up confused, hung over and with bloody knees. My high heels were still on my feet and I wasn't sure what happened the night before. Just like every other night for the eight months before that. I woke up with a daily nightmare to face. The difference this time was that I intentionally set a goal for myself. I went out with two friends the night before and told them I would have one drink only. Just one.

I don't know where this moment of clarity began. But I'm grateful it hit me that day.

I stepped into the bar, leaving the warmth of the summer behind me on the pavement. The barman handed me my regular drink before I even requested it. They knew me well. As soon as the cider touched my lips, it went down as quickly as a glass of water would after a long walk in the Sahara. Almost immediately, I started making excuses to order another drink before finishing the one I still had in my hand. I got another one. I couldn't stop myself. I sat on the bar chair looking at my empty glass with surprise. As I turned to my left, my two friends were still nursing their drinks. I realised they hadn't even begun. They knew what I said; only one drink, and they could have only one. I couldn't ... I had to have more. I had to keep drinking and I had to drink fast. Before I knew it, and despite their despair, I ordered again. I had lost my ability to choose.

I was afraid.

I was in a relationship with an alcoholic I met in a bar. He was a big, emotional Croatian, twelve years older than I. He had no job and a midlife crisis. Victor and I fell in love in an instant. We were two sad, dysfunctional, co-dependent people looking for affirmation. It was a batter for disaster. We moved in together after just a few months. I felt out of place in his house. He had been married for a long time and his divorce was finalised just after we met. I ended my previous relationship – with an abusive drug addict – shortly before I met Victor.

I was a functional alcoholic and drug addict. I call it functional because I worked as a financial administrator at my parents' company. Between my previous abusive relationship and moving in with Victor, I lived on my own for a while, trying my best not to use cocaine. I succeeded a little, but I smoked weed every day. I agonised my days away, yearning for the flood of peace my many joints would wash over me in the evenings.

Victor was in rehab for alcoholism (his third try) on the day I decided to have one drink only. I woke up with fragile and broken memories the next morning; images of the night before flashing in and out. I wasn't quite sure what I did, who I was with, how I got home. My ruined cell phone flashed on the pillow next to me. There were throbbing gashes in my knees. I was still in my work clothes from the night before. Hung over, sore and scared, I made the decision. I was done. No more terrified staring into the mirror, looking at my lost soul. No more glaring into my eyes and looking, searching for life, when the only thing I saw was death.

This was the end of the self-destructive cycle that started five years earlier. I was in a drug and alcohol induced haze for those five years; hiding and avoiding any emotion, because the one thing I feared most was to feel.

This is not a story about drug addiction and alcoholism only; that is merely the beginning of the story. My journal entries between 2012 and 2018 are the foundation of this book. Why? This story is like any other. But some stories are just stories – they don't say much about the truth. Our own absolute truth is what brings us to the root of ultimate healing. This is my understanding, and this is how my spirit grew through the experiences I've had. I have had quite a life. I tried to reflect that life with truth in my journal.

I follow a thing I call Universal Truth. It rings clearly. Sometimes it's hazy; at other times I hear it with clarity. What I do know is there are some things I tried earlier in my life that I enjoyed, but never followed through on. I would find an interest such as yoga, running, or painting. I would enjoy them for a while and then the fun suddenly evaporated. I incessantly compared myself to others. The obsession to drive myself harder became unbearable, and I stopped. I do allow myself to do these things nowadays, and I follow through on them. When – after a lot of practise – I do things merely to enjoy them, it is easier to maintain them. The Universe always takes me where I belong when I do not offer resistance and when I follow the tingling sound of its truth. This is when I find joy, expansion and magic in my existence.

I decided to keep as much of the integrity of the original dairy entries as possible. It shows a clear progressive transformation and healing as it wounds its way from the beginning of my spiral into addiction to where I'm today. There was obsessive thinking and a great deal of pain. Especially in the beginning. I'm a completely different person now. I experience and perceive my reality differently.

It will all become clear as the book and journal entries unfold.

You are more than welcome to read my diary.

CHAPTER 1

Immobilised

In 2012 I booked myself into the rehabilitation centre. I was hooked on weed (the green stuff, marijuana), cocaine, and alcohol. I thought the lovely people at the rehabilitation centre would teach me how to drink properly and drug responsibly. This is a story about recovery, but more than that, it's about how I rediscovered myself and what life can be about. I may have taken the long way to figure it out, but it was the best way for me and I'm grateful for it. I hope I may help someone else with the knowledge I gained. I'm still not perfect. I have my off days, but I'm sober and the change has been exceptional.

I made profound discoveries during the last six years. I believe self-love and self-compassion are two of the secret keys to life. Without it, I repeated my mistakes over and over again. When I finally accepted and loved my multifaceted self, I came to understand where I fit into the Universe. I realised there was something important about me. The great Powers That Be loved me beyond anything. I understood that Source or God or The Universe – or what I were to name That Power – had their gaze upon me with pure unconditional love. I saw my worth and could co-create my life along with That Power. I became part of the world, whole, and truly capable of the things I was meant to achieve.

The following entries were made in the rehabilitation centre and, after that, the halfway house. When I read them now, I'm fascinated by the disorientation and confusion and fear I experienced. The fear was the worst part of it all. I can still remember the constant feeling of anxiety and panic that the world could crumble around me at any moment.

Isla Stone

There was a psychologist at the rehabilitation centre who I idolised. She was the most beautiful woman I had ever seen and was everything I wished I could be then. Smart, thin, gorgeous, educated. She changed my life with a few words, but those were the words I needed to hear. The last two of the sentences of the poem touched me.
'He pushed them over the edge
And they flew'
I had to learn how to soar.

2012/03/10

Today is a new day, a fresh day with new outlooks on life.

Well, I felt pretty sure about it this morning. On Thursday – two days ago – the therapist gave me a new perspective in my session. My outlook completely changed; the penny dropped. I decided to go to a halfway house when after rehab and to break up with Victor. I called the halfway house and spoke to a woman called Samantha. I called Victor in his rehab and broke up with him. I felt good. A weight had shifted off my shoulders.

However – obstinately – Victor decided to refuse hospital treatment by signing himself out of his treatment facility and then arrived at my rehab centre one late afternoon. Luckily my mom was there for our weekly visit and I ran to the front desk and asked the woman at reception not to allow him in. He left me a letter. Apparently, he is broken.

2012/03/15

I feel like doing my nut! I'm going crazy with all the same people around me all the time.

It was a long day. I tried to organise being discharged here on Saturday evening, with the intention to spread two days' worth of events into three. I want to pack the things that I might need for the halfway house, get settled in there over the weekend and do my disciplinary hearing on Monday. Then maybe I can get Tuesday off because Wednesday is a public holiday. I want to get into a daily routine of Bikram yoga and meetings.

I'm tired, but I have felt this way for the last five days. Drained and worried. Living one day at a time is such a challenge. But I must learn. I figured out that I was the biggest manipulator of all. I disgusted myself. I've been this way even before I started taking drugs.

2012/03/16

Today was my last day in groups. It's funny how so many people choose to be unhappy. Surely, they know everything that has happened was the consequence of their actions? Why can't people accept that? If you did the crime, you do the time. Sure, it's easy to blame everything on the situation, but that only just shows a lack of character.

Maybe my consequences have not been that dire, yet I know my selfishness put many people in awkward and uncomfortable situations. I'm facing a disciplinary at work, I screwed up before I left. Yet again I must win back my boss', my stepfather's, and my mother's trust.

Victor is being selfish and manipulative; but I continued with the relationship in the time that we were together

3

when I full well knew I shouldn't have. I hurt him more
than I needed to by breaking up with him when I did.

The days in the rehabilitation centre were tough. It was the first time I had to face what I had done, who I had become as a blackout drunk. It was the first time I had to confront myself without alcohol. Boy, was my perspective skewed! I was deeply resentful, manipulative, angry, wounded. The things I thought bothered me the most weren't quite the problems I blamed my life's dysfunction on. I resented my biological father for his absence when I was a child. I thought I suffered so much because of the gap he left. During my recovery I recognised that there were many other issues I ignored. As I unravel the complexity of these dark secrets, so the book unfolds.

I was a blamer and a victim. Initially I regarded myself as a wronged Angel who tried to help the world. I thought I did the world a favour by keeping the peace and being a martyr.

Even after a while at rehab, I was still not completely coherent. I tried to understand what was happening. Because of the physiological damage addiction caused in my brain, I got to grips with reality slowly and in little waves. I lived in denial and fear my entire life. I was constantly in survival mode. Now I had to throw myself into a space where I had to tackle my reality in the deepest, scariest sense. I woke every morning at 3.00, a chain-smoking ball of anxiety and dread with an unstoppably racing mind. Thoughts sped through it; an endless train without brakes. Sounds echoed in my head. I felt like a madwoman.

I listened with envy to people at the support groups. The journey to recovery resembled a gigantic mountain full of obstacles and hardships. Would I ever be capable of walking out of the treatment centre and not drink again? Would I disappoint everyone I met there? I had a creeping doubt about whether I had a drinking problem at all. Mine didn't seem bad compared to those whose stories I heard? At times I felt like a fraud for getting this help. I wondered if someone else might not need treatment more than I did.

On the last day in the group, the facilitator asked me to be honest instead of to people-please. I had to tell a group member whether they were going to 'make it' in their recovery. He said if I was honest, I would have a chance myself. Statistics show that about 40–60 % of addicts relapse. The spotlight was on me, all their eyes were on me, these people I spent the last twenty-one days with, crying with, smoking with. I scraped up the courage, I honestly did not think this girl would make it. But I also really wanted her to be fond of me. For the first time in God knows how long I put myself first. I told her I thought she would relapse. I tried to sugar-coat it, but I said it. It was hard. Maybe my opinion dissuaded her from remaining sober. I don't know where she is now.

Towards the end of my time at the rehabilitation centre, they suggested I should go to a halfway house. Here, they gently reintegrate patients back into society, while the facilitators assist them to apply the new tools they have gained in the rehabilitation centre. There would be support meetings to stay sober while dealing with everyday life. My counsellor at the rehab suggested I should go to Samantha's halfway house. It feels like a lifetime ago. I stood at the communal phone box, nervously holding the little paper with Samantha's number. I can't stand speaking on the phone, especially to strangers. When I spoke to her, she sounded lovely, and I pictured her to be this hippy-like fairy.

2012/03/19

I moved into the halfway house yesterday and had a freak out. I could not be here anymore. I wanted to utilise other resources for my recovery. I felt scared and uncertain.

Samantha spoke to me. She said I must just take it easy – that I should give it a few days. So, I settled in and went to lie down.

Waking up today I didn't feel too bad. I still feel uncertain, but it comes and goes in waves. Waves of yes and waves of no. Yes, I want to be here; and no, I don't! I want to climb in my tiny silver car and drive. This changed after process group.

I went to work at 13.00, got there at 13.30. Did the disciplinary hearing and it wasn't as bad as I expected. My mom sat in on it, and all I got was a verbal warning.

God created the Universe, the earth and all of us. His energy went into us; energy can't be created or destroyed. Everything, the Universe, God, is inside us all, so He could enjoy the human experience through us. That must mean everything, everyone is connected. Everything that has energy shares a common denominator: God. I'm forced to conclude everyone has a reason for being here, because God wants to experience our lives through us. God is within us to be here, whether we are good or bad. God is not separate from us; there is no divide between us and God.

My mother was a complex human being. She was brilliant and analytical. She was a fine-looking woman for most of her life and even in her later years had a regal appearance when she made the effort. She supported me – in her way – through all the drama of my rehabilitation and recovery. Despite her care, she also created heaps of chaos and unwanted experiences for us. She was attracted to broken men who needed mothering. She was a fixer. Unfortunately, this impacted on our lives as her children. In the process, it broke us. When my mom was in her early thirties, she met John, who became my stepfather. We moved in with him when I was eleven years old and he has been part of my life ever since.

My recovery journey unsettled my mother. Nevertheless, she stood by me. She was horrified when I told her I was booking myself into a rehab for drug and alcohol abuse. She attempted to convince me that I was just going through a bad patch.

I was anxious to leave the safety of the rehabilitation facility. My fear was palpable when I walked into the halfway house. It would be my next step towards becoming whole.

When I met Samantha, my jaw dropped. She wasn't the hippy I had in my mind's eye. Radiating professionalism, she was shorter and more petit than I imagined. The passionate fire in her eyes showed her to be a force to reckon with. She wasn't going to be a walk-over.

The house was lovely. Many striking paintings and other art that made it special. My favourite was a large double-panelled painting of an African woman. The paint was layered on the canvas in impasto. The colours were rich and almost fragrant. Several astonishing textures made the painting come alive. The rest of the house was decorated with photos of previous housemates and similar art from the same artist. The furniture was splashed with warm colours, and I glimpsed the possibility of feeling safe there.

Samantha showed around. There was a single shelf in the refrigerator with my name written on a label, stuck on the end of the shelf; there was a dark nook in a cupboard where I could put my coffee, or dry foodstuff. I had a bed in a room that I shared with two other women. I was given a little cupboard for my clothes. I placed my belongings on the floor. We had an en suite bathroom. That was a relief, but I still felt uncomfortable because I hadn't yet met the women I had to share it with. My car was in the driveway, but I could only use it to go to work or a meeting. They took my cell phone and medication. Terror pressed down on my chest like an immovable weight. The world closed in on me; I felt claustrophobic.

We had to be at a process group once a week on a Monday evening. On a Tuesday we had a house meeting to talk about the structure for the week and the rest of the week we had to go to support meetings. I had to plan my whole week on a weekly planner, and we received a sheet every week to fill in our plans.

That first day I wanted to run. I wanted to grab my car keys and escape this reality. I wanted to drive and drive and drive. I understood for the first time: this was my life for the next few months. I had no freedom and freedom was what I valued the most. I realised that my life would have to change. I would never drink again, drug again or party again. I did not know who I was or what I wanted, and I was lost. It was overwhelming and I wanted to die, to disappear, to not exist.

Samantha will always tell anyone who doesn't know me how I have changed, and giggle when she tells the story about my first day. She spoke to me when she saw that I wanted to scuttle off like a squirrel. She sat me down outside in the tranquil garden after my mom left and said I should lie down for a while and get some sleep, that even though this feels overwhelming, it will pass, and I would feel better. I listened to her, because I didn't know what else to do. So, I climbed under the warm fluffy covers of my new bed, and a few minutes later this larger than life girl bobbed into the bedroom. Her energy was that of an atom bomb. I was a mute mouse. I lifted the blanket to cover my nose, and just my watchful eyes peeped out to keep guard over this biped creature, in case I needed to dart out of the bedroom to a safer corner in the house. She asked me who I was, I mumbled something from under the comforter, and she said okay and walked out. She was called Barbara (or Barbs) and we became friends after a few weeks.

2012/03/24

I miss Victor. I miss his smile, his warmth, his love, his presence. I look around me and there are so many men, so many fish, but in the end I'm the real problem. I screwed up a wonderful, loving relationship because of my selfishness and manipulation. I know he carries fault too; it wasn't a healthy relationship. Even though I miss him, going back to him is not the solution to the agony or the loss I feel now. The loneliness is slowly getting to me. I desperately want to expand my energies elsewhere, and to stop focusing on myself only. Expanding my energies elsewhere is surely also not the solution. I should be patient; I must not distract myself from my own growth.

I'll probably get hold of my sponsor tomorrow. Finally, I'll make some decent progress in the Program. I've been to quite a few new meetings. The people from the house and I got lost today but made the best of it by finding our way around Northcliff.

Lara came to visit me. We had a treasured sisterly heart-to-heart. I said I was sorry. I really want this time to be different. I don't want to let her down again. I've been selfish and have not been around for her as someone she could look up to. She was worried sick about me. It's difficult to be here, but it gets easier every day although I still feel as if I'm trudging through tar. It's more comfortable to go to meetings, especially the new ones. I've become quieter to share. I feel inadequate to share now. I'm sure as I progress through my recovery it will become easier.

God, please help me to surrender, to accept things as they are where I can't change them.

Please give me serenity and inner peace.

2012/03/25

I struggled today. My insides were an amalgamation of fear, anxiety, uncertainty, insecurity, and emptiness.

At times I feel I can't stay here, but I know I have no choice in the matter. I must do this for myself. I know

I'm strong enough to do it. I need the support; I need the therapy; I need the structure. I can't do this on my own.

I saw Victor at a meeting. It was hard. My heart ached. Every now and then I look at my phone and think that one text won't do any damage, but I know what that will lead to. It's not worth it.

He said our cat and dog had separation anxiety now that I'm gone. Although I understood this, I giggled. Seeing him there made me happy and sad. I'm happy that he comes to meetings and sad because we had to break up.

I told to the boys from the halfway house how confused I am about where home is now. I'm homesick, but I don't know where home is anymore. Victor's house is no longer my home, but I never really settled in there. I felt like an intruder. My parents' home is home, but it's such a toxic place. It's unhealthy there on an emotional level and I'm uncomfortable there, I don't belong there. I have deeply damaged my relationships with my family for such a long time. I have damaged myself. I'm floating around in limbo. I'm getting myself right somehow. Though it might be in vain because my mom and John are destroying each other. Not that worrying about it makes any sense. I should be building on my self-worth and doing it for myself. It's easy to forget.

2012/04/01

Being sick kicks you off your pink cloud. Beauty is not lost to me though.

I did not write about the beauty I started seeing in the world. I used to wish the day away in the past. Then I thought, 'if I don't get through today, tomorrow can't come'. A day, I realised, is akin to a flower. A bud in the morning reveals itself as the day progresses. The day blossoms and every part of it as it unfolds has its beauty. Interactions between people, the birds, the wind, the clouds, events – whether good or bad – are connected, and lessons are learnt from them, feelings are felt from them.

I had a sense of gratitude and peace. I can't change things the past or the future. All I can do is look at me, love myself and my value. I'm part of the wonderful tapestry called life. There was no mistake that I was put here. I know that now. I have a purpose even if for now it's just to experience the beauty around me. It's funny how I'm creating bonds with others. Well, it's not funny, but it's new. They're not deep connections though. I still protect myself and my intense emotions.

The first days in the halfway house were dreary and difficult, but incredibly eye-opening and comforting too. For the first time in my life I realised what unconditional acceptance was. I was worthy of someone else's love without having to do something for them.

For the five years prior to recovery, I saw in greys and blacks and whites. There was no colour. Suddenly, my world expanded into vibrant and dancing hues and it was amazing. There is colour here!? One unremarkable day while driving on the highway I glanced up and saw some birds flying; I saw the clouds and the colours of the sunset. Suddenly I had this emotion, it felt good. I smiled and my eyes welled up with tears. This felt warm and gentle, kind and compassionate, I was alive and appreciated seeing with new eyes for the first time. It was gratitude. This was my first aha-encounter with gratitude, and

I wanted to feel it again and again, this absolute contentment in a moment, this joy in being aligned with everything around me. That's what I had been after all this time!

Despite my new-found vivid gaze and gratitude, I had to accept many hard things too. My life had been driven by denial. I believed my own illusion that my family was a happy little group with a few kinks, and that I was the black sheep because I could not fit into that unit. I also believed I was a screw-up and a complete failure. Oh, the things I thought ... The lies I lived with.

For me, it was hard work to connect with people; I had an interpersonal barrier wall higher than the Great Wall of China. I don't open easily. People struggled to speak to me because I created awkward silences. I still sometimes do. It was a big deal to trust others. I've had this difficulty in most of my relationships. Friends, family, intimate relationships. In intimate relationships I just didn't know how to love myself. Those relationships were very co-dependent.

Most of my life, I suffered from deep anxiety. Even as a child, I would pick at my cuticles until they were sore and bleeding. If I found a striking piece of cloth, I would rub it until I felt the texture perfectly. I still do that and have done it my whole life, since my father carried me around as a two-year-old.

I'm the eldest of three children. My clever, funny, lovely brother Alex is sixteen years younger than I. He is a handsome blue-eyed hunk with thick blonde hair and the features of a model. Lara is the middle child. She's a package of dynamite and can easily be set off by a comment she doesn't approve of. Her long, silky, gorgeous strawberry red hair glistens when it's caught in in the sun's rays. Her fair skin is sprinkled with a couple of freckles. She might have been an elephant in her past life – she has a tremendous memory! We've had many arguments and fights, but we have many dear and special memories too. The day she came to the halfway house I realised the significant damage I had caused with my behaviour. She was disappointed in me and it felt as if there was a wall between us. I thought that because I was now trying to change myself, she should just accept it and forgive me for the last five years of destruction and harm. I was sorely mistaken. There was a long path of healing ahead of me and my close family members.

My father and I have a very strange relationship. He is a bit juvenile, and despite his absence for most of my life, he knows me better than anyone else on an instinctual level. It's kind of weird, but that's how it is. He is a short, strong man. His curly hair has been greyed by the many years of anxiety and fear he has lived with and is living with. He has an adventurous spirit and a wonderful sense of humour. He has had quite an exciting life, and at times I envy his ability to just turn his back on the world to have his next adventure. He was absent in my earlier childhood. He used to promise me the world and then never deliver. He would make dates to visit but would not arrive. On the very few occasions where he did pitch up, he brought sweeties and dolls and doll house accessories and toys. He was an absent father, but I loved him, and I still do. I always looked for his face in every man in the shopping centres as they walked by while I held my mom's hand ... I missed him terribly and my heart deeply ached for him. Little Isla would sit in the large driveway of our home and rip frangipani flowers apart, playing 'He loves me, he loves me not, he loves me, and he loves me not'. I would ensure the flower petals got him to love me, because if he didn't then I would get very sad and cry. I always wondered why he didn't want to see me and why I felt he didn't love me.

One of my uncles on my dad's side of the family sexually molested me when I was about four or five years old. He called me to his room at the outskirts of the large estate where the extended family lived. There were pictures of animals on the wall and a boma outside his window. He closed the curtains. Why would he want to close those blue curtains during the day? The room became shaded, with the light prying through the material. Afterwards he said if I told anyone I would get into enormous trouble.

My great-grandfather (my dad's grandfather) walked down the path towards his front door after my uncle let me out of his room. He looked a bit cross and asked me what I was doing there. I said nothing and ran away. I told no-one until I hit puberty. When I was about 10 years old, my mom decided to tell me about the birds and the bees one rainy afternoon. She gave me a book and sat with me while we read it together. I told her what happened at the plot with my uncle. She drew her body into a tense ball and tried not to cry. Now she knew.

The main themes in my life were these two things: my father's absence and my uncle molesting me. I focused on this often and blamed my dysfunction on it.

A year before I stepped into the dark depths of drug and alcohol abuse, I was taken into the psychiatric treatment section at the same psychiatric facility where I recovered from addiction, for anxiety, depression, and the desire to commit suicide. This was in the spring of 2006. I didn't use much drugs or alcohol then. I was just disturbingly depressed. I was at home during the day after having missed too many classes at university. I planned my suicide for a long time. I stopped taking my psychiatric medication and saved all the tablets so I could overdose. I wrote a very comprehensive letter of how I was thankful to everyone in my family for everything they did for me. I wrote that I was now going to end their suffering by ending my own, that I was very sorry for being such a disappointment and a lot of other gloomy things. I then decided this letter was insufficient. I had to write one letter to each person who contributed to the goodness in my life. This was obviously ironic because my suffering was about to end. But then it seemed to be so much work to write these long letters. I commenced with the first letter. I got as far as 'Dear Grandma', then gave up and called my mother. I asked her to help me write my suicide letters. She told me to wait a little while. She would be right there. To my surprise, I was booked into a psychiatric ward a few hours later.

When I came out of the hospital, I had a confrontation with my father at a coffee shop. We used to meet at cafés and restaurants to chat. I did not often meet him at his house because he lived in another province. When he visited Centurion, he stayed in hotels or rented places for short periods of time.

We met at a shopping centre, one of our regular meeting places. We met every two months or so and he would give me money whenever I saw him. If he didn't have money, he couldn't bring himself to meet me. I didn't care about money, I just cared about seeing him. I told him this on a regular basis; it finally did penetrate his mind, but only years later. I was zoned out on masses of medication and feeling uninhibited on the day I left the hospital. I just had a great deal of therapy, but none of the scars they opened were contained properly. My father and I drank coffee in the smoking area. I wasn't smoking yet. He was a smoker since I could remember. Our conversation was slow at the beginning, but I ached to ask him the one thing I always wanted to know. With my chemical lack of inhibitions, I had the courage to ask him why he was never around when I was a child. Where was he when I needed him the most? Why would he never give me answers on these questions? He stared at me with his large green eyes and tried to skim over the conversation. I don't remember much of it. What I do remember is a lot of shouting. Across the open-plan space of the shopping centre, I screamed and sobbed at my dad on the opposite side. He looked like a deer in the headlights. He wasn't sure what to do with me. I'm sure he wanted to run; he didn't. He hugged me. I went home and slept. One of my biggest fears was that I would live a life where I would not get to know my own father. That he was alive, but that I wouldn't be allowed to spend time with him or get to truly know or understand him.

During my childhood I spent tons of time with my mom's mother. I call her Grannie Martha or Grannie. My petit Grannie is a strong and amazing woman with wisdom in her twinkling eyes. Her insight is subtle, and she will guide you without you realising that she is doing it. People are amazed when they hear how old she is; she looks far younger. I was a colicky baby, and my mother suffered with postnatal depression. My Grannie mothered me quite a bit.

My mom divorced my father when I was a year old. She then moved in with my dad's father, my paternal grandfather. She was in a pickle. Not long after I was born, my Grannie experienced a debilitating bout of depression. She was in a terrible relationship, after she was windowed the first time and she had four dependent children still living with her. When Grannie's life became unmanageable, she had to focus on her own healing, and my mom had to step in to help her. My mom's four younger siblings were still in school, ranging from high school to primary school. My father wanted my mom back, but she did not want to go back to him.

One day my mom came home to find the cupboards open and everything thrown out around the house where we lived. I couldn't have been older than 2 years old. We were still living in the house after her and my dad divorced. It was a burglary. The only strange thing that she said the police noticed about the burglary was that her wedding dress was beautifully laid down on top of the heap of clothes on her bed. She had a friend in the police. He was a detective and he told her to move out of the house. He said this wasn't a break-in. It was a threat.

My paternal grandfather offered her financial security and safety. He was also a predator. My mother had nowhere else to go with me and her siblings.

She was manoeuvred into the relationship with him; she was young and naive. Because of the absence of my father, I had already displayed emotional problems as a toddler. Psychologists told my mom that my grandfather was the best replacement for my father. So, she went with it for a while. My mother looked after people, she never looked after herself.

During the time with my grandfather, my mom experienced enormous turmoil and difficulty. He was difficult to live with and he had high expectations of my mother. He made it tough for her to leave him. She fought hard for her freedom, but she eventually got away.

After my mother managed to break away from my grandfather, she got involved with a man named Francis. She always claimed him to have been her only true love. He had the disease of alcoholism and unfortunately to date has not recovered. He is Lara's father. The five years with him taught me I wasn't worthy of being picked up from school on time. I learnt to care for myself and my sister. In the early days of living with him, my mom would work late, and Francis would be out drinking. He often left me and Lara alone at home. I was around seven years old, and Lara was a toddler. I would call my one aunt or my Grannie to fetch us for company when it got dark. They could not always do it, but it helped when they could.

One afternoon as I was walking home from school after a grade two class, my pigtails bobbed with joy when I saw someone I recognised on the corner of our street. My dad! He stopped and picked me up. My heart pulsated with elation. I was euphoric. My father came to save me. We giggled and spoke and hugged. He told me he lived on a farm with his new family now. He didn't apologise for not being around for the last two or three years, but he said he missed me. I sort of believed it, but I struggled. I was just ecstatic to see him. It was lonely to live with my mom and Francis. I had no friends; I didn't know how to connect. By this time the safest bet was to live in my head.

My dad hung around for a day or two. He signed me into aftercare and from then on I had to go there instead of going home after school. My mother asked him to pay for it every month because he never paid maintenance. I hated aftercare. It was horrid. It was dry, the grass was dead, they made me say my times tables and I froze. I didn't know what to say. They asked me if I was mute … I tried to memorise the answers because I couldn't think when I was called to stand up. My breath caught in my chest and I went red, I couldn't breathe. Those rulers they used to hit you over your knuckles with when you got the answer wrong stared at me. Memorising worked sometimes, other times I don't remember, I've blocked it out. The smell of stodgy spaghetti bolognaise still makes me feel sick.

One day, I was the only child left at aftercare. Again. Eventually the last teacher there asked me if I knew our phone number. I had it and called our home number. This was probably around 18.00 or 19.00. Our phone line was cut because my mom did not have enough money to pay the bill and I could not get hold of them in any other way. Cell phones did not exist in our world in 1994. The teacher had to leave eventually, and she offered to take me home. I reassured her they would come. They didn't. When it got dark, I decided to walk. I knew the route home. If no-one would fetch me, I would get there myself. So, as the sun finally set over the suburban horizon, I started walking the five odd kilometres home. It was far for a kid with short legs. When I got home, it was dark. My mom and Francis were yelling at each other when I reached our fence. I opened the gate and walked in to find my mother in tears. They had a misunderstanding. Francis had to fetch me, he got drunk and forgot. My mom worked late. They did look for me apparently.

I reckoned I had to be my own guardian. These two did a bad job, so I decided to look after myself.

We stayed with Francis for about five years. Eventually my mother gave up. His alcoholism had reached breaking-point and we moved to my Grannie.

2012/04/15

> *Time goes by quickly in this place. Time flies in general. I gave up my first sponsor because I felt I couldn't trust her. Barbs told me she was a gossip, and she (my sponsor) kept pushing for my life story. I don't know why she was so insistent to get my story, and it made me feel uncomfortable.*

> *In this morning's meeting we spoke about Step Three: 'I've made a decision to turn my will and my life over to the care of God as I understand Him'. The woman who shared her experience of Step Three gave me such a feeling of peace and tranquillity while she spoke. I saw pieces of her aura, something I haven't seen in a while, since being in rehab. She made me think.*

The hardest thing to do is to surrender self-will and the need to control the direction your life moves into. I found God and his Angels and His Universal Energy last year. My first step was to learn how to ask for help. It came in wonderful shapes and ways. I'm grateful for that. I'm grateful for the help I had in the past year.

Doing this – the Program – has made me realise so much more. The connection I have craved desperately with my Higher Power is slowly blossoming. Giving up on controlling everything, surrendering and allowing God to truly take me on a spiritual journey I could only have imagined is happening right now. I must do the work; I don't have to control the course.

I feel a bit down now because I just can't seem to get the whole structure thing right. Every week I fill in a schedule. Then I don't stick to it. I suck at it! Today I want to go to yoga, but I'm tired and emotionally drained. We're having a braai and they asked me to make a potato salad. Now the bunch of them have gone shopping and goodness knows when they'll be back. I'll only be able to make the salad when they return.

I just don't have energy (or will) to freak out and speed through the whole recovery thing. What is wrong with me? I don't know. Maybe I'm depressed? I don't want to be.

I just feel like I'm going through the process, moving through time. A shadowy figure amongst passing colour. Tomorrow will be a better day; this I know. Spiritually, I'm more than my emotions. I don't have to define myself by my emotions. What I feel at one time does not sum me up in my entirety. As my Spirit Self I'm here to find pleasure in the human experience.

2012/04/16

I'm fucking infuriated and frustrated! I want to scream until I explode into a million pieces. Then it wouldn't matter anymore because I'd be in a million pieces.

I went to yoga yesterday. It was wonderful. I managed to pull myself out of that feeling of despair and frustration, and I got there, and I did it and I felt awesome. Now at the halfway house it feels as if I can't go to do these things because there are so many people to consider for meetings. Planning was never my strongest point. Now I must plan things in advance, and I suck at it. I'm stressed out, but I guess I must learn to do this.

*Second entry of the day

What a bipolar day. I'm sitting here thinking and grieving about Victor. Everyone in the house dislikes him and so do I, but it still doesn't take away the memories we created together. The laughter; the love we shared. I left him for a reason, but the heartache bubbles on the surface when I hear Adele songs or when I see his face. The dreams we had together were fantasies we both revelled in. We loved each other. It became increasingly arduous.

The memories of us, so very co-dependent, yet so comfortable and with the illusion of being safe. Smoking in the car, lighting a joint before we got to our destination, my hand on his leg while we drove to Hartebeespoort.

Fear and peace wrapped in such a neat little package. Fear because we drank like fish and because the coke usage increased and started destroying our relationship, and peace because we thought this septic relationship would last for life. I genuinely loved him – I still do, or maybe I just love the concept of him. I don't know anymore.

2012/04/18

It's hard for me to explain how I feel. Last night Sam (Samantha) spoke to me. I came to realise some scary things about my life. In the process group today, we also spoke about consequences in finances and about saying goodbye to my drug of choice.

On my way to work I started feeling. It began in my stomach. I sensed the emotional monster I've been hiding from for the last five years. It's coming back. While I sat with the boys at the house, one of them played a song from the Dave Matthews band and I cried. I couldn't stop myself. I can't control that build-up of raw and unmasked emotion – the thing I'm petrified of. It's exquisite to feel again, to cry without numbness. It's also fucking scary. All I want to do is run.

2012/04/19

Feelings.

They resemble colours. Fluid ribbons of colour flows through every part of me. Through my veins, my blood, my heart, my diaphragm. They are beautiful, but at the same time they are scary.

Isla Stone

Before my initial stint in the psychiatric hospital I was in my first long-term relationship. Matt studied towards becoming a geologist. He was a metalhead and while we were together he covered his arms in tattoos and got several piercings. He would have enjoyed tattooing his whole body. I carried a front of being 'hard core'. I met him in a heavy metal club where I used to headbang and wore a tough girl mask. We danced to a Chris Chameleon song and then we had a drink. Before he knew it, I was over him like stubborn fluff on a jersey. What was supposed to be my first one-night stand became a very volatile four-year relationship.

I was young, and I had no idea why I was miserable and depressed constantly. I did not know why it was such a challenge to pass technikon exams or why I could not contain myself. I had no idea why I was the way I was. I just felt stupid and tried to compensate for it by being increasingly hard core. I attempted to put up a façade to hide my feelings. I felt inadequate and terrified. I was afraid of this self-fulfilling prophecy of not being good enough, smart enough, attractive enough, thin enough or blonde enough.

I compared myself to every person on the street, to everyone at technikon, and I just could not see myself as adequate. I thought of myself as a nothing, a meaningless failure. I proved this repeatedly. I was enrolled for a diploma in Nature Conservation. I really wanted to be a Veterinarian. My maths marks were horrific, and I did not get into a B.Sc. course. No university would take me for the degree I wanted to do. I could get in for a Bachelor of Arts, but that wasn't good enough. Thus, I decided to do the diploma in Nature Conservation.

At the onset of my studies I lived with Grannie. I liked living with her less at this time than I did as a child. I couldn't do the things I wanted to do. She was a bit older now, and overly caring. It baffled me slightly. She fussed about what I ate, she worried about my results, she was concerned about who my friends were, she even cared about my body odour. It overwhelmed me. By now I wasn't used to a great deal of care. I took care of myself; the way I did it was by not taking care of myself at all. I wanted to self-destruct, and she was in the way.

But we still had our little jokes, our special things. We used to watch *Days of Our Lives* every afternoon and after that I think it was *Egoli*. She lived in a suburban area filled with complex housing. There was a field two complexes away from her home. We could see into it and every day at exactly 17.00 an ostrich walked along the fence. We would wait for him to walk across the field every day, watching him with pure delight. One day, the ostrich did not arrive. Later that week, we found out someone had shot the poor creature in the head. We were distraught.

Not long afterwards, my stepfather offered to buy me an apartment closer to the technikon. My Grannie disapproved. I felt guilty, but also elated. What a joy! My own apartment!

It backfired. I couldn't look after myself financially, physically or emotionally. I pushed my friends away and my Grannie too. I found a job at a restaurant and worked as a waitress to earn extra money. My parents did give me a monthly allowance, but it wasn't enough for food and toiletries and the things I wanted, such as petrol for the daily 30km drives to see Matt. I eventually fell into a deep depression.

After having a bath one day, I just lied down on the carpet in the living room with a towel over my body, unable to move. I was in agony, and the fear of feeling worse immobilised me. I lay there for close to four hours. I spoke to my mom about my experience, and she took me to my first psychiatrist. I never took psychiatric medication previously. I didn't know I could say if something wasn't working for me, or when I felt negative side-effects. I didn't tell anyone about the electric shocks in my brain. I didn't know how important it was to take the medication daily. The negative side-effects became so overwhelming that I stopped taking the medication. I suspect this contributed to my spiral of terrible and unmanageable sadness.

The fear of feeling was so real to me, emotions got me into dark pits of despair, and my early adult life was a vivid piece of evidence that I couldn't deal with the immense intensity of my emotions. I did not understand them or how to cope with them. I once told my aunt that no-one in this world knew what I felt or grasped the intensity that went with these emotions. They were killing me, and I did not know how to stop them.

At the technikon I passed some of the courses and failed others. Around my second year I had to retake a few subjects and I started to give up. Despair began to swallow me whole. My friends tried to keep me afloat, but I sank deeper into hopelessness. After my second year at technikon I dropped out and applied for a Bachelor of Arts at the university where Matt was studying. A change of scenery would be better for me and a university is far better than a technikon. The fickle mind amazes ...

Matt and I partied often. I drove us to the parties because he did not have a car or driver's license. He drank a lot, and I didn't at that stage. I had to be sober to drive and was still semi-responsible. He didn't believe in depression or anxiety. He told me to pull myself out of it.

That year was a hit and then a huge miss. I missed so hard my teeth clattered. By the end of the second semester I was admitted into the psychiatric facility for the suicide letter saga. Matt was in London for a conference at the time and broke up with me.

A few days after I came out of the hospital, I began to cut myself. I figured if I could lacerate the outside of my body, the pain on the inside of my body would subside a little. I would forget to wash the scissors and mostly did the cutting in the shower. My sister would find the bloodied scissors and shout terrible things at me while I was half naked. As I did the deed, I would scrunch up my face and say 'ouch, ouch, ouch'. Eventually I got a huge cyst in my armpit and had to get it cut out. Unfortunately, or fortunately (whichever way you want to look at it, I prefer fortunately) the local anaesthetic did not reach entirely into the pith of the cyst. Tears streamed down my face while this intern doctor cut out pieces of my epidermis. After the little surgery, I walked out of the emergency room wracked with pain. I realised how ridiculous I was to put myself through agony by cutting. What on earth was I thinking?

When I made up with Matt and we were in bed about two weeks later, I told him I didn't want to die without trying drugs. I didn't care what drugs, just, drugs. He figured LSD and Cat (Methcathinone) was a great first time. My downward spiral was set in motion there. It was the start of five years' worth of numb emptiness.

At least – I thought – I was numb.

2012/04/23

> *And so, it's come full circle. I'm depressed. My muscles feel heavy, my heart is bleeding and giving up. Still, I must remember that I'm more than my emotions.*
>
> *The last weekend was difficult. We went on a camping trip. Once we came home and I drove out of the gates I had an anxiety attack that lasted the whole weekend. I spoke to Victor and told him I felt vulnerable.*
>
> *Frida – one of the psychotherapists here – said he could be a sociopath and joked that he probably eats children's spleens.*
>
> *She's right. He probably is a sociopath.*
>
> *I became aware of my freedom today; of how lovely it is to have just me to worry about. Worrying about myself is much worrying already, but just for now until I get this right – which might take some time – I'm grateful it's just me.*
>
> *Me, me, me. Isla. That feels weird.*

Isla Stone

2012/04/25

Sleep well my dear friend, may your agony and fear now be released forever.

A friend from the rehabilitation centre passed away eleven days ago. He was a good man, a genuine human being. Sure, he had his faults, but he was depressed and in lots of pain. I think he gave up a long time ago; he lost hope. It kills me a little inside. I'm confused. In a way I don't understand why he didn't want to fight. I suppose I saw his resistance. Maybe he was just tired. I know he is in a better place now. In the spiritual plain, with no material attachments, no physical ailments. Just peace.

He touched many with love.

2012/04/26

Sixty Days.

I'm sitting in half-shade, half-sun under a tree in the middle of the garden. I see yellow-orange flowers when I look up. Some of the petals have reddish-maroon coloured flecks and streams on them. Ants crawl up and down the tree in a neat little row; frantically doing their part for their colony. The sun is warm on my back and a soft breeze is caressing my wet messy hair. The house's dog sits diagonally left ahead from me. She has serenely also chosen a half-shade, half-sunny spot.

Today I went to the Big Book meeting. One of the guys from the house joined me; no-one else in the house seems keen on Big Book meetings. I enjoy it because the chairperson is funny but speaks the truth in his humour. I saw Victor there, but I didn't really speak to him. I saw someone I knew from high school today. She never struck me as the addictive type, but life is full of surprises. She has had twenty sober months, which is cool. I thought I'd be embarrassed, but I wasn't. I took her number and I think we'll go for a coffee sometime.

I feel this urge to exercise, to get extremely fit. Sam and Frida are both fabulous and fit. I suppose in a way it's good that I look up to them. I know I tend to want to do too much. I over-dedicate myself and my time to a rigorous exercise regime and because it's insanely intense in the beginning I never keep to it. Then I beat myself up because I can't keep to it. It's that insanity, the obsession of addiction.

Now I'm too scared to dedicate myself to anything. What if I over-dedicate, what if I under-dedicate myself? Then again wondering about what ifs will not get me anywhere. I'm seeing my new sponsor today. She was referred to me by Barb. I'll write about that when I come back, I may have some clarity on this.

2012/05/04

Boredom.

I once heard from my stepfather that boredom was only felt by boring people. Well, I'm at work now. I've done all my work. Okay, I can do some more of my work ... But I don't have the comprehensive information I need to do everything together. I prefer doing my work in a certain

> *order. I guess it isn't boredom, but rather my mind that won't stop.*
>
> *If I want something to happen, I want it to happen now. I'm impatient in that way.*

2012/05/13

> *Right now, I have a heavy feeling in my chest. It's painful. I realised today how many times I have manipulated my mother to get what I wanted in my own selfishness and self-centredness. I'm sad for her because her idea of socialising is going to the pet shop and having a coffee with people who see money whenever they see her coming. The reading this morning was about allowing other people to take responsibility for their own shit. However, it does not take away the many times I took her for granted. I want to run away from recovery. It's difficult to see the wood for the trees. And there is no way I can take away this pain. It boils and festers under my ribs. I'm a crappy sponsee, I'm not doing enough for my recovery.*
>
> *Overdosing on viral guard is not an option, it won't work, and I must face this feeling of inadequacy. This was a shitty weekend for me, I won't lie. When will I learn?*

The first time I met Frida, I thought I met a fairy. She had an air of magical sweetness. Her shiny hair was long and dark, her face round and friendly and pretty. Her penetrating brown eyes saw right through me. She had boundless energy and spoke with an air of knowledge and love. It felt as if she knew me already. I did process groups with her and Samantha, and I had one-on-one therapy with her too. She believed in me and supported me with such unconditional love. She has helped so many people like me with her work and still helps countless people who are new to this journey.

For the first three months in the halfway house I still struggled with disturbing images, where I had killed myself, deadly images of blood and white skin and dead eyes. These scenes in my mind were explicitly graphic, and I had those most of my life. They seemed tangible to me, and I couldn't get rid of them. I hung from the magnificent old tree in the middle of the garden at the halfway house under a grey sky. Someone found me with slit wrists in the bathtub. I drove off cliffs, into barriers – graphic, graphic images of death and destruction. Three months into recovery these thoughts subsided, and suddenly, I didn't picture them at all. Slowly, but surely, I was getting better.

I've seen and heard countless painful stories during my time in recovery. Many people die from this malady. Addiction is a disease. Tortured souls fight with themselves throughout their lives. The alcohol or drugs are merely an outlet for the problem. The problem wasn't in the drugs and the alcohol it was in me. I had to find a solution to my 'personality' problem. My fear debilitated and consumed me. Over time I realised much of it had to do with self-perception. And a lot of the perceiving was quite obsessive. I tend to be self-centred, self-absorbed and self-serving. When I get out of myself, and I remove myself from the obsessive thoughts, I can live life more easily. Those obsessive thoughts were the basis of my fears. Every bit of it had to do with my ego. When I was egocentric, I was fearful of how I would be perceived by others. If they disliked or ignored me, it caused more fear, because I needed people to approve of me. I did not approve of myself. When I did not feel affirmed by others, the fear of not being good enough engulfed me and I was washed over with inferiority. I had to embrace and understand that I had a purpose, that I was good enough, that I was deserving, and that my haphazard attempts at controlling others were futile. I could not change how other people saw me, but I could get down to start valuing myself.

Isla Stone

2012/05/18

This is a shitty day. I want to run away from everything and everyone. To date this is the worst I've felt in recovery. My mind throws absurd thoughts around. I want to be normal! I want this to stop! I'm tired, and I don't know where to turn!

I feel scared and frustrated. Last night I dreamt about my child self, and I woke up dazed and vulnerable.

In a sense I've trapped by myself in a glass box. It has to do with my self-esteem and my inability to confront people when I feel they are invading my space. Just writing about it makes me want to explode and scream for days!

I have created this for myself, when I knew when to stop! But I couldn't. There is no-one else to turn to that I once trusted before.

2012/05/21

Here and now, not worrying about the future and how I want things to happen. I must let go of self-will and come to terms with how my Higher Power wants my life to pan out.

Letting go and not worrying about things I can't control has given me a deep sense of calmness. I've been considerably more grounded lately. There is a certain peacefulness, a serenity that has passed over me like a warm blanket even in this cold weather. I have also learnt there is no such thing as getting something wrong in recovery, but it is merely exploring your new-found skills and knowledge. Testing the waters to see, there is no failure, there is just getting it right the next time around.

2012/05/22

Mother of God. I can be a bitch, a sneaky, mean one at that. There is an irritating new guy in the house. He annoys the living crap out of me. I need some music to get out of this place in my head.

2012/05/27

Ninety-one Days.

I've avoided writing, I've avoided step work, and I've avoided speaking to my sponsor. I've gone to meetings and I did therapy with my counsellor from rehab and Frida. It's been an intense three months for me. It was my Ninety Days yesterday. I'm amazed. Three months of solid recovery, no alcohol, no drugs, no sex. I can honestly say it has been incredibly challenging.

I feel guilty because I could work my recovery harder. Step work is going very sluggishly, and I must do my life story by the fourth of June. That is soon.

I'm seeing my sponsor on Saturday though. Awesome!

My counsellor suggested I should write as soon as I wake up in the morning. I love that idea. If I wake up early, have a coffee and a smoke, I can easily write something while I'm sitting on my own, after meditating.

I had a random thought that scared me the other day. One of the housekeepers poured cleaning chemicals into a spray bottle and I had this deep sense of comfort and satisfaction. I knew there was something to help me end it if life became unbearable: those sweet chemicals.

Grim thoughts of suicide had left me for a while. Gradually they may have crept in here and there. That morning, they barged into my head with a vengeance.

FUCK EVERYTHING

2012/06/18

I haven't written in a while, I've allowed things to slip, insidiously. I'm clinging to a ledge, and blow by emotional blow, my fingers are losing their grip. I'm lonely and sore. Very, very sore. I feel dreadfully panicked and sick and tired. I want to kill myself, but I know I shouldn't. I hate everything about the pain in my life. I'm not working the Program as I should, I know that I would probably deal with this soreness a whole lot better if I worked harder. I had to start my life story today, I hate it. It fucking destroys me, one little bit at a time.

We had a family meeting last week and so many sick realisations came to me with Frida today in therapy. Things I really don't want to deal with.

I wrote an email to the Dean of the Science Department at UJ, trying to get into a B.Sc. for next year, I haven't received a reply yet. I want to finish my studies; I want to get a degree.

I ask God to help me every day. I guess if I don't put in the work, I won't get anywhere.

I acted out this weekend past. I visited Victor and kissed him. It approximated a relapse. Fuck! I miss him, I miss his face, I miss laughing with him, I miss being held by him and fucking him. I miss everything about the guy. I still love him, a lot. I had this fairy tale in my head that he would be clean and working this amazing Program, but he isn't, he has relapsed. He will be the death of me. I hate everything about my dysfunctional life now. Fuck it all.

There are two of me. One wants to break free from this insanity; the other wants to deal with the whole lot of shit. Two walls are squashing me. I'm going to splatter, and it would be cool if I did.

My brain won't shut the fuck up. So many plans, so many ups and downs. One day it's just great, the next it sucks. Sometimes I wonder if running away won't work better. I guess it won't. Moving away never works, I'll be taking myself with me.

2012/07/14

Today is a good day. It is cold, however a good day. I'm lying in bed all cozied up, thinking about how wonderful everything is.

These days were emotional and dark. I found something. I didn't know what it was, but little realisations began to explode like spats of popping candy in my mind. I was just rediscovering emotion and all the therapy loosened certain blocked memories. Some things were routine memories, things I automatically remembered. But then there were the hidden memories that started surfacing. Those memories were tiny splotches of clarity that lightened up the grey corners of my cluttered mind.

When my mother left Francis and we moved in with my Grannie it was wonderful. I was about ten years old. She drove me and my sister to school with our little packed lunches in our school bags. Those were the only packed school lunches we ever had, before or afterwards. She baked us special biscuits to take to aftercare. I didn't even mind aftercare. I made friends and knew everyone at school. I did athletics, played netball, and participated in gymnastics. Life came together, and I was happy. We lived with my Grannie for a year. Before that, I went to two other schools. First an Afrikaans and then an English one, when we still lived with Francis. While living with my Grannie I was in an English school, and by this time my Afrikaans accent was a whole lot less evident, no-one knew I was Afrikaans anymore. I loved being ten, because I was safe.

My mother worked in Centurion and we lived in Vanderbijlpark. She travelled between the two cities every day and yet again I hardly saw her. She would kiss me good night and by the time I woke up in the morning she was gone. She had to miss the traffic to get to work. I suspect that this was a difficult year for her. Towards the end of that year (1995) we went out for dinner one night and she told me we would be moving to Centurion. Not too long before this she introduced me to a new man she had met. He eventually became my stepdad. He was okay, I had met him once or twice before at her work during the holidays. They spent a large amount of time together and sometimes she slept over at his place. One day she took me over to his place, and we slept over. He had a little flat on a busy road in a bustling part of the town. It was very neat, but the furniture was old.

When the day came that we had to leave Vanderbijlpark, my heart was destroyed. I had to leave all my friends and the school I loved. I had to stop doing gymnastics and my netball team needed me. My haven was taken away from me, this safety that I finally found in the world that previously did not make any sense.

We packed our things.

We moved.

CHAPTER 2

In the East

Before I walked into recovery, I discovered a movie called *The Secret*, then I read the book. It made me feel incredible and elated me. I loved the idea of being the creator of my own destiny. I went for it, wanting it desperately. But I was lonely and confused. I used a lot of drugs. It was impossible to decide what I wanted, because I didn't know who I was. It moved me to such an extent, I thought I would test it. It was worth a shot. I missed Victor, who was away at rehab. I lived on my own and one evening I really craved a visit from him. I wanted it to happen for the greater good, in the best interest for all concerned. I hoped he would complete his treatment; but I also wished there would be some cause for him to pitch up at my place. For some good and pure reason.

I forgot about it afterwards. I smoked so much pot, it was easy to forget things. The next day after work, I settled in for the evening when someone knocked on my door. I was confused, normally people must ring the bell at the bottom of the stairs. I wasn't expecting any of my regular friends. I opened the door to a huge woman with long hair facing away from me towards the courtyard. I said hello … She turned around, and I gaped. It was Victor. I had asked for this the night before! It happened almost immediately! He pranked me with a long-haired wig, he was a bald man. I laughed uncontrollably. I was in shock about this miraculous manifestation. He told me he had to come to a sleep therapy clinic in Centurion as part of his treatment, so he decided to pay me a quick visit. I had pressed on the button of Universal Law for the first time.

I continued exploring the Law and its intricacies for a long time. I went to rehab a while later, and then to the halfway house. After seven months at the Halfway House, I moved back in with my mom and John, still intrigued by *The Secret*, and still discovering my own mysteries and riddles on route to my ultimate destination – a place of wholeness.

2012/08/03

> *Okay, I'm feeling dreadful and have been driven to write down my thoughts again. I'm scared I may be losing my mind. I moved out of the halfway house, back to my parents. I've been practicing positive thought, but it's disappointing. Here's the deal; I believe The Secret. I believe if you really put your mind to something it will materialise. I bought a few lottery tickets and am hoping I'll win it, so I can get away from home. I deserve independence, I deserve success, I deserve freedom and choice. Being at home does not offer me all of that, it does not offer me humanity in its entirety. I should not be prevented from helping others. In this household I'm told what I can and can't do. John has prohibited me from attending recovery meetings. My wings are clipped. The reason I can't live on my own or share a place with someone is, of course, financial. I have debit orders screwing me every month. I'm extremely sexually frustrated. I'm oozing hormones and I could fuck anything with two legs. I want to help others with my lottery money too; I'm still practicing positive thought. Maybe I live in my head; discarding reality. I don't believe life must be hard. I don't believe the Universe or God does not exist. I believe – and I want this life to show me – that anything is possible, because it's true. I believe it in every part of me, in every cell of my being, my heart and my soul and my spirit.*

Life should be lived with happiness and fearlessness.

2012/08/18

I have much to write about. I went through a hard time since I left the halfway house. Last week I slept with Victor. I used him for sex, a feeling of connectedness and trying to simulate what we had before. It didn't work. I felt guilty for using him yes, but also for dragging myself down. I don't mean that in a harsh way, I just mean it in a sense that, well, I let myself down because I knew what I did was wrong.

It's difficult to live with my parents again, and last week I did online research to check how many of my tablets would kill me if I took an overdose. I'm can't wait to be independent once more. I totally believe in good things. I thought about my Higher Power, I reminded myself of the wonderful people I've met on my journey in recovery and how I have plenty to give this world. Last weekend I was given The Secret book and DVD. I was thrilled, because I wanted to read the book and watch the DVD again, ever since my initial little miracle with manifesting Victor on my doorstep. I believe in manifestation. It's not complicated, but it's hard to practise if you're not in a good space.

So, I started reading it again. I have an ideal. I want to win the lottery, buy my own house, own a car and a dog, go on awesome holidays, pay for my studies and help people in the Fellowships with my new-found and growing wisdom. I have many ideas of where I want to end up. When I have abundance, I can be independent and work for little money (or none at all) spreading a

message of love, joy, strength, and – most of all – hope.
This has been a process for me, a slow progression. In the
beginning, before knowing enough about The Secret, I
got no numbers right for the lottery. Now I've won a little
bit of money. Yay!

It helps to be grateful, rather than dwelling on the things
that make me miserable. It takes a lot of practise. I never
realised how negative I could be when I'm in a place I
don't want to be in.

I know this will work and I'm grateful for this learning
process. Gratitude is cardinal and a great daily practice.
One should write about being grateful for what you want
as if it has already materialised.

We moved in with John in 1996, when I was eleven and Lara was five. My mom was exultant to have the lot of us together in a little happy family. It was okay to live with John in the beginning. It was fun. He had a weird sense of humour. He always tried to make us laugh, to win us over with his humour. He charmed us and sucked us in. The new primary school wasn't as nice as the previous one. The kids were different. They weren't as friendly as the kids from the school that I came from in Vanderbijlpark. It was difficult to make lots of friends, but I did eventually make one or two friends. One of them remained a close friend until the end of high school.

John started telling me I had to do exercise, because I was approaching puberty now. He said the boys would notice me if I had a nice body. He always found little faults with my looks. My mother told him to leave it, but he didn't. I listened because I wanted to please him. He was my stepfather after all. During those days at his house we'd play soccer, and if we could kick the ball past him, we'd get chocolates on Thursdays. We had a housekeeper called Rose who lived in a cottage behind our house. Some evenings after work or weekends my mom played music. Lara and I would sing along jubilantly. We listened to Les Misérables and Lord of the Dance, to Queen and Pavlov's Dog, Jimmy Summerville and Toto. We danced and sang and laughed, and John would join us.

Those were good times. John and my mother worked long hours for the same company. My sister and I shared a bedroom, but we would wait up for them in a homemade tent in the lounge. There were bad times as well. My mom and John often had screaming fights. There were times my mother ran into our bedroom, throwing a bag on the bed, declaring we'd move back to Grannie. I wouldn't mind; I loved living with Grannie. One Sunday my mother and John went at it again, yelling at each viciously. I walked into the kitchen to ask if everything was all right. John told me it wasn't. He held my crying mother from behind while she tried to break free from him. He said she was losing her mind. He shouted a warning that she was going to shoot me and Lara. My mother yelled at me not to listen to him. Something in me snapped. She owned a .38 revolver ever since I can remember. It was hidden under one of the kitchen drawer panels – we didn't have a vault. I ran down the driveway into the road. I sat on the pavement and asked some of the people who were coming home from work – on their way to the taxi rank – to please, please call the police. I said my mother wanted to shoot everyone. I needed help. They stared at me incredulously and kept on walking. I waited for the gunshot, shaking, thinking I was selfish for leaving my poor sister in that ominous house. I was too scared to go back inside. After a while, Rose fetched me. She said my mom was okay and lying down. I was in shock. My whole body trembled and shivered. John dragged me into their bedroom to see my incoherent mom. He asked me why I was shaking, but I was too traumatised to explain this to a violent adult man. I just said I was scared. He told me I was stupid and that my mom was okay. She just needed to sleep. I kept shivering. My whole world was shaken.

After that night I pushed towels under our bedroom door as a barrier. If my mother came in while we slept, I would wake up and tell her to kill me instead of Lara. I kept a rock under my pillow; if she got in, I would hit her over the head. How horrific to feel this way about the woman who used to be my main caretaker! She had suddenly turned into my enemy. No-one seemed to understand the impact that night had on me. I dreaded Sundays; waiting in angst for another episode. Every night without fail, I pushed the towel under the bedroom door until I was about sixteen.

The years with John became increasingly more difficult. Sometimes it felt as if we were a family, but most of the time it was troubling. He scared me. He had ongoing one-way shouting matches with me when I didn't do things his way. It usually lasted about twenty to thirty minutes. He steamrolled me with rhetorical questions and I learnt not to answer. Engaging with him would just drag out the fight. During one of these altercations, we stood in the portal of a new house we had moved into. He was screaming about my bad maths marks. He said I was stupid, and that I would end up at a teller at a supermarket. I believed him.

My mother was the eldest of five closely knitted siblings. She would often take us to Vanderbijlpark to see them and my Grannie. After my mom came my Aunt Elizabeth, then my Aunt Marietta, my Uncle Anton and then my Aunt Anna. I love them dearly. They were an integral part of my childhood. Uncle Anton was a magnificent martial arts fighter; he has many blackbelts in various disciplines, ranging from Karate to Tae-Kwondo. His light-hearted humour always cheers me up. Aunt Marietta has displayed many of her incredible paintings in art galleries all over the country. She is colourful. Motherly and loving Aunt Elizabeth's compassionate soul has helped many people. Aunt Anna is a butterfly. She is the youngest and always on the road. She lives her life with enormous freedom.

We would go visit them over weekends. Initially my stepfather would come with, but then he started to stay at home. He would often complain in the evenings when we returned. My mom and John had monumental fights on those nights. He would say my mother didn't care about him and claimed she loved her family more than him. He started isolating her from them. In time, the excursions to the family became fewer and further between. My mother was trying to soften the blows while John was grooming her to be devoted to him only.

Earlier, when we still visited the family regularly, the countless hours we drove between Vanderbijlpark and Centurion were exceptionally special times. I waited patiently for my younger sister to fall asleep, and then my mother and I would have deep conversations about the times she had with my grandfather and my father. She told me grown-up stories about her life when she was younger, and about my Grannie's life. I felt needed and loved while she spilled these heavy emotional dramas into my cup. I was so young, but I felt the love and closeness I desperately craved from my mother. I was a little adult at those times.

I still went to visit Francis every second weekend; sometimes we'd also visit his mom and grandmother. They played a central role during my younger years. I spent much time with them. Gran (Francis's mom) and Gran-Gran (Francis's grandmother) worked hard to make me feel welcome in their family. I never did feel quite at home with them. They were English and Anglican. On Sundays there were roasts and mustard sauce on the formally laid table, set with pretty English china plates and grand cutlery. We were often bundled into the car with the two of them to join the Sunday school class at the Anglican church before lunch. Gran-Gran loved working in her fragrant and lovely rose garden. I always felt uncomfortable and unable to communicate with Francis and initially, I felt the same with his mom and grandmother. I grew up in an Afrikaans environment; the change to this new way of life was perplexing at times. I did not like going to church and I was scared to break some fine and delicate thing in Granny and Gran-Gran's house. The house had a stagnant, old energy. I often felt as though I could not see through the haze of time. Granny and Gran-Gran lived together all the years. Gran-Gran passed from old age eventually; Granny died of cancer not long after that.

2012/08/27

Today I'm so happy and grateful. I've won the lottery! Today I'm so happy and grateful that I'm a millionaire.

Today I'm so happy and grateful to own my dream home in Sandhurst. Today I'm so happy and grateful that I can buy my own car.

Today I'm so happy and grateful to go on beautiful, exciting holidays all over the world!

Today I'm so happy and grateful to pay for my own education. Today I'm so happy grateful that I have made a good change in the world. Today I'm so happy and grateful that I'm successful.

2012/09/03

I woke up this morning feeling incredibly energised. Today would be an exceptional day. I have an intense feeling of gratitude and peace, but most of all, excitement. I put both my feet on the floor as I got out of bed and said, 'thank you!' with a huge grin on my face. I checked myself out in the mirror with a smile while I took my clothes off to jump in the shower. The water was cleansing on a physical and spiritual level. I felt utterly serene. I got dressed and put some make-up on my face – today I would be in charge!

I drove to work feeling grateful and excited. I kept saying to myself. 'I'm so happy and grateful now that I'm rich and wealthy!' I felt it, I truly felt it. At work, I did my usual thing – switched on my computer, made myself a

*cup of coffee and sat at my desk. I opened my emails,
and what do I find ... I received my support email from
the lottery company, officially stating that I had won
the lottery!*

I won it!

*I've become a multimillionaire. Couldn't contain myself,
I gave a squeal of delight! My hands shook, my heart
beating a million miles a minute. I'm so grateful in my
heart for this!*

The more desperate I became the harder I tried. I didn't know it was at the mere start of my journey. I attempted to simulate the experience of winning the lottery. From what I had learnt and how I absorbed the information, I believed if I modelled the experience of what it would feel like to win the lottery, it surely would be mine. I'm generally quite impatient. I want what I want when I want it, and I want it now. Having said that, I was also in a quandary. Back at home, I felt trapped and afraid. I hadn't been home for ages, and I now realised to what a large extent my mom and John's relationship had deteriorated.

I discovered later that trying like hell does not lead to manifestation. You relax into what you want; you know it's yours; you must be patient and enjoy the journey. It's about your vibration, like attracts like. There is a lot more to it too. Those are a few of the many things I learnt along the way. I did not win the lottery. After this experience I decided I would create my own riches on a spiritual level.

My childhood anxiety intensified when I was in high school. Later, I would understand John's influence on the severity in which it manifested itself. We experienced abuse on many levels at home. The one-way shouting matches continued. My art was always a subject of contention, my maths marks were always a subject of contention and my weight was always, you guessed it, a subject of contention.

In high school (well, in my most of my life) I read many books. I delved into the joys and hidden worlds of Enid Blyton, Judy Blume, J.R.R. Tolkien and many other authors. The time I spent in the library was just about the same amount of time I slept. I loved escaping into the worlds of magic and adventures of running away with a group of friends to find peace and tranquillity, to find exciting adventures and islands. Robinson Crusoe; oh, how I dreamt of climbing on a boat, drifting off to an island far away to build a fort and live with birds, insects and lizards. I fantasised about anything and everything to get away from my grim life where I could not live up to any of John's expectations. I wanted to be accepted and I tried with every inch of my being to be acceptable, to be good enough. It was never enough.

The escapism became worse later in high school, when the first *Harry Potter* book was published. I read those books in one or two days as soon as they were released. Then I would read them over again and again. I read them in class, and I read them in bed until the early hours of the morning. Obsessive escapism. I had a wonderful imagination; it carried me through many things in my life, especially as a child. Based on the historical disappointments with my father, John confirmed every one of my suspicions of not being good enough. He insisted the reason for all my failures was laziness.

John's adoptive father was a cartoonist. John was also a relatively good artist, but never made much of an effort to develop it, except at the beginning when my mom encouraged him. When I drew something or completed something, he would look at it and call it mediocre. He would sneer about there being no real skill in it. He reiterated my own thoughts about my stupidity and said my marks were not up to his standards. He said I lacked discipline. I started lying to him about school to avoid the one-way shouting matches. I couldn't handle the screaming, the shame, the anxiety. I couldn't stand the deep, penetrating sense of fear I constantly experienced around him.

As a youngster I loved diarising my daily experiences. I had a little journal with a lock, and I would write about this boy and that boy, about my friends, and this and that. One day I had written about an argument my mother had with John. He brought it up in a conversation a while later. It was strange because I didn't mention it to anyone; I had just written about it in my diary. He was reading my diary. He would then use that intimate knowledge to pick fights with me. I didn't really consider the implications of this until later in my life, when it made a lot more sense.

2012/10/12

> *Two-hundred-and-twenty-eight Days. Clean and sober.*
>
> *Loads of things has happened since I last wrote. I did not win the lottery. I suppose I could wish until I'm blue in the face and this dream won't become a reality until I've set my shit straight. Money isn't everything. All I wanted to be is free.*
>
> *Freedom comes in many forms and I suppose I'm as free as I choose to be. I can let many things rule me; the things I want control over but in the end will never have. When I choose to let those things go, to let God take care of it, not expecting a result I have created in my mind – I'll be free.*
>
> *I still can't say I know what I want, where I want to go, or what I expect – but I know one thing: I must act.*
>
> *Sometimes I wish God/Angels/Universe/Source would guide me about the right decision to make. I can study full-time. But what should I study? I suppose, inevitably it's entirely up to me. I'll make the right choice. I was obsessed with winning the lottery. I spent a lot of time and energy wishing it would happen. A close friend of mine says if you don't desire an outcome it will come*

to fruition in the long run – the same as the Buddhist principle of Lojong – abandon all hope of fruition.

Where does hope come into it though? I'm not even sure. But I know there is a power within me that I'm yet to harness.

2013/01/29

Eleven Months and Three Days.

I'm feeling vulnerable. I'm feeling scared. I'm feeling sad. I'm feeling anxious. Today I moved back into the Halfway House as a patient for a month. It is frightening and frustrating not to be able to see beyond that. I applied at a good University to study a B.Sc. as an occasional student and I don't even know if they've accepted me yet. Even that scares me. I've made this elaborate plan in my mind – how I want everything to work out. I have fallen into the trap of wanting to control everything. Living at home with my parents scares me. They need me there; I need their money. It's kind of sick, but I thought it would work out.

I hope and wish and pray to find another solution. Looking at what I'm writing I realise how meaningfully I could practise the Third Step here. Turn my will and my life over to the care of God as I understand Him. It's hard to work on faith because you think you have it waxed and then, well, then you don't. You never have this thing waxed. There is never an easier or softer way. My life is filled with exhausting choices and challenges. I decided to move back to Sam's Halfway House and to try to get my unravelled mind into a cohesive mode again.

I should work on a plan for going forward. I've spent too many nights and days on unrealistic expectations of what I wanted life to be. Unfortunately, this is not the reality and I have completely misunderstood the concept. I won't win the lottery because I try to manifest it. There's God's will then there's mine. It's hard to give up the notion that I'm the creator of everything in my life. Now it's time to let go and let God. Fear won't get me anywhere, obsession won't take me forward, anxiety won't fix me. It's my greatest wish to relax and let go of the all-consuming worries.

I'm afraid of my stepfather; he has given me everything and I know he can take every bit of it away. He sets traps for me in conversation. If I say the wrong thing, he can manipulate and mutilate me with his words. He does inappropriate things. He lifted my shirt to see if I was wearing a bra, and I aggressively pushed his hand away. He was furious with me the whole day after. He is nosy about my sex life. That's not on! He threatened me with peanut butter and said – with a creepy leer – he would paint it on my body while I was asleep. I'm allergic to peanut butter. He wants me to know he has control over everything I do. It hurts me, and it scares me, and it fucks me up.

So, here I sit trying to make up my mind about the rest of the year. It terrifies me that I must make the sacrifice to live at home with them if I want to study. Studying is the one thing I really want to do for myself.

Or nothing?

Isla Stone

2013/02/07

> *My most wonderful dream yet! I dreamt a cool thing. I don't want to write about it yet. I'm ecstatic!*

2013/03/22

> *Three types of birds are singing their own individual, beautiful songs. The wind is gently caressing my face. I'm wearing a loose pink shirt with LOVE printed on it. I've come to visit Grannie and Uncle Marius at Uncle Marius's farm in the bushveld with La, Ally and my mom. Uncle Marius is Grannie's wonderful partner. They have been inseparable since they met again after many years at a high school reunion three years ago.*

> *I'm sitting on the old white steps of an unattended rondavel. The almost overflowing river is so close to me, and the ancient trees are watching over me. Uncle Marius calls them bushveld trees. I still feel a little sick. My stomach feels uncomfortable. I'm calmer and far more at peace, though. A lot has happened over the last two weeks. I realised my deep despondency only two days ago. I felt helpless, afraid, angry, sad, and resentful. Then I got sick and it made me tumble into a black hole of self-pitying despair, which made me even more ireful and helpless and unmanageable.*

> *The light has finally dawned somewhat. I have awakened from darkness and gloom. I hope and pray with all my heart that it has.*

> *So, let's go back about two months ago …*

The Friday I got accepted! I was offered a spot as a B.Sc. occasional student. I was overwhelmed. It was a miracle! Better by far than winning any lottery. I got another chance to make things right for myself. I took a leap of faith.

After the eons of toil, regret, self-destruction and self-hate, this is my chance. This is an opportunity to make things right with myself because I'm worth it. I'm intelligent enough, I'm good enough, I'm beautiful enough, I'm strong enough. Now is the time to rectify all that hateful internal ranting at myself. I know it won't happen overnight. I still do it. It's undoubtedly the biggest problem I have with myself.

As I said, I took the leap of faith. God wants something great for me, I just need to want it for myself. I reached into the inner strength that Barbara says I carry. I had a mini freak out from the start. Everything moved rapidly. I wanted this. I want this!

I managed to complete some assignments, but not all of them. I went to many classes, but I did miss a few. Then last week, the week before, it started. The pressure cooker. I thought I was okay. I studied hard for chemistry. Wrote it on Tuesday then studied hard and wrote Biology on Thursday.

I failed chemistry. Biology I don't know yet. I must focus. Every second counts. Then I got sick. By Monday I pooped water. I had an essay due on Tuesday for Biology and bunch of other work for the lab. I spiralled and freaked out. I didn't see my Chem tutor on Wednesday.

> *How badly do I want this? The negative inner dialogue needs to end. Time management and routine is key.*
>
> *Dear God*
>
> *My last prayer was about gratitude. With this prayer I want to ask for help. I do get help from You daily and I'm truly grateful for that help. But, will You please help me to not to be so hard on myself with negative self-talk? Please help me to find a strong and balanced routine.*
>
> *Thank You.*

After a family meeting at the halfway house where Samantha called in John and my mother, things went pear-shaped. John was restless and kept pushing me to move back home. He insisted on me finishing my studies, and he made promises that he would pay for it if I played by his rules when I moved back. His conditions included that I do not go out, that I study diligently, that I do not socialise. Even recovery meetings were a problem. Mainly it entailed doing everything his way.

I could live at home, he had paid for my car, so my expenses were minimal. During the time I spent at the halfway house I realised that the amount of control John had over my life was unnatural and unhealthy. During the short time I lived back at their home while I attempted to study, something irked me, gnawing at me. I felt restless and uncomfortable.

Studying was difficult. I spent years using drugs and drinking; my thought processes were incoherent, and I was still obsessive and in a space of healing. I repeatedly sat myself up for failure. When I was at my weakest, I would set the biggest challenges and watch myself fail majestically. Then I had every reason to acknowledge what a failure I was. I had moved back in with my toxic family, while getting back on my feet for the first time after years of drug and alcohol abuse, and now I wanted to conquer a science degree. Could I do it?

We were driving on our way somewhere when John solemnly asked me whether I had won the lottery. A chill went down my spine. I wrote the bit about the lottery to simulate the feeling I would have had if such a miracle occurred. It was my private entry and part of my attempt to manifest abundance. The reason I'm sharing it here, is to express the insanity I experienced at home. The only way he would have known was if he had read my diary. I asked him how he would have known something like that; he started explaining and said a woman at work told him. I told him he was lying. For the first time in my life, I directly confronted him on what he had done. I told him it was unacceptable. He wasn't allowed to read my diary and I wouldn't stand for him doing it again. I was driving, and in control. He couldn't do much, so he apologised insincerely.

There have been many other altercations, too many to mention, too many worth mentioning. Thinking about it now, I laugh out loud. It was hilarious. This man thought I had really won the lottery; I most certainly wrote about it quite convincingly.

The journey born out of my first dealings with *The Secret* was a vital part of rediscovering myself. Many will say that alcoholism and drug addiction are partially forms of a spiritual malady, a disease of the spirit. I believe every interaction, every experience and every moment are of complete value and filled with a lesson if I look for it. In my life when I find a saying, or a YouTube video, a song or lyrics, a book, or a person with wisdom that rings true to me I absorb the information and call it Universal Truth. It makes me feel incredible, it puts a grin on my face, it lightens my heart and tells me that everything is in Divine Order. It has taught me to love life, to take myself less seriously, to walk with a forgiving heart and to let life take me where my soul wants to roam.

CHAPTER 3

A Spiritual Rock-bottom

2013/03/09

> *I'm feeling full and tired. I'm back at the halfway house.*
> *I've moved out of my parents' house for good. I realised*
> *John had molested me and my sister from a young age.*
> *The complete picture fell into place. It's sickening. And*
> *I'm not sure if I've processed it. I was eleven when we*
> *moved in with John. After seventeen years of difficulty*
> *and pain, I still couldn't quite pinpoint the exact nature*
> *of my distress before now. The realisation has opened*
> *a floodgate of pain. I never understood my feelings. He*
> *took so much from me. He took away my ability to find*
> *good healthy relationships. He took away my outlook on*
> *what intimacy is supposed to mean to me. He blurred my*
> *boundaries. He manipulated me. He gave me material*
> *possessions to get power over me. He has taken my*
> *family from me. I couldn't write in my diary because he*
> *would read it. I'm free now. I can make my own choices,*
> *live life for myself, heal. Now I'll take back what he took*
> *from me. With love and forgiveness in my heart. I'll find*
> *peace; I'll find serenity.*

At the time I lived with my parents again, I had some safe space to clutch in the early evenings before John came home and I had to walk on eggshells again. One night, I was watching television when he came in. I tried to evade a conversation, in case he wanted to fight. He said he had a date with some woman that evening. He was callous enough not to care about the feelings this might evoke in me. My mother and John had been working together for many years and set up a successful business together. She still ran after his every whim and tried to take care of him. He liked to discuss private things that no child should hear about their parents' relationship. I did not want to discuss his flights of fancy about going on a date; I felt upset and knew I had to put my boundaries down. I said I felt ill and left the room. While he was in the bath getting ready for his supposed date, he called Lara to have a 'chat'. I heard my sister's escalating distress. She shouted at him, and I could hear the enjoyment in his voice as he responded to the drama caused by his provocation.

Lara came to me while he was still dressing up. She exploded with anger and said she had much to deal with and didn't want to handle this shit as well. The worst part was how she had to look him in the face every day, knowing he had molested her. Those words halted the world, the Universe, the earth, the water, the planet, the air I breathed. That moment unlocked years of abuse I had edged around, tiptoed from, closed my eyes to, and avoided. Memories engulfed me; the truth was a horse that kicked me in the forehead.

My sister spoke on. I gasped for breath. How could she casually mention molestation? Then again, how could I just block it and hide it from my memory? I hid the truth of his behaviour for such a long time. I knew my life would change forever as soon as I acknowledged it; as soon as I put a name to it. John had abused us sexually.

After Lara went to sleep, frantic memories inundated me. A good deal of the pain and agony started to make sense. Neatly hidden pieces of the puzzle suddenly fell into place.

The next day I went to Samantha and I cried; oh, how I cried! A river of seventeen years of distress and anguish. Twenty-eight, actually. Seventeen years of abuse from John, and eleven years of random mistreatment before that. She looked at me knowingly; saying she had wondered when I would acknowledge it. She suspected it. Frida and my counsellor too. Lara (who is my sister, for God's sake!) knew. All of them were privy to this essential information, but me.

Somehow, I missed that very important memo; now I know I was just not ready to acknowledge it.

They never told me getting honest with myself in recovery would be this hard.

It was a troublesome situation. John payed for my studies. I had given up my job at their company. I had no money. My car and my clothes were my only available possessions. John bought them for me. Most of my furniture was in a storage facility my mother payed for. I wasn't independent; I wasn't paying my way and I was controlled by my stepfather. I was exactly where he wanted me.

The thing about the beginning of this journey is that I had developed or rediscovered some values. I knew I had to look after myself and my own well-being. I was coming to understand this concept slowly. I had never done this before. Leaving home again was one of the first steps I took to solidify the value I see in myself.

Samantha let me sleep at the halfway house that night. We arranged that I would stay there for a while until things had settled down. It helped me immensely. A star in my dreary darkness. The following day I went back home with Barbara to collect my clothes. I hoped beyond hope that John would not be there, but he was. I packed only what I needed and left, giving him a tense kiss on the cheek, saying I would visit the halfway house for a while.

I did not return until a year later.

2013/06/23

> *I suppose I wrote about moving back to the halfway*
> *house. It has been a rough and interesting ride. I've not*
> *been faithful to this diary – I scribbled incoherently in*
> *other A4 books too, because I had to get rid of a load of*
> *emotions. I had to air out the dusty parts of my hidden*
> *soul. Life will never be easy for me. I guess I knew that*
> *since the day I left my mother's womb. My soul chose a*
> *difficult path; it's hard to learn the lessons I selected for*

this life, but it makes me grow and mature on a spiritual plane.

It's not up to me to determine my fate. God always knew the plan. I've learnt to do my best and then turn my will and my life over to the care of God as I understand Him. The outcome is not up to me. Sometimes it's tough, and I must take this action daily. When I do it, miracles happen.

Dear God,

Today I want to thank You for my journey thus far. If it were not for the sum of my experiences, I would not be the free, strong and independent woman that I am.

Thank You.

2013/06/24

I'm a little down. I could sleep even more than I have already. I've been in touch with Matt. I'm lonely and filled with remorse. I feel guilty because I'm clean and sober and he is still using. I know I'm playing a dangerous game. I eventually came to my senses and told Matt where to get off. I may have sounded a little pedantic, telling him what I think about him. He is an addict. He refuses facing it. It scares him to even consider the possibility. I guess I had to learn the hard way, and now he too must break his legs to learn how to walk again. I can't sit around and watch him do it repetitively.

I despise the cold when I can hardly feel my frozen toes. When my nose is so cold that every breath of air is an icicle. Parts of me have died away and other parts have flourished. I don't know why I get so morbid these days. Maybe it's the dark side of me trying to balance out the light side. Sugar also seems to be a problem.

I miss my mom. Samantha said I miss the idea of my mom more than my mom herself because she was never there for me. I was always there for her, which is also true. I suppose it's okay to miss the illusion of the mom I created? Her little wrinkly face and blue eyes and scrunched up shoulders. That description depresses me. She's immeasurably better than that.

Dear God,

Please remove this feeling of morbidity from my heart. Please help me to feel light and free and happy.

Thank You.

2013/08/07

I'm sad and sore. I felt the ache of a lifetime of dysfunction. I wish I knew what to write. I wish I knew how to fix myself quickly, but I know I can't do it on my own. My life has changed substantially during the last five months. I read my Angel Cards compulsively. Maybe I sometimes misinterpret them or interpret them the way I want to. I'm sitting with the loss of my family, of my childhood, of the time between being a defenceless eleven-year-old girlchild, and now being a fucked-up woman at twenty-eight. I sit with insecurity and fear of these changes. Change was never a bad thing. But I miss my mom, I miss Lara, I miss the security, I miss elements of John, and I miss Alex most of all. I'm powerless over the change. I'm confused about missing parts of John, but also hating what he did to me. This is part of the intricacy of having been abused by a trusted person. I can't explain these emotions. I sometimes wonder why this has happened to me. Is it fair? I don't know. Was I so terrible a human being when I was using drugs that I deserve every bit of this? Then, looking back, I can see how the abuse brought me into active drug addiction. In the end the destruction of others' emotion brought me to my knees. Yes, I blame my mother for all of this. Her choices and decisions brought me to this desperate painful darkness.

None of this is fair.

I'm too tired to fight any more, to be mad any more. I don't know if the exhaustion means I've given up emotionally. I've frequently seen how pain creates growth. I can't say I'm tired of growing, but I'm tired of being angry with my mother and John. I'm tired of being angry with myself. I'm absolutely tired of fearfulness. I get irritated with people if they don't do what I think they should. Maybe that makes me judgemental? It does. I don't want to be tired any more.

I was distressed after leaving home and I did not speak to John after that. I was terrified of him. As in any other abusive relationship, I was the victim. But I was breaking free – I was rescuing myself. This was a new thing to me, and it shattered my world.

On a Sunday after I moved into the halfway house for the third time Barbara had bought us tickets to watch a show at the Barnyard Theatre. I was on edge the whole afternoon. My worst fear came true when he started calling my cell phone. I did not answer. He called again. I did not answer. There were about twenty missed calls. He was scared, but I didn't know that at the time. It's reminiscent of the snake and human analogy; they're more afraid of you than you are of them. He is the snake.

I called Frida in a panic, she said not to be afraid, that I was being courageous. He was scared and trying to intimidate me. If I look back now, I'm grateful for these humans. They were the Angels who saved me from darkness. That moment when I broke free, my life finally started.

A few days after I moved out of my parents' house, I arranged that Lara and I speak to my mother. I wanted her to understand what happened and why I moved out. Her response surprised me. I expected her to kick him out immediately; to send him on his way and protect her daughters. I was bitterly disappointed. That was one good lesson: one must never have expectations. In shock, she started blaming me. She asked me why I didn't say anything sooner. She told me I should have known I was being abused, seeing that it happened to me previously with my uncle as well. She was accusatory and said that if I had done something sooner, she would not be in the predicament she was in now with my brother. She made it my responsibility that she did not leave John years ago. Her priority was to protect my brother. I was devastated by her words.

She stayed with John. To me and Lara, it felt as if she no longer cared about anyone but our little brother, Alex. My mom's life neurotically revolved around Alex and John.

I was fifteen when my mother discovered she was expecting a baby. She took a pregnancy test in our bathroom. Those years we were still a family in some sense. She hollered something and John ran into the bathroom. They closed the door. Lara and I stood outside. I looked at her and said, 'mom must be pregnant'. Ten-year-old Lara giggled with delight. I couldn't keep my excitement from showing either. We wanted to play doll, and this would be loads of fun! My mom and John emerged from the bathroom with huge grins; they were pregnant. My mother looked flustered. She was thrilled. She held the pregnancy test and then put it in a plastic bag. She kept that test in her handbag for a while as a reminder of her joy.

They got married soon afterwards. We wore gorgeous purple dresses, my mom looked radiant and beautiful. She was close to popping by the time the wedding came around. Alex came into the world as a soft little lump of joy. He giggled and had the tiniest nails on his fingers and his toes. His enormous blue eyes absorbed every ounce of information from his small world. He brought a new-found joy into our home. He also brought sleepless nights. Alex was a natural born insomniac. From day one, the child had pains and aches. My mother discovered he had low muscle tone in his back, and she started looking for other potential problems. She did some research about Asperger's and autism. But she never discovered what was wrong with him until years later. The long nights took its toll.

As the years went by and Alex's sleep deprivation started touching the rest of us in the household, the family unit, instead of standing together, started pulling apart. John blamed my mother and moved to the couch permanently. He refused to sleep in the bedroom with her. Alex slept with my mom in the bed, and John chose to allow it. My mother did not know how to deal with this demanding child, and she also did not know how to deal with the more restless older male she was living with; her husband whose mental deterioration accelerated every day.

2013/08/11

> *I have this bizarre need to listen to Vivaldi's Four Seasons. It's in my head. Somehow, listening to it will release something in my soul. A tight chested, breast hugging emotion.*

> *I've been told that I'm intelligent. It is a gift. I want to let it out. I don't believe it myself. I want to remember the things I learn, I want to use it, access it, grow it.*

Maybe this is why I truly want to be a doctor. I'm selfish and self-obsessed. I want to grow for myself. I have no romantic notions about what it means to be a doctor. If I try, through some Godly miracle, maybe I can study in China, or another country. Yes, I do want to grow. But I also want to help people. Others have told me there are different ways of helping humanity. I agree. The difference is that I could save lives if I became a doctor. I could advocate for others. I want to believe it's possible. I'm standing on this wall – the one side is belief and the other is reality.

I live in a halfway house; I've lost my parents and family. My soul is broken, my bank account bare. I'm following my mom's bad example by staying in a job where I hate what I'm doing. I promised myself that I would never just settle for a job that comes along because I must pay bills and make ends meet. I believe this is part of the reason why my mother has always been so unhappy. I'm becoming my mother.

People say I should never give up on my dreams, they also say I must be realistic. What a contradiction! I want to be my own person; I want to believe in my own possibilities and abilities. I want to break away from others and their opinions of me. I'm Isla, I'm me. Today I want to believe in my potential. Today I'll advocate for myself.

After a few months of feeling terribly sorry for myself – and heaps of drama – a Pharma company offered me a small project. I had to create a PowerPoint presentation for them for a planning session they would have in Dubai. The woman who asked me was a friend of Samantha's. During the few months I was staying at Samantha's to get my mind and emotions together I did some administration work for her. The presentation project was different – I had to go to this corporate company and portray myself as a professional. For the interview I met up with Samantha's friend at the Pharma company to have a meeting with the General Manager who requested the project. I misunderstood the scheduled time and arrived an hour early, at 6.30 instead of 7.30. Finally, after waiting in angst, Samantha's friend arrived, and we went up for the interview. The General Manager was strikingly attractive and immediately became one of my role models. She knew what she wanted and how she wanted it, but she had a sense of compassion about her. What an amazing human being! I completed the project successfully and she mentioned an interest in hiring me for longer-term jobs. I told her I was still enrolled at university for the year and had to go back to study. At that point I didn't know the funding for everything would be stopped.

A few weeks after I left home, John sent my mom and sister to collect my car. I didn't have a car for a while but mentioned it to Aunt Anna, although I told no-one else in my extended family. The car was released back to me a few days later. I now know my aunt spoke to him and he did not want to be seen in a bad light by my mom's family.

I was fragile and could not see a way forward with my studies without funding. I was terrified without my safety net. The General Manager asked me when I wanted to go back to my studies. I walked into her office, and she asked me what was wrong. I wonder if you know that huge lump in your throat, or the feeling of your forehead going red, the feeling of begging yourself not to cry now, but you feel those tears welling up and you feel so helpless? I burst into tears and told her I wouldn't continue my studies. I said my parents and I had a fall out. I had a set of morals and I did not agree with their stance on the matter. I did not see eye-to-eye with them any more. She told me to wait right there and called the HR Director. They offered me a month-by-month contract in the Finance Department. I met the Financial Director and Maureen, the Planning Manager. I would report to Maureen. That day I knew I would always be okay. The company came to be my second family. They were amazing people.

I detest the word 'discipline' – John used it repeatedly and continuously to prove my unworthiness to me. I prefer terming it 'self-love' instead of 'self-discipline'. I realise that these are not the same though. Someone recently helped me to see it differently. Discipline comes from the Latin word *discipulus*, directly translated means learner, student follower. I like to see myself as a student of life. I can't be disciplined in one area of my life and not the other because then I am not allowing myself to learn as much as I can about myself in situations that challenge me.

The Pharma company and my new family of colleagues played a huge part in teaching me how to practise this kind of self-discipline. To do things when they should get done, to be brave, to be an adult. It taught me I'm radically more than I ever imagined. I'm capable of more than I ever thought possible. After a year of being contracted to them, my responsibilities increased. They'd seen what I was capable of, and I was given a permanent position as a Financial Analyst.

The family I found there was close to me, and I still love them all.

When I got the initial contract, I decided to pay Samantha some money for my stay with her. I paid several of my other expenses with money from my provident fund as well. My petit Aunt Anna with her sweet pixie face helped me through that testing time. She always looks fresh, as though she had walked straight out of a steaming shower. She has loads of secret knowledge and is my mother's youngest sister. Anna has always been a little different. She didn't conform to the expected path for Afrikaans women of her generation. She is still not married and doesn't have children. She has insisted on finding the right partner, not the convenient one.

I would visit her, and she became my surrogate mother. She stayed at Grannie's home in Vanderbijlpark and worked for my mother and John's company in Centurion. We watched movies and talked for hours about beauty products, family sagas, our histories, and addiction. We spoke about everything. She made us warm mugs of milk or Milo before bed. She allowed me to use her beauty products. It was my hide-out, my safe place. Maybe she had no idea how to deal with this situation; it must have been difficult for her. But she helped me immensely with her innate spiritual wisdom. I admire her strength, her fairness and her love. She held me together.

I still had a dreadful opinion of myself and I sucked at asking for help or emotional support. I didn't realise how much my family loved me, and had difficulty to connect with them, or even to allow myself to be open to them in my most vulnerable time.

I was fuming about my mother. Now it seemed Lara had turned against me too. I felt immensely betrayed. They took John's side, and I felt shunted to the gutter because I stood up to the abuse we experienced. My mom blocked me from seeing my brother. My sister avoided me, and she had much anger towards me. My mom blamed me. It was a dark time. Secretly, though, sometimes my mom would send Lara to the halfway house with money I could use for food and toiletries. John never knew about this.

My mother loved going to Port St. Johns on the Wild Coast in the Eastern Cape province. We'd been going there for years. It's the most magnificent, wild, and generous coastal landscape surrounded by conservation areas. An estuary mouth snakes out from the landscape surrounded by cliffs and luscious vegetation. One year while I was still a full-on junkie, she bought four beadwork owls there, one larger than the other three. These owls signified herself as our mother, and Alex, Lara, and me. Her three children.

One day, not long after she forbade me to see Alex, she messaged me and said she had put my owl on the grave of my grandfather. She could no longer look after me. She was sorry. She asked my grandfather's spirit to please help, because she didn't know what to do any more.

I said this was preposterous. I can look after myself. I told her there were many people who cared about me. Also, my Higher Power has never let me down. I decided to speak to my Aunt Elizabeth, who is the sanest member of our family, with her feet solidly on the ground.

She wears her golden blonde hair in locks around her shoulders, and her blue eyes are filled with welcome and comfort. Her motherly beauty and loving way have kept us all warm during hard times. She has the softest way about her, but also does not take shit. She has an acid undertone when she gets irritated and has been pushed too far. I told her what happened. She was speechless with shock. I said she shouldn't worry about it but asked her to help me find my grandfather's grave. I didn't know where it was in the graveyard and I didn't know who else to ask. Elizabeth and I used to be attached to each other. Years ago, she looked after me as if I were her own. After the owl story, we reconnected. She took me to my grandfather's grave, and we found the owl. She held on to it for a while and took care of it. It was then passed on to Anna. My owl now has a view of the beautiful Stellenbosch.

CHAPTER 4

A Miracle

I moved into my own place after working at the Pharma company for a few months. I needed to get on my feet properly for the first time. It was daunting. I was on a dark ocean, on an abandoned ship, the sails set high, the wind screamed in my ears; I navigated the storm by myself. I discovered a therapist who has played a huge part in my recovery and rediscovery. Gabriel has been described as a teddy bear with a hand grenade. I told my mother to pay for the therapy. I didn't care what she said. She agreed.

And finally, I had my own space again! It was a small cottage on a farm. It had an open-plan kitchen and lounge, one bedroom, and one bathroom. It was fantastic to finally have my belongings in one place again. The last time I had everything in one place was before I moved in with Victor. My mother had been paying for my storage and I collected my furniture from the facility. I moved the rest of my stuff from my mom's house and picked up the bits and pieces at Samantha's place.

It was easy to get to work from my cottage – I drove against traffic most of the time. I left quite early and always arrived at work before everyone else. I got home late. The evenings were wonderful. I didn't even own a TV. I read books, wrote in my diary, and healed. At times, I cried. But mostly, I was delighted. I sat outside on a blanket under the stars and spoke to God. I loved being on my own. I needed the solitary interval. I learnt to accept my emotions, no matter what. I was okay; it was okay to feel so intensely. Nature heals, and I mended many parts of me there.

But I was too isolated and soon started obsessing.

Isla Stone

2013/09/03

Loneliness.

Am I the only one on the planet today? Anna was supposed to visit today. She drives everywhere all the time. She has other friends in isolated places. When she told me she wanted to come past me today, I was sick, but I said yes. I missed therapy and work because of that. I went through the trouble of cleaning up extra properly. Then she called to say she had missed my turn-off. She blamed me. I felt terrible, but Sam said I must not take it on. It wasn't my fault. At least Samantha's helped me to not feel so damn guilty. Still, it's rotten that my mother is ignoring me. My father is going through his own shit. And the one person I'm connected to in my family just told me off.

It's harder than I expected to live on my own. I was excited by the notion, I still am, but I live far from everything. Now I'm not sure if it's a good thing. Will anyone want to come visit me?

I'm second-guessing my decisions again. Two women at work asked me where I stay, and they seemed shocked when I told them. I guess if I earned what they did, I wouldn't have to live so far away. But I love it here. I adore the monkeys, horses, and pigs. The mountains inspire me. I enjoy the open space and I like nature. Even if I earned a million fucking Rand a year I would still live here. So, fuck all them all! I enjoy aloneness. I get to listen to Beethoven. Who else listens to Beethoven?

70

My mother isn't available at all. Samantha is always available, my sponsor is always available, Barbara tries to be available. There are many good people in my life. It's time for me to stop focusing on the people who aren't there for me, and to start focusing on those who are.

I must do step work.

2013/09/05

Sometimes I go on and on. I charge ahead, and I push severely hurtful things to the back of my mind. These are the important things I should concentrate on. My brother is important to me.

When I push along in this vein, one day, if I have a bad day, a really horrid, stressful day – boom – I'm fucked. Then the smallest thing can bruise me. Hearing my brother's voice in the background during a conversation with my mother over the phone can put me in agony. I feel an abundance of love for that sweet, innocent little child; and huge sorrow because I haven't been allowed to see him for such a long time. Knowing what I know about the emotional abuse both he and my mother experiences at home by my stepfather and feeling frustrated because there is nothing I can do about it. My sponsor told me that pain is growth. I guess I'm growing. I had a sudden bizarre urge to drink today. But I didn't.

2013/09/15

Something broke inside me today. I listened to Josh Groban and started dancing slowly, powerfully. Tears streamed down my cheeks while he sang about loving a woman who is still the same, despite the hardships she was dealt in her life.

The last time I danced like that I must have been nineteen. In my own room. I realised there is still me in me. It's beautiful; I haven't lost myself. The bitter-sweet tears won't stop. Sweet because I haven't lost this delightful piece of me. Bitter because I've missed her immensely. What a strange and engulfing feeling! I'm jumping out of my emotional skin. It's magnificent.

I drove home from work on the N14 one day. The rain always seems to be worse on that side of town. Dark clouds loomed, and then broke. Lightning sizzled; thunder went off all around me. The highway was filled with water. I could not see far ahead and crept along with my hazards on. I hoped to survive this raging weather. It was by far the worst storm I had ever driven in. My car aquaplaned a few times. Electric thunderbolts rode the clouds, and I followed them while they barged across the dark sky. They were so close. I moved my eyes to the left; just across the horizon, a lightning bolt hit the ground and a strange silence fell. Suddenly an aurora of colours emanated from the skyline. I was breathless at this beauty. I told myself repeatedly I just had to get off the highway, and then I'd be fine. Once I got to the offramp, I whispered 'just ten more kilometres'. Halfway to my home on a stretch of pot-holed road, I noticed a telephone pole that must have been struck by lightning. There were sparks flying everywhere, it was comparable to watching a movie. Two seconds later, a shadow passed in the corner of my left eye and a large white owl came into view. It flew over the flashes, spreading its majestic wings over the spectacle. I knew it was a message: I wasn't alone in my personal storm.

2013/11/19

It's a waste of time to worry. It doesn't change anything. It clouds my judgement and I end up making terrible decisions or no decisions at all. I sink deeper into the pit instead of getting out. Avoiding things also doesn't help. Everything seems to be falling into place, slowly, but it's getting there. I stare into space and think about how worry depletes me. I muse about how exhausted I am of not having money, how bushed I am of holding on to my mother, Alex and Lara but not having them at all. I'm wearied by my self-pity. I'm tired of always being positive and smiling while the worry machine churns inside. Will I have a job a few months from now? Will I make it out of this financial dump? Will I ever be able to buy a new cell phone or get a new lease on a place? I worry about whether I'll ever find a husband, I agonise that I may not be good enough for God, I worry whether … This apprehension is such a waste of time and energy. It wears me out to even write about it.

I'm good enough for God.

I'll have a great job in three months.

I'll become financially independent in the next three months.

I'll buy a wonderful new cell phone on contract for myself in the next three months.

I'm healthy right now.

I'll find someone wonderful and amazing to marry.

> *I'm letting go of my worries and handing them over to God.*

In my early twenties, whilst studying Nature Conservation at the technikon, I made three friends. Two of them became a couple soon after we formed our group. They were the smart people in the class, with ridiculously amazing marks for their exams and projects. Despite my best efforts, I saw my own work as mediocre compared to theirs. I felt less intelligent than them and did not imagine myself ever getting as far as they would in life. The last part of our quartet was a different story. He failed year after year, but he was stubborn and persistent. He got his diploma a couple of years after I dropped out. We stayed friends throughout the years, and he pursued his career in conservation for a while, then gradually moved into the more lucrative mining industry. Our friendship lasted for about twelve years after our studies. While I lived in the cottage, he often visited me. He would drop by and take me on fishing trips, or just come and chat. His friendship pulled me through that time and helped me while I was trying to isolate. He refused to leave me alone as often as I wanted to be. He became a good friend.

But things are not always as they appear, and I'm exquisitely talented at hiding the truth from myself. I lost his friendship because of my blind stubbornness. The end of our friendship was awkward. I realise that he became toxic over time too. Maybe he had a low self-esteem, maybe it was because he was surrounded by toxic people in his workplace. One weekend we went away to a lovely camping site in Clarens. There were many birds and a huge river where we could fish. I was in a bad way emotionally, and he treated me with a lovely dinner. When it finally came time to turn in, he came on to me sexually in the tent. I said no. When we got home after the weekend, he tried to kiss me, and I lost my temper. I couldn't understand why he refused to accept my 'no'. I did not realise that he was in love with me. I saw him as a platonic friend and always will. If I had known it earlier, I would have walked away from our friendship. I would not have broken his heart. The friendship ended there. Everything happens for a reason and we interact with people when we need to learn the biggest lessons from each other.

2013/12/04

Acceptance.

It's the day before Lara's birthday and I feel like a stranger to myself. Completely unfocused on anything, I bought more Angel Cards. These are directed at dealing with energies and the universal.

Maybe I'm feeling strange because it's almost Christmas time. This is the first year that I'll be on my own. I saw Gabriel today and he said I was like a character in a sitcom. He told me I wasn't engaged in our work and if I wasn't serious about therapy, he would kick me out. That woke me up from my unravelling. I'm bursting at the seams; the emotions don't want to surface properly. I cried on my way home. At least something came out. I grasped to what extent music holds the key to my emotions. Queen played on the radio and I recalled how my mom used to sing. She would perform with such passion and gusto! I was close to her in those cherished moments. Now I'm no longer a part of her world – in fact I'm apart from her world.

Tearing myself away from the co-dependent relationship with her helped me to develop into the person I need to be. At the same time there is a big gaping mother-shaped hole left where she used to be.

Feeling lonely again. But I know self-pity won't improve things. It is okay to feel sore and sad and to have a sense of loss. But I don't have to delve into purposeless misery. There is a big difference between the two.

2013/12/15

Mistakes.

It's stupid to go to clubs to show my sister that I can 'Party' without alcohol or drugs. It's a lie and mistake. Not because I can't, but because I don't enjoy it. I don't want to be untrue to myself any more.

This weekend I went clubbing with La and her friends. It was a bit of a time warp. The names of places have changed, the clothes have changed, but the empty, soulless, meaningless existence of everyone is still the same. Doing those things no longer impressed me. I disliked every moment. I felt shame and guilt this morning as though I had used. I felt sick the whole day. I still don't feel great; shaky, sicky tummy, sinus, prickly eyes. Who knows what they put into those smoke machines? The music was too loud, the energy affected me. Now I know how my body reacts in memory to those surroundings. It triggers everything I did in the past.

It's not me any more, I don't want that type of affirmation, I loathe the scene. I've grown up. I value myself beyond that setting. Now I must just find what it is that I do enjoy.

The journey of self-discovery had finally reached a certain momentum. After I lifted the unbearably heavy anchor of my past, a clear blue sky emerged from the depths of this storm I was riding on my lonesome ship. One afternoon, my Aunt Anna called. She finally had the opportunity to move back to Stellenbosch. My heart sunk into my shoes. I was happy for her but miserable for me. Why did she have to leave? I needed her to mother me; I needed her to guide me. Who would make me warm milk and talk to me about my trials and tribulations?

Samantha asked me to be a House Manager at the halfway house quite often, especially over weekends. I made extra money doing this and I learnt a lot about myself and how well I managed stressful situations. Addicts do weird and wonderful things.

When Anna left, she came past the halfway house where I was working that afternoon. We met in a nearby park. Her two dogs waited in the car, already tranquilized for the one-thousand-five-hundred kilometre road trip. I thanked her, and she showed me the owl. She took it from my other aunt, Elizabeth. Anna promised to look after 'me' in Stellenbosch until I can join her. I cried. It was the end of a journey. She left a little hole in my soul. Looking back, I know I wasn't navigating this ship on my own. Anna, Samantha and Gabriel were at the helm with me. They helped me to steer the ship in the right direction.

The Universe had never abandoned me.

CHAPTER 5

A New Season

The Pharma company had a pleasant canteen with a bottomless pot of filter coffee and good food. The staff got a monthly canteen fund. I gained weight there initially. I fancied the muffins and the scones way too much! In the mornings when I felt upbeat, I would switch on my laptop and greet whoever was there. On vulnerable days, I kept my head down, got coffee, and traipsed downstairs to have a smoke.

Initially, as I settled into my new post, and prior to being appointed permanently, I obsessed about their impressions of me. Eventually, I was appointed as a Financial Analyst although I didn't have a degree. My desk faced the door and colleagues who passed by could all see me. I would sit nervously and imagine 'They think I'm a fraud'. Or 'They think I don't know what I'm doing'. 'How will we ever get rid of her?' Those thoughts crossed my mind every single time someone sauntered past the doorway. It happened all the time and it exhausted me. At the end of the day I would get home, sink into bed and beat myself up about all my failures. I dropped out three times in uncoordinated attempts to get a qualification at respectively two universities and a technikon. My maths marks were dreadful at school. I deemed myself less capable than others. My mistakes enraged me. Regrets engulfed me. My mind was my harshest adversary; my way of thinking was my worst enemy.

One day on my way upstairs after a smoke break, my phone rang. It was my cousin Lily, my Aunt Elizabeth's daughter. I was the first of the children to arrive in this generation within the family on both my parents' side and Lily is four years younger than me. Before I could even greet her, she jumped in and asked if I wanted to move in with her. She had recently broken up with her long-time boyfriend and she needed a place to stay. I was drained from driving such long distances between the farm and the city and my current lease was about to expire, so I agreed. It happened in an instant; we made the decision to move in together in November 2013. For the next two months we looked for a place, but the right one eluded us. On a rainy day close to our due date a rude woman showed us an expensive duplex in an upmarket suburb in Centurion. It was splendid! It was also close to the school where Lily would teach, and we convinced ourselves to take it.

We had the most exquisite view – there was a nature reserve opposite the road, and we were right next to a river. The ambience was therapeutic and calm. Our home had a wooden staircase, two bathrooms, two bedrooms and a lovely living area. We had a balcony on the top floor and another one at ground level. I got the upstairs bedroom. We had more than enough space for the both of us to have our own 'me time.'

My move was sudden and unplanned. A friend out of the support groups agreed to help me. While I tried to sort bits and bobs on a blanket at the old place, the guy came and took all four corners of the blanket. He wrapped it up and threw it onto the back of his truck. My bed was a problem because the staircase in the new house was too narrow. I had this bed since I was sixteen. It was old, but the frame was still perfect. I was amused and chilled at the same as I watched them hoisting my big bed between the two balconies with a little bit of rope and a lot of shouting.

Despite our lovely new home, I was still not in a good space.

2014/01/04

> I feel out of sorts. Who knows why? I'm gloomy and
> morose; nothing I do or nothing anyone else says can
> me make feel any better about where I'm in my life. I
> suppose I can view it as a positive; or a negative. I'm
> breaking away from the abysmal waters I've ever been

in; a yawning black hole forcefully pressing down on my chest. It's getting lighter now, but I'm weary, exhausted, and hurting.

This may simply be a pity party. It's an endless struggle. I don't feel sexy. I'm lonely. My room is not how I want it, my clothes are dirty in the corner, I have one cabinet with most of my life still in boxes packed away where I can't see it. Beloved books in boxes. Things on the floor. My bed a lonely flat thing. Nothing fits, nothing is perfect, and I guess it's just so me. Organised chaos. I don't know what I'm planning this year. I'm not sure what to do.

John doesn't respond to my messages. It makes me feel rejected. Why should I feel shunned? I miss my brother. I don't want to apologise, I refuse to. I feel like crap for being decent to John. I'm done with sending messages to him now. Why should I be civil with a man who destroyed me and my family and took my innocence? Let it be as it is. I have forgiven, I've tried, I've asked for help from the Divine Creator of All Things. Nothing more is required of me. I don't have to feel guilty. I have done nothing wrong. I'm more than capable of achieving what others think is impossible. Whatever my path may be, I'm already at the perfect place and the right time doing the right thing. My perfect moment is now, even though it is hard to accept.

The first rule in recovery is to not get into a relationship in the first year. (Well, there are many rules, but this is one of the big ones.) Barely out of recovery, we're still somewhat unaware of who we are and what we want. We're damaged, and our bodies and minds are still healing from the many hours of chemical abuse. Therefore, rational decision-making about relationships is impaired.

I went to meetings frequently and keenly. I met a much older man at a meeting. A much, much older man. I wasn't in love or even especially attracted to him physically. His knowledge enchanted me. I wanted to know more about the Program, and I wanted to know more about spirituality. I thought I would get to understand things better if I got to know him better. Before long, we had sex. We did have a soft spot for each other, but wisdom and knowledge are not sexually transmitted. There were additional reasons for my behaviour: self-destruction, acting out, neediness, father issues. The list goes on.

2013/01/13

> *I feel guilty and terrible about myself. I feel irresponsible and careless. I know I'm none of these things.*
>
> *Over the weekend I looked after the halfway house. I was already quite tense because I had just finished a shift there last Saturday. I recently moved into a new place and nothing is organised yet. My life is unsettled and messy, confused, cluttered. I'm dog-tired. On Saturday morning I went to my first CrossFit training class. I'm super motivated and still have remnants of the energy running through my veins. I enjoyed it and felt rejuvenated. I also went to see my mom and Lara. It was a nice visit, but then the day went downhill. My dad called me to say my grandfather has passed away. I felt bleak, but promptly pulled myself out of the pain. I had to look after the house.*
>
> *I chilled at the house and waited for Barbara; she came to visit at about 17.00. One of the guys was troublesome because he had to face the consequences of his addiction. He was demanding, but he didn't act out as such. When Barbs arrived, he asked me and Samantha for*

permission to go shopping and we both agreed that he could go. Barbs and I went to buy pizza a bit later.

We came back with pizza and watched a movie. After a while, the same guy asked to go out again. I said yes but gave him a time limit of ten minutes. He came back in good time. Barbs and I came out from the room after about an hour to get coffee. The boys walked in from the darkness in the back yard. It seemed suspect, like they did something they weren't supposed to.

By Monday the guy went AWOL and relapsed. Should I have been more vigilant? Harder? More forward? Or would this have happened anyway? On Sunday I told Samantha what happened the night before. She told me to always be honest with her if I notice anything untoward. I was distraught and asked her if I could leave the house for a while. I went to see my old friend to speak to him about step work. We had sex. Maybe this is where all the guilt comes from. Why do I still do this? Even after all the therapy? Am I imbecilic? Is it because I have guilt around sex? Why? Guilt and shame, embarrassment for allowing myself to let it happen again. Anger because he wouldn't respect my wishes. He just pushed ahead. This guy is dangerous for me. He is detrimental to my recovery and my path with him is over. There is no need for me to feel guilty. I'm not perfect, I acted out, but that is okay. I accept myself; I love myself with all my imperfections and perfections. I'm a good soul. I'm full of love. I'm love and I'm loved. To be honest with myself is to be honest with God.

In my case, I had – apart from father issues – obviously also grandfather issues …

My grandfather owned a plot on the outskirts of one of the cities and a game farm in the Bushveld. In addition to being his romantic partner after splitting up with my dad, my mom used to work for him. We would often go to the farm. I sat in the back of the car while the car flew across the landscape to get there as quickly as possible. She would pay the staff and do the other business she had to do there. Because I used to get carsick, she would often drive at night while I slept.

The farm was wonderous. I loved seeing the wild animals, the giraffe, zebra, kudu, and impala. There were chalets close to the river, and the grounds were fully equipped with trampolines and tennis courts. It ran as a lodge with people booking for a weekend or holiday getaway; some people came to hunt. My younger uncles would often take me along when they went hunting. We'd drive back with the kill on the back of the truck. Once, I freakishly pushed my finger into the dead eye of an animal; trying to will it back to life. Preparing the meat to make biltong, they would systematically cut the skin from the body, then remove the insides, then cut the flesh while the bodies hung from a hook on a tree with the smell of death in the air. I could not have been older than four or five.

In the evenings when my mom had to entertain the guests around the fire, I would socialise along with her. They thought it was hilarious when I pulled off my underwear to moon everyone. I was often naked in the bushveld when I was this age, on the rocks by the river or between the trees.

I loved my grandfather when I was younger. I was still too small to see his dysfunction. I merely saw a kind-eyed old man who loved me. He gave me hugs and would do anything to keep me happy. He really cared for me when I was small. I remember how I *felt* about him when I was younger. Not who he *was*.

My grandfather had many children from many different women. My dad and his brother and sister are the eldest. After them came three more, and then another, and then the youngest of the eight children. My father struggled as much to be present with integrity in his own life as his own father had. My dad fought for many years to get the affirmation he pined for from his father. Even with his shortcomings, my dad was a better father to me than his dad was to him.

I was heartbroken about my grandfather's death. As an adult, I had difficulty coming to grips with the fact that he wasn't a good man. My belief in his goodness was based on the emotions I experienced as a small child. One night when I cried forlornly about my dad, my grandfather came in and sat on my bed with tears in his eyes. He promised me to always be there for me, no matter what. He said he would never desert me. He would never do what my father had done.

When I grew older, I began to consider why my father might not have wanted to be around then. He felt that my mother had betrayed him. And my grandfather mislead him even more. The resentment hurt and embarrassment might have been too much for my dad. Without excusing or condoning his behaviour, I'm considering how bizarre this situation was, and what his experience may have entailed.

My grandfather was undoubtedly a piece of work. The last time I saw my him, I was around fourteen years old. Our interaction was uncomfortable. He didn't approve of my upbringing. I said something he was annoyed with. In his later life, he took on a sour, choleric stance on other races, religions, and cultures. He was a prejudiced old man who would say terrible things based purely on his anger and resentment. This is where I came to believe that resentment and fear set people apart more than anything else.

In my early teens, I got to spend time with my dad more often. Our relationship started mending slowly. After his second divorce, he lived on the farm with my grandfather when I was a teen. It seemed that time had healed my father and my grandfather's relationship. My father lived in the one house. He ran a newspaper printing company from this house. He had his own printing press and used to print stories, shirts and business cards. My other uncle was a mechanic who worked in my grandfather's workshop. My grandfather received a subsidy from a business partner. Many years earlier he started setting up the farm by revamping the chalets and lodge area. He had big plans to transform the lodge into an international conference venue fully equipped with all the trimmings. When President Nelson (Madiba) Rolihlahla Mandela was set free in 1992 and the South African political landscape changed forever, my grandfather's international investors pulled out of the venture.

Suddenly he was stuck with a half-built conference centre with no funding and no means to continue with the tourism venture he had in mind initially. Because he kicked off with a full renovation and not a gradual change, he was left in a lurch. I suspect he gave up, or had his mind set on only one way of doing things. As time passed, he filled himself with ireful stories and miserable feelings. He worked against the people who lived in the areas around him, and they pushed back. Eventually the farm became a dark energy of shadowy has-beens and could-ifs; only a memory in the mind of this earth child who learnt how to love the smell of the wild as a small girl on the banks of the river.

2014/02/24

> *I worked at the halfway house again this weekend. It was exhausting, and when I'm so tired it's hard to see how my work there contributes to the meaningfulness of my days. I have to remind myself that it helps me grow. It solidifies my ability to calmly confront certain situations I would never have dreamt of facing previously.*

> *Barbara has been in a bad space. I worry about her. The weekend was taxing at the halfway house because she helped me catch a guy who might have been using since he got admitted to the house. We found a condom with piss in it – right out of his bag. Unbelievable.*

2014/02/25

> Guilt.

> *I dislike the medical aid health card and assessment. I fear I may have damaged my body irreparably with a chronic illness because of reckless sex. I feel guilty about having loveless sex and for not treating my body like a temple.*

2014/03/07

> *I'm exhausted, beaten, sick, lonely, and grim. I've lied to myself again. I recently met a man. I liked him from the word go. He wore an old pair of rugby shorts and a t-shirt when we met. This is the second time Lily and I went to listen to live bands together. We love it, but I'm probably asking for trouble. Hang out in a barber shop for long enough and you will get a haircut. I became slightly reckless with my recovery. Looking on it now it scares me because I might have relapsed so easily. Exposing it here makes me feel safer and I'll speak to Gabriel too.*

> *We sat on the grass listening to the music when a group of guys invited us to sit with them in the shade. We happily accepted. This guy likes drinking. I understand this is a test for me. I know what I want. He wanted us to visit him at his place, but we declined. Already I wasn't sure about him, I had my doubts. He drinks, he has a low self-esteem and a shitload of baggage. He boldly says he can't be trusted, yet also claims to be honest. How contradictory ...*

> *He did not contact me for some time, then texted to*
> *wish me happy Valentine's Day. After about three weeks*
> *of silence, his name suddenly popped up on my phone*
> *again and he asked if I wanted to go out. Lily has a crush*
> *on him but she's trying to pretend that she doesn't. It's*
> *irritating. I'm keen on him and her coyness pisses me*
> *off. He is playing a game. Night three I slept with him,*
> *thinking he was interested. I was sexually frustrated,*
> *vulnerable, and exhausted. I blithely spread my legs.*
> *Just like in the old days. I'm annoyed about still doing*
> *destructive things to myself.*

Lily filled the hole Anna left behind. I didn't quite see it then. I don't think she did either, but we needed each other. We both had to heal the wounds we carried then. We were the perfect partners. We had some hiccups initially. She wanted a large dustbin; I wanted a small one. She wanted to cook dinner every evening; I wanted everyone to starve. She wanted the dishes to be washed; I wanted them to chill in the basin until they got green fungi and grew legs. I had a bit of growing up to do, and so did she. She had to grow in areas I already had growth spurts in. I needed to grow where she had already grown. I helped her with communication. I showed her how to facilitate healthy confrontation. We taught ourselves together about this new thing called self-love. She was on a more religious quest, whilst I leaned more towards a spiritual one. I read many books about positive self-regard.

I focused on Louise Hay and Osho. That positively started shifting things. Previously, I understood the concepts intellectually, but I wasn't yet ready to apply them. I have several historical journal entries where I write about spiritual growth, about looking after myself in the right way – these entries were written in 2010 when I still used drugs, drank and binged on food. Self-destructing at my best. However, until I made the first decision for me that showed a drop – an inkling – of self-love and self-preservation in a time of absolute chaos I wasn't able to change things for the better or grow the way I wanted to. That decision was getting sober and starting my spiritual odyssey.

Lily loved her church, she dragged me along once or twice. Aunt Anna was a devoted Christian as well. It was uncomfortable for me, I felt as if I was doing something wrong or being disloyal to them, especially Anna. I was afraid to burn in the damnation of hell for eternity. Still, I pushed Christianity aside. I have an aversion to organised religion; I grappled with many concepts in it. The Bible was difficult to understand, and every time I read a piece in mine, I felt flagellated. My dislike was of course related to the way in which religion was forced on me as a child, as well as my grandfather's fire and brimstone view of religion.

When I was in primary school my mother sent me to Sunday school on my own. One day they spoke about Revelations, the end of times. They said the good people would be swept up to heaven, but the bad ones would stay behind on earth. It scared me witless and stuck with me for many years. Whenever I shared a bed with my sister, I would make sure our feet touched. If she disappeared in the middle of the night, I would know right away. It's terrible that a little girl of eleven should carry this fear of being left behind and this burden of feeling sinful.

I know my Higher Power is unconditionally loving and forgiving. I know I'm always safe and protected. Even though I make mistakes, it's okay that I learn from them and do my best to change myself for the better daily. I'll always be loved no matter what happens. I can have dreams and aspirations. I'm more than capable of achieving them with my Higher Power's guidance. My Higher Power is on time, holds my hand and encapsulates me with huge amounts of love beyond my comprehension. But I can feel it in wonderment. I don't have to go to a place of worship once a week and when I open myself up to my Higher Power, I can always be connected if I choose to be. This love is unconditional. I'm one with my Higher Power – I experience joy, freedom, and elation when I'm in alignment and in the right vibration. I'm a co-creator with my Creator. It's fantastic to be joyful, happy, and jubilant, but it's okay not to feel that way too. Life's contrasts help me to understand where I want to be. It creates ways for me to get there. The Law of Attraction does not require constant elation for successful manifestation. It's cardinal to release judgements about happenings, and the cause of events, and why one feels a particular way. I continually learn how to change the thought patterns I established from my early life, to the ones I have now, to the best ones I hope to have in the future. It's crucial to understand that loving myself is part of this spiritual process. If I grasp and live this lesson from my Higher Power, I'll grow exponentially in this lifetime.

Lily and I shared a straining neediness for men. This is where my obstacle became clear to me. I edited a few of my journal entries – they were too painful to share. I would obsess about a guy here and there. I would then become horribly embarrassing, leave notes on their cars or bump into them on purpose and blush profusely. I had no confidence about my ability to communicate with the opposite sex. My therapy sessions focused on this extensively, especially because my previous behaviour was utterly dysfunctional. I either scarcely met someone and slept with them while incapacitated (before my recovery), or I slept with them while not drunk (in my recovery) before the first date had even started, or I just slept with them. There wasn't anything in me that said, 'Isla you are worthy and worth more to a man than sex. Intimacy is more than just having sex. Sex is not the only way that a man will see you or appreciate you. You are more than a sexual object. You have a mind. Words come out of your mouth. You have a personality.'

At the beginning of my recovery I abided by the rule of not falling into a romantic relationship. No-one came near me, mainly because I kept my head down. Besides, I have a stupidity about me when it comes to men. I never quite knew when a guy came on to me. However, when I had to start working on it, it was a different story.

2014/03/30

It has become increasingly demanding for me to write during the last few months. Mainly because I have so many mixed feelings. Invariably I'm left with an empty pain because my self-worth and spirituality has reached an all-time low. I guess it's a vicious circle: I feel this way because I stopped writing and am not allowing myself to put my thoughts and feelings down on a piece of paper.

How is it that after all my work I still end up with a sense of uselessness and desertion? I'm deserting myself in the same way everyone else has deserted me. I've tried to do the right things, to take the right actions – but looking back maybe I tried to serve myself only in this whole saga. I'm not a victim; I'm a survivor. I said this the other day, but some days I feel like a child filled with fear and doubt. Dwelling on my behaviour, trying to analyse every thought, makes me feel egocentric and self-interested. Why am I allowing myself to freely delve into now irrelevant pasts?

I have constructed walls around myself, especially with my family and the eons of thinking no-one appreciated me. That self-centred wall kept me from appreciating others. It is still difficult to change, to not feel the way I do when I'm around them. It helps to write it down. Then I face all the weird emotions and clean my chest cavity.

I must remind myself regularly that I'm good enough for me, I'm strong enough, I'm intelligent enough, I'm radiant, I'm compassionate and loving. If I don't do this, I end up blocking myself, my soul and my love from shining as it should.

2014/03/31

Soaring.

If I could have things differently, or if I could choose my life with no limitations, no fears, no hardships or past pains, if I could have all the wisdom in the world, all the resources at my disposal, all the freedom I ever wanted. What would I choose?

I would choose to pursue my passion to study nature. To do research in the rain forests, in savannahs, on mountain-tops, in deserts. Absorb everything the earth has to offer as it was meant to be and understand it. The grass, the trees, the soil, and the animals. The grand crescendo of life.

If I could go back to when I was twenty-one knowing what I know now I would see how much I must be grateful for. If I could grow from there again, I would be where I want to be today. I've pleased others far too often and never allowed myself to get what I deserved. I hurt myself. I'm done with that right now. At this moment I have all the resources, wisdom, and freedom I need. I choose to let myself be who I was meant to be all along.

2014/04/06

So many ideas, so many things I've wanted to do. However, at the end of all those ideas was an ego. A greedy thirst to be perceived as something that I'm not.

What do I want to do? What is my life purpose? Those questions bear no answers; they are the questions of the ego. How can I serve? If I help others help themselves am I not in essence helping myself? If I look after myself and develop a strong, loving relationship with myself, I can achieve that.

I've always craved finding my life's purpose. I had this idea that anything – no matter how impossible – is possible. Anyone can reach their dreams. I would reach a point of getting so close to making up my mind that *this* is what I wanted to do, that *this* was my life's purpose, that I was finally doing something to make all the blocks fall into place. Then, after some time, it would fizzle out. The thing I was pursuing no longer fuelled the blaze of passion. The roaring, sparkling flames turned into embers, then into ashes. Every time, I was left feeling empty and unfulfilled. I would desperately move to the next thing insisting that I must surely have a purpose. I was adamant to have a meaningful career because I considered myself unimportant in my role as family member. I also reckoned the other spheres of my life were relatively pointless. It was crucial that my profession – what I did to make money, but also how I served others – should be meaningful. What purpose could I serve? I couldn't decide. Psychology came to mind. Or perhaps becoming a doctor. Or a veterinarian? What about being an ecologist? A Palaeobotanist possibly …

I was a terrible student. I had anxiety problems. I struggled terribly with my self-worth, but there was a fundamental error in my ability to find the inner self-love to do the work for myself. I did it for everyone else. Not for me. I wanted to be recognised for what I achieved. It's like anything else in life: if I do something for someone else, for affirmation and not for my own well-being, I'll fail. The only course I ever finished was a massage course that I attended for six months in the middle of active addiction. That didn't mean much to me. I always had these outstanding ideas about how great it would be to finally allow myself to be what I thought I wanted to be, an academic of sorts. I now realise it would have bored me to tears. I find ideas and concepts irresistible for a while, but then I become saturated and move on to the next intellectual thrill. I had to find my own interests. My interests lie in spiritual growth, in life, in everything.

When I still drank like a sailor with Victor, we ran into a woman he knew. She was a seer of sorts. She looked at my palms and said two things to me. She said, 'Your father loves you, and you need to start living life'.

Those two statements unsettled me.

I've had this recurring topic of my father in my life, and the living life thing. That touched a nerve.

CHAPTER 6

Disillusionment A Moment Back in Time

At the age of nineteen, after high school, I took a gap year. I didn't know what to do with the rest of my life. I had several romanticised ideas about how the world worked and decided to do volunteer work abroad. I found a UK-based youth development organisation doing worldwide charity work. I decided to go with them. I wanted to go to Malaysia in Borneo for three months. It would be the longest time I'd ever been away from home.

I was so nervous that I broke into hives before my first telephonic interview. With a lot of support from my mom, I managed to fulfil the prerequisites, complete the interviews, see to the banking requirements, visas and all the rest. There were trips to the travel clinic and health assessments. There were swimming tests.

I had worked for my mom and John's company for a while to save money for my trip. I also raised some additional funds. I wrote a letter to one or two of John's colleagues to request their help. I managed to make up more than half of the monies and fortunately my parents helped me with the rest.

No-one thought I would really follow through with this larger than life thing I decided to do, but I had made up my mind. My mother was in a daze while she helped me pack my rucksack. I could only take five sets of clothes. I was a shy, frightened little girl and I would travel across half of the planet to do this thing that I had no idea about.

My Grannie, sister, mother, John and Alex came to the airport to say goodbye to me. I sat next to Grannie, holding tightly onto her hand, as I always do when I'm with her. She tearfully handed me a little teddy bear. She told me to hold on to it if I got afraid. I held onto it a couple of times during the trip. I felt small when I shuffled steadily through the gates at the airport, waving goodbye to my family. I was alone now.

It was an extraordinary experience. This is who I was planning to become! A traveller. An explorer, an adventurer. This would be me. I was almost there. I wasn't sure how it would happen, but I was on my way to the seas far away.

Little Isla never dreamt much about her many future children, or about a picturesque wedding to a perfect man. I didn't want a house with a white picket fence. I wanted to climb on a ship to sail across the seven seas or trek through unexplored tropical jungles. I wanted to explore new terrains and meet fascinating new people.

My first adventure was about to commence.

I'm sharing some of my writings from then to give you an idea of who I was then. There were two journal entries and a letter I wrote to my family. I intended diarising the whole experience, but we were constantly in the damp, humid jungle and relentlessly busy. Yet, this trip signifies the start of the beginning of my life as a young woman who thinks for herself. It signifies the realisation that there was more to life than the toxic, tight-knit family group I was enmeshed in. I had a rocky passage to truly understand what it meant to accept and love myself. This trip was a tiny seed that had now grown to become a little tree.

2004/10/2nd night

> *It's the second night here. Finally, I got to borrow a pen.*
> *I can't concentrate much. They're playing the bagpipes*
> *now. The people here are fantastic, and I've met so many*
> *already.*

Tomorrow I'm leaving this camp. We will go on a trek for the first time. It's exhilarating! I'm just worried that it might rain heavily.

The hammocks are cosy and unexpectedly easy to set up.

2004/10/3ʳᵈ night

We went to jungle camp yesterday. I took a few photos of the vegetation. It was amazing. There were no leeches up to now. I made a local friend; his name is Henry. He wanted a friend from South Africa, and he took my email. I took a photo with him.

The trip of three months was broken down into three phases. First, it was the adventure phase, followed by a phase of community work and then concluded by the third phase, where the focus would be on the environment.

During the first phase we first did a twelve-day trek through the Borneo jungle. The jungle was thick with luscious vegetation. Its mysterious beauty overwhelmed me. There were fourteen of us in the group and we were taught how to use the radio system. We each had our own hammock that was easily set up in the jungle for sleeping at night. You simply tied it between two trees. We tied a tarp overhead like a little roof to keep the rain from soaking us at night. Before we left for our trip, we got the food we had to carry with us. Food parcels carpeted the floors in the meeting area of the place where we were staying. The man handing out the food made a comment to me about my peanut allergy. Peanuts are high in protein and easily dispensed as peanut butter – all the groups got peanut butter for meals. Our group could not get peanut butter because of my allergy. He said, 'The difficult ones are always the ones with food allergies'. I was embarrassed, but there wasn't much I could do about it. I die if I eat peanuts. We got chocolate spread instead. Every group had to be given a certain number of calories per individual per day.

Most of the people who were part of this excursion were from the UK – I was the only South African. It was quite a challenge to understand the array of different English accents. The Liverpool bunch had me especially confused!

We had no access to any roads during the trek and carried everything we needed with us. There were so many river crossings and mountains, and so many crystal-clear pools to swim in. We walked for hours at a time every day. It was exhausting! Our food was most definitely not meant for connoisseurs, but it sustained us. The rivers, streams and paths crawled with leeches. I would often see blood on my pants by my ankles, knowing a leech had found a delicious morsel. Initially it freaked me out. All of us, in fact. Once, after a few hours of trekking, something wriggled down my bum crack. I had a heart palpitation. There was no way I would allow a leech to stay there. I pulled my pants down in a panic and asked a girl I had become friends with to check out my bum. The fourteen of us collapsed with laughter when she reported it to be trickle of sweat. Of course, my white peach-shaped bottom became an ongoing topic of conversation after that.

Because we shared hardship in combination with fun, joy, and adventure we had a close bond from the start.

I almost killed myself twice on this trek. Once I walked with the rest of the group on the edge of a sheer drop with turbulent waters below. We followed a guide in single file, carrying our heavy rucksacks filled with food, gear, and hammocks. I lost my footing at the edge of the drop, then slid down. As I kicked my heels into the soil, I felt the weight of my body and my rucksack on my thighs. With all my might, I managed to push my legs up straight. Just in time, a couple of people grabbed me under my arms and lifted me up before I could slip further. If they hadn't, I would have fallen into the water.

The second time, we were at a river crossing. Like most of the Malaysian men, our guide was short, strong and muscular. The river rushed tempestuously at the crossing. It was raining upstream. These crossings made us all nervous. The group leader asked who wanted to go first and I volunteered. The guide helped me to cross while I held onto the rope he had tied securely from one tree to another across the river, but I lost my footing. The water swept me off my feet. My rucksack went into the water. It dragged me down as it absorbed water. The torrent pulled me down further. After what seemed like minutes, I felt an arm pull me up while I gasped for air. The guide dragged me back to the rope. He pulled me onto my feet, and I managed to cross the rest of the way.

After the twelve-day trek they swept us off to an island called Mamutik. This was part of the adventure phase where we had an opportunity to do our open water divers licenses. We spent more than a week learning how to dive. We had our own island. I wanted to stay there for the rest of my life. I fell in love with diving in those warm waters. It was a miracle to breathe under water. The flamboyant fish blew my mind. I would lay in a yellow hammock on the beach every day at sunset, drinking in the beauty of the colourful clouds on the horizon. I became quite dreamy and peaceful. It was an intensely serene space and for the first time in my life, I felt a sense of spiritual connection with anything.

I also fell into a deep infatuation with my diving instructor. It lasted a short while.

After the diving, our next quest would be to climb the highest mountain in South East Asia. Mount Kinabalu. I wasn't impressed with this. I wanted to stay on the island.

We got onto the boat, then onto the bus and off we went to this huge mountain in the distance. It was awfully daunting. I stared up at the endless, gigantic rock thinking it could not possibly get as cold as they said in the brief. Here, at the foot of the mountain, the vegetation was dense and tropical. I was sweating as much as I did on the first day I arrived in the country. We had to bring very warm clothes and thick gloves. The gear was in my bag waiting for the cold while I scratched my prickly, overheated skin.

As we climbed higher and higher, the air got thinner, more fragile, and the surroundings changed into a desolate, rocky moonscape. It took us two days to climb that mountain. Some people got altitude sickness. They had to stop their ascent. My stomach churned a few times, but I managed to scale the beast. The climb was long and tiring. I put my head down and put one foot in front of the other. Again, and again.

We stayed in an uncomfortable, rat-infested lodge below the peak that night and woke up at 2.00 to watch the sunrise from the peak. I didn't get much sleep. My thoughts crawled back to a story I had read about how rats nibbled at children's faces somewhere in another part of the world. I felt miserable and exhausted the next day. But oh, when I got to the top and saw the sunrise, I felt alive! It was fabulous on that mountain-top.

Hi Mommy, Daddy, La and Ally

> *I miss you guys! Just managed to speak to mommy on the phone, waiting for her to call me back.*
>
> *Hope you're all okay. I've had an adventure and a half! Wow. My first phase was the adventure phase. This is probably the most physically demanding of all the phases. The first bit consisted of a twelve-day trek. We trekked through pure jungle and stopped off in small scattered villages along the way. It was tough though because we had to carry twelve days of food with us for eleven people. I managed of course to dislocate my knee on the second day. I gritted my teeth and carried on for the other ten days. I took a picture of my knee and how bruised it was. It was probably the most painful experience of my life. The second bit of the adventure phase was learning how to scuba dive, and then to help with reef checks. It was incredible. For the duration*

of our course and the reef checks we stayed on a small island called Mamutik. To give you an idea of how small this island is, we basically walked the length of the island to get to the bathroom. Utterly marvellous. I woke up every morning at 5.30 and watched the sunrise on the dock. I was barefoot constantly. Six days of heaven.

But then ... dum dum dum the mountain of terror. Mount Kinabalu. After the six days of bliss we were dragged off the island. More specifically, I was dragged. I was the only one disappointed to leave, everyone else was bored. The mountain laid ahead. We climbed half of it on the first day and slept in a hostel full of rats until 2.00 – yes that is correct! – to climb the rest and worst part of it. It was terrible at the time but seeing that sunrise sort of (not completely) made up for it.

I'm sitting in a room at the Borneo Paradise Hotel now. It's pure, lush luxury. The last twenty days I have not had a warm shower. The water is always bloody cold, in this climate not always a bad thing. But after trekking for twelve days it tends to become more of a necessity.

I've made friends with a handful of locals. Bruno was one of our diving instructors. He is nice. Mae is another brilliant diving instructor. I got an 86 % on my test. So, luckily, I passed. Could have done better though. It's astonishing to breathe under water. And the equipment is cool. Please tell Anna I got my open water divers license. Now we can go diving together. I did mention something to mommy about getting a voluntary job here for a year. I think it's an excellent idea. They need people to work for a longer period, and they'll appreciate it if I stay for a year.

This letter is written in different spaces of time, so sorry if I confuse you!

I spoke to Drew. He said a Japanese or Chinese organisation will take me on to teach English. It might be a good option, because I don't need any qualifications.

After changeover we were put into different groups. Now I'm in a new group where I don't know anyone. These people are cool, don't worry.

We've set up camp. We have a little kitchen and a living area (obviously all in an open space). We get water from the river. We're supervising the project more than doing anything, only because the villagers have taken it into their own hands.

This part of the letter is written two days after leaving Borneo Paradise. I got to speak to Grannie!

The second of the three phases was the installation of the gravity water feeding pipes for communities without running water. It was incredible to stay and work as part of the community, getting to know their charming family-oriented culture. Generation after generation lived in the same home. The people were friendly and warm. They would invite us to their homes for meals and laughter. We played a game that was similar to football, but the ball wasn't allowed to touch the ground, it had to be kept up in the air by kicking it. No hands could be used either. I played with the locals and some of the team members in the afternoons. The men took control of the village matters, whereas the women took control of the family matters. The food was distinctly different to what I was used to. We ate bamboo stalks, squirrel meat, and – infrequently – chicken. The chicken didn't taste like the chicken I was used to. It was always chopped up into small pieces and every piece of meat had a bit of bone in it.

This phase kept us tied to one place for a long time. It got painfully monotonous in the end. We bathed in the river. It was delightful, but I also got a horrible infection on my ankles from mosquito bites. The longer we stayed, the more uneasy I felt. I tried to bond with the other people from the group, but I was timid, and had no alone time. The work was stressful because we had a deadline. The gravity water feeding pipes had to be installed by the end of our phase, the taps needed to have running water by the end of our stay. Everything had to be completed on time. Enthusiastic villagers helped with the digging and installations. Thankfully by the end of our three weeks, after much worrying and strain, we managed to complete the project with the villagers' help. On our last day we left the taps open. No water came out. Then the rain came and after an hour or so, that sweet water gushed out of the taps. We celebrated with so much joy! It was brilliant to know they would finally have running water. When we said goodbye, the women of the village gave me a beaded necklace they'd made for me. I still treasure their gift.

After I got back from this trip – at change over at the hotel – I experienced an inexplicable bout of depression. I was cross with myself. I was on this ideal, breath-taking trip and I felt down? Why?! The more I thought about it the worse I felt. I just pulled straight into myself and did not attempt to make any conversation with anyone. I felt left out and could not bring myself to connect to the rest of the group. I didn't know what to say. I was in paradise, but I was blue. I missed my mom. I found reasons never to go back home. I wanted to teach English in Borneo. If I didn't use my ticket, I may have been stranded there, but I thought if I went back home, I would never get away again. I contemplated my next move. I spoke to my mom during that change over. She would hear nothing of it, John told me I had to study. My notion that going back home would keep me from ever setting foot on this dazzling piece of land again came to fruition abruptly. I was too afraid to go against them, especially John. I didn't want to hurt my mom.

The third phase was the environmental project. We travelled off-road through a forest for several hours to get to our workplace. It was magnificent and awe-inspiring. Gargantuan trees majestically towered above the clouds. Vines swung from the trees; ferns splashed everything with their opulent shades of green. The floor of the forest was littered with old dead leaves and moss. We had a little bunker set up, a longdrop toilet in the distance. We strung our hammocks to trees on the bank of the river. I used to sit there and watch the river or swing in my hammock. Feeling nature. Being alone. I walked blissfully barefoot most of the time in that forest.

We assisted with the building of a basic research facility for scientists. There was virgin rainforest on the other side of the river, and they were studying and discovering new species. We were manual workers for that time. I learnt how to use a hammer and nails. I banged nails into wood, hoping for the best. Every day like clockwork it would rain at the same time, at around three. We would get our soap ready and shower in the rain. Other times when we wanted a thorough clean, we would go down to the river to wash ourselves there.

In the evening I would walk down to a clearing in the woods and sit in the dark staring at the fireflies and the yellow, reflective eyes of the various hidden creatures amongst the trees. I was in a piece of heaven and my heart fractured on the day we left. I knew it was the end of a magnificent adventure. I did not know what waited for me at home and I did not know what I would do when I got there. I held onto hope for a miracle that would allow me a longer stay in Malaysia.

The last celebrations happened where the whole group went to a lodge on an island. By this time, I had managed to lose all my shoes, including my costly trekking boots. I felt a sense of loss. Everyone played around and had fun. I tried my best to take part, to laugh, to look forward to going home. I didn't really. I didn't know why. I did not sleep that last night; I sat in the water off the island with a friend I made and a few other guys. We watched the sun rise in miraculous colours over Mount Kinabalu while the small fish darted around us in the water.

Eventually, we had to get onto the busses. Many of the other folks would travel on, but I didn't have the funds to do that. It was the end of the year, and John and my mom expected me to enrol for a degree the next year. My heart was a heavy boulder when I climbed back on the plane. I cried when the it took off and the woman who sat next to me told me gently that I would be back soon.

She was wrong. My life took a different turn.

CHAPTER 7

Continuing the Journey

In the first six months of living with Lily I frequently worked at the halfway house to supplement my contract work at the Pharma company, where I wasn't yet employed full-time. The halfway house was chaotic. It was an emotionally taxing and exhausting job. I stayed over on weekends. When I slept there, I did not feel rested because I had to sleep with one eye open. I was responsible for these people under my care. They had to be kept safe from each other, and – even more so – from themselves. Samantha trusted me, but I often didn't trust myself and I lacked confidence in my abilities. Whenever I was around someone I had pedestalised in the industry, or a person with loads of experience, I became timid and insecure. I didn't believe much in any of my gifts, and was especially vulnerable when it came to something I was passionate about. Samantha and Frida said I had a gift to work with others in these settings. Nevertheless, it was hard to be confident in real-life situations where I had to say things to participants in groups when others observed me. I knew what to say when I was alone with them, it came naturally. But whenever there was an expectation that I should operate as a leading voice in a group of people, I clammed shut.

Terribly dispiriting things happen in this industry. I've known a bunch of people who did not make it. They are the gratitude stones, the people who make the rest of us appreciate the fact that we're still in recovery; still alive. They encourage us to keep going.

It is as it is.

Some people get help, some people get help and then go back, then some people don't get help and die.

Isla Stone

2014/05/01

> At this moment I'm cosy and warm in my bed. Many
> things happened in the last month. I may be in the
> middle of a transformation, a progressive, magnificent
> change, but I'm in danger of relapse if I don't stay entirely
> focused on myself, my needs, and my growth.

> This spotlight on myself – this self-love – has ignited a
> revolution in my soul. There's a vivid, bright, generous
> red rose opening up in the place where the emptiness
> in my chest used to live. Vibrant colours resonate
> from the aura of this rose, filling my veins with hope
> and contentment. It scares me. It's almost unbearably
> peaceful, here in this moment. But I appreciate peace.
> So, why is it excruciating now? Maybe it's because I'm
> making choices that are in contradiction to my path ...
> There was a moment where I thought I might finally
> find my way if I cut off my bond with my mother. Our
> relationship sat at the heart of so much despondency
> and unmet expectations. I was right. It feels harsh and
> wrong. Right now, I see this inner conflict. I can love
> myself and serve my Higher Power. Or do the same thing
> repeatedly whilst expecting a different result.

One day I received a message from John. He asked me to meet
him at a restaurant. My heart fell into my feet, but I decided to go. It
felt as if I would be facing the devil himself. I asked Barbara to go with
me. He was unstable, and I didn't know why he wanted to see me. We
met at a place close to his office. I was scared stiff. He said he knew
why I left. He told me I hurt him to his core because I lied about him.
I would only be welcome at the house again (and only be allowed to
see Alex) if I apologised.

I said that I remember what I remember. I refused to apologise. John claimed I left because I failed at university. He said I used him as a scapegoat. I nodded mutely. Again, I would not allow him to provoke me into a debate. I had to keep my wits about me, and all I had to remember was that there wasn't anything to apologise for. I did nothing wrong.

Eventually he said I could go to the house on condition that I inform him before I go. He did not want to be there when I was there. I conceded. I didn't tell him about my feelings or my fury because I still had a massive fear of him. I wasn't brave enough to confront him directly yet, but at least I faced him and stood my ground. I survived.

On the 3rd of May 2014 for the first time since I walked out of my parental home, I saw my brother again. His weight gain and the dark rings around his eyes shocked me. There was an anchored heaviness in his eyes that seemed far too much of a burden for a child of thirteen years. He was painfully unhappy and lost. He attempted suicide during my absence. He was preparing himself to jump off the roof of my parent's home, but my mother managed to get him down before he hurt himself.

He was in pain spiritually, it seemed to me that he was screaming for help. This was just one of his many attempts at self-harm throughout his young life. The lack of sleep that haunted him from birth was one of the key factors in his misery. After my return I saw a definite change for the worse in him. As I understand it and from what I heard from my mother, John told Alex I had to leave home because I had seduced him. Alex was confused and hurt about his blood sister seducing his father. He couldn't understand why I would do such a destructive thing.

I had mixed feelings on the day I saw him again. We always had a close bond. He felt like my own child. He was born when I was sixteen. I fed him often, changed his nappies and took care of him when I could. Don't get me wrong: my mother did most of the mothering, but I was a devoted, attentive older sister. I knew we were similar from the day he was born. My mom would often comment about me and Alex being the same. We have a soul connection.

Alex was understandably hurt about my year-long absence as he and I were and are very close. I couldn't tell him why I left because it involved his father. I felt guilty and angry. I was furious with my mother for not letting me see my brother. It took a long time for our relationship to mend and for him to trust me again. If I look back now, I don't think I could have done anything differently. Not in the space that I was in. I had too much emotional trauma to heal while moving into a healthy life.

My brother was anxious and depressed. He hated school and skipped it as often as he could. My mother had a battle to get him to his classes. He constantly played computer games. His behaviour escalated to such an extent that he was placed in the same psychiatric clinic I went to. They booked him in there in 2016 for his addiction to video games. John's verbal and emotional abuse became worse with time.

When I re-entered my family's lives, they told me John was terminally ill. He was born with a heart defect and his heart had now taken a turn for the worse. He started with experimental treatments in 2014 already. They told me the prognosis was bad. Whenever I visited my parents' home that year, I had a huge sense of guilt about John dying. I felt guilty because I had so much anger and resentment towards him. I experienced many paradoxical emotions, including being distraught at the prospect of losing him. I broke down and cried at work the one day. This is the man who abused me. He took away my innocence, but I didn't want him to die. I saw him having an attack one day. He went pale and trembled. Apparently, this was what happened when his heart speeds up. He said it was extremely painful. Both of my closest work colleagues consoled me, they didn't know what to say. I didn't tell them the whole story, but they knew parts of it. I thought he would die soon.

He survived that year and many more. Every so often he would act in an unacceptable way. His abnormal behaviour became a norm for my mother, but I got better and knew how wrong it was. He cheated on her. He treated her and my brother badly. The more I knew the less I wish I knew.

Alex was mired in telling himself how useless he was. The cycle was repeating itself – Alex would have to kick off with a healing voyage similar to mine. He had to do all the hard work from scratch, for himself. I couldn't do it for him.

Two weeks after our reunion, my mother, sister and brother got me a ginger kitten. I was lonely, and they saw it. The animosity between us had settled by then. I named him Ginja the ninja protector of souls. He is my little ginger life-saver. Initially when Lara put him in my arms, she beamed about him being one of the 20 % of female ginger cats. When I took my supposedly girl cat to get neutered, the veterinarian turned Ginja's orange body around and pinched a tiny appendage at the feline's bottom end. The vet asked me what I thought it was. I figured it must be a vagina, but the vet laughed and said it was Ginja's testicles. He then went on to tell me that whoever sexed my kitten at the pet shop was an incompetent oaf.

When I held Ginja in my arms, he looked into my eyes and climbed into my soul. He kept me sane in the times that I thought I would lose my sanity. Lily wasn't impressed when I brought this little treasure home. The reunion with my family was special, but still full of hurt. We tried to move forward without facing the elephant in the room. My mother's excuses for not leaving John ranged from finances to her being Alex's protector.

2014/05/16

> *I step back now and look back at my earlier entries. I've*
> *come so far. I've grown so much and experienced more*
> *than I ever dreamt of in my recovery. Certain entries*
> *remind me of how hard it was to accept my disease. How*
> *I did not believe in myself and the beauty within me.*
> *I'm electrified by what is yet to come. This is still the*

beginning. There are aspects of recovery I'm not paying heed to. My recovery isn't always balanced, my focal point is mainly on meetings. Sometimes speaking to my sponsor and doing step work falls by the wayside. I must take it one day at a time. Other entries remind me of how I used to loathe myself and speak down to myself. I had to learn how to surrender to acceptance. I'm blessed and singularly grateful for this path. I am alive.

2014/06/02

The last weekend was the best one I've had in ages. I chose to let go of fear and to embrace passion. On Friday evening I received a text message from Barbara to ask if I wanted to visit her with Samantha. I said yes. We had a lovely sleep over. On Saturday, although I felt lazy and unenthusiastic, the plan had been to go rock-climbing with one of the guys from the house. Instead of choosing to rest, read and sleep as I normally would, I chose to go out. I wanted to embrace the experience. Boy, am I happy and grateful and blessed! What a superb day!

We met up at the house and then drove in convoy to Krugersdorp. We stopped off to get something to eat along the way. I was delighted to see this piece of perfection in the middle of suburbia. Proper nature; perfect rock-faces to climb. It would be foolish to think I'm particularly observant. If I choose to be open-minded, willing and adventurous, I'll discover many more hidden treasures.

I came home exhausted that evening, but also felt strangely refreshed. I had more energy left and went to watch a movie at Monte Casino. On Saturday I ticked several items off my to do list. Payed rent, got Ginja

*vaccinated and chipped. Also got a massage desk with
wheels. I have many things still to do for Indigo Moon.
A logo, a flier, business cards, and a website. I've got to
get the required materials. One of the women from work
has resigned. I'm elated on her behalf. I'm happy and
grateful for my life right now.*

Fear.

In one of the Fellowship support groups they say that an alcoholic
suffers from an unnatural fear.

While living with Lily, I was astonished at how much she got
done. She went to church and took part in life. She met friends for
coffee, she is a talented musician and the most delightful tunes would
come from her room at night. She had a passion for life. I sat upstairs
in my room, avoiding life. But life was calling me. Lily encouraged me
to live and to embrace my talents.

I considered what my talents were, but I wasn't sure if what I was
looking at were talents or a self-imagined delusion. She pushed and
pushed, and the more she pushed the more I pulled into my shell. The
one thing I love about Lily is that she sees my soul the way I see hers.
I would occasionally slip out of my shell. It felt incredible. I would
connect with people when I didn't try to, and then magical things
happened. When I said yes instead of no, I switched on my experience
of life again. As soon as I realised I was enjoying myself, a fear set in,
and I retracted like a tortoise. It was a painful process. This fear was
inexplicable, intangible. I could not quite get a grip on it or understand
why I was afraid to live and to enjoy life. Why did it frighten me to feel
passion? Sometimes I still experience this difficulty. Inside me, there
is a wall holding back my wishes and a river of suppressed zeal has
built up over the years. This passion started leaking out. I could not
stop the leaks any longer. I didn't want to. The dam wall was springing
leaks, but the concrete was still tightly packed. It helped me to see the
leaks of passion, and I wanted more of it to fill my life. I wanted to feel

it, to live it. So, I set off to crack open that wall with more growth, more understanding and more self-love.

The more I saw Lily enjoy every moment the more I wanted similar moments for myself. I began to draw again, but it was hard. The distant voices in my head said I was wasting my time. I showed some of my pictures to Lily, and then I shared them with my mom and my aunt. I still had an emptiness in my stomach. I needed to affirm myself.

I had many ideas about how to help my fellows. One of them was to open a massage business to help others with touch therapy. I enjoyed it and I saw and believed in the value of massage. On the other hand, I told myself I wouldn't be good enough. I thought my qualification was inadequate. I ruminated about my possible lack of skill. Then I came up with other excuses – my hands would suffer with the massaging, my wrists would get arthritis, the energy of others would intertwine with mine. I told myself I might not know enough about energy work. Massage was probably inferior to physiotherapy? The little leak of passion reminded me about how people enjoy my massages, how they fall asleep. How they tell me about their experience of relaxation and peace under my hands.

However, I had my excuses and I would stick with them.

Gabriel tried to help me push through my feelings of low self-esteem. I kept pushing back.

2014/06/14

> I just had KFC at the halfway house. A prior housemate died two weeks ago. My heart is sore, my emotions are confused. All I want to do is sleep or relax. This is my second week at the halfway house. I got some delicious cake as well. I want to go to Rio de Janeiro. It makes me despondent that my old friend and both prior housemates died in such close succession because of this

disease. It doesn't seem fair. But in it there is a lesson. We do this for them.

The sun is balmy on my legs as I scribble this. My mom went to Howick with Lara and Alex. She didn't invite me. Not that anything would have changed if she had. I'm not disappointed. I'm fighting the co-dependency.

I detest TV. I used to watch too much of it, and I think it figuratively allows people's brains to swell and explode into uselessness. When I'm at the halfway house I watch a lot of TV to keep myself occupied. I also write in my journal and read, but it becomes easy to just get swept up in the mindless, emotionless screen when my mind is so full.

2014/07/15

My life has changed for the better in the last week. My world has always been filled with countless lost possibilities. Now it has exploded with a wonderful blessing. Today a year ago, I started working at the Pharma company. I was insecure and doubted myself. Far down I knew I was capable, but I usually I didn't grasp opportunities, because I feared failure. I always saw a helpless child in the mirror. A sore, sad little girl child unable to grow up.

After a year of at first filing, photocopying, then taking on a few more tasks, and then some more and then ultimately piles of additional tasks, they've offered me a job as a Financial Analyst. Wow, a title and a great salary! All the tears and elbow grease, and all the exquisite transformational emotions of the past year

> *has brought me to this point. A moment for me to accept this prospect of success. What amazes me and makes me feel grateful is that I've not only gained this job, but everything I learnt on the path toward it. I'm thankful beyond measure. I'm really feeling the gratitude. I never want to forget this.*

2014/07/25

> *I'm at home. I've fought off the flu for a week and haven't looked after myself. I've tried to manifest love into my life. A relationship. I'm frightened by this. So, I guess the manifestation will take a while. I know why I'm fearful: because I must get in touch with my sexuality again. In my active addiction I switched into another personality when I drank. I became a different creature. Antonio used to call me Paige at those times. I was vindictive, bitchy, and manipulative. I became powerful and I used my powers to get what I wanted without taking heed of whether I hurt others. Gabriel said I must look at what I became when I took on that other persona. It shows how I suppressed certain parts of me that scared me, or that I considered to be 'bad'. It's that concept of light versus dark. You can't have light without dark and you can't have dark without light. What scares me the most about me is the other part of me: my power. My power and my sexuality.*

My sexuality has gotten me into a lot of trouble in the past. I get nervous and sick to my stomach when I think about this. Maybe it's past trauma. The molestation when I was five was linked to my sexuality. When I lost my virginity my world fell apart, and this related to my sexuality. Coming out to speak the truth about John (and the rejection from everyone involved) was coupled with my sexuality. One ex-boyfriend, Antonio, blamed our poor relationship on my sexuality. It led me to the active spiral of drug addiction with Matt. We weren't in a real relationship, we just fucked and got high. Becoming sexually intimate with me has given more than one man the impression he had the right to tell me I'm fat. My sexuality fired up a fear about pregnancy and sexually transmitted infections.

Of course, my sexuality wasn't the cause of any of these things. I made bad choices when I chose men for relationships as I was traumatised and had no other solid foundation against which to choose a good male template from. Fear and obsession are integral parts of being an addict. Nowadays – slowly, gently – I control those neurotic thoughts. They don't control me any longer.

I dated Antonio before my relationship with Victor back in 2010. We started dating in 2009 or 2008, after I broke up with Matt. This was another lethal relationship where I deepened my acute spiralling into active addiction. A lot of my chaotic behaviour started whilst in it.

Before I met Antonio, I still had sex with Matt occasionally, although I also tried my utmost to get away from the toxic relationship with him. I blamed my drug abuse on him – I had a huge co-dependency problem with him. He had an enormous hold on me. At that time, I thought of Matt as my first love.

One December, we house sat for a friend in on the Westside of Centurion. We used Cat every day for the month, and I was working at a business as a temp. When I got paid on Fridays, we'd drive 25–30 km to another part of the city to buy drugs. Back in at the house we'd smoke hubbly and use drugs. We'd trip and talk until the birds started chirping the next day. The feeling still sits with me today. It's horrendous to come down from Cat. Anxious, in a miasma of rancid sweat from a whole night of using drugs, then realising with a shock that it's morning because the birds are making a noise. I would have a bit of Cat left to get me through the day, and then it would stutter to a destructive start again in the evening.

By end of the December, my heart was on the verge of exploding. I decided I was done after a huge binge on New Year's Eve. We went home with a girl we knew after partying at our favourite club (the one where we met). We sat on her bed where I pretended to fall asleep. I didn't want to be sociable any more, and I didn't want to use any more. I blamed Matt for my drug problem. I stopped answering his messages. Finally, I thought to myself, I was rid of this toxic relationship of almost four years. I went to see my psychiatrist. My medication was adjusted. I stayed with my parents to clean up. My mom knew something was wrong, but she didn't realise I was using hard drugs and I didn't tell her either. I lied by omission. I told her I was smoking pot, but not about the 'hard' stuff. I said I needed her help. My mom always bailed me out, she was always there when I needed her; especially when I messed up. Matt told her I owed him money. She paid him off.

Once I finally cleaned up and felt semi-normal again, I occasionally went out to a local pub with one of my childhood friends. I managed to find myself a proper gem of a human being during one of our outings. Or that's what I thought. The gem was actually a stone. I can laugh about it now.

As alcoholics and addicts we develop these homing devices that eventually assist us to find the most maladjusted, sick, and toxic people. People who dance the same dances we dance. His name was Antonio. Antonio was, as I said, a stoner. He had an unconventional upbringing. His esoteric out of the box views were decidedly different from the intellectual views I had grown used to. I began to smoke pot with him, because he smoked pot. Cocaine became my preference, because he loved it.

Antonio was a first-rate victim. He often fought with his mother in the most terrible way. I kept telling myself that if you want to know how a man will treat you in the future you must look at how he treats his mother. Since I was mostly drugged up, I didn't realise he treated me in the same way. It was a psychological war, and I was losing. I gained a lot of weight. He was an expert at making me feel as if I was in trouble. As if I did a terrible thing.

Our relationship started off in a swampland of poison. I struggled to pull myself away from Matt. There was a part of me who wanted to hear from him, while another part never wanted to see him again. After a while I got in touch with him again, and we met up. While Antonio tried to convince me that our relationship was my destiny, I visited Matt on the sly. Eventually Antonio found out. There was hell to pay and I obviously had to stop seeing Matt.

I stayed with Antonio for three years, and he would constantly drag the cow of my unfaithfulness out of the ditch. He had no trust in me. I wasn't wise enough then to realise that if a relationship is damaged to such an extent, it would never mend again. I was in active addiction. Some of my worst experiences happened during that relationship. I was just as much to blame for them as he was.

Three things are central to my memories of our relationship.

The first was when we decided to go to a new music festival. We thought it would be a fun. He had a group of old friends who went with us. Before the festival I decided to get in touch with Matt to find out if he would be there. Antonio told me what drugs we would buy. Despite my co-dependence and strong need for affirmation, I've always had a strong personality. I hate being controlled – John controlled me for years and I had enough of that. I became rebellious when they did not give me a choice in the drugs they bought with my money as part of the pool. I had rapidly developed a preference for cocaine as a party drug, especially after Antonio opened the coke door that I entered through so willingly.

I heard Matt would be at the festival too. Now I had an excuse to see him. I still clung to him somewhere inside. I wanted his affection. I asked him to bring me some cocaine, and we met up there. I introduced him to Antonio, who freaked out about it. His reaction baffled me. 'Fuck him', I thought defiantly. I spent most of the music festival doing drugs with Matt, although I managed miraculously to be present every time Antonio and his friends took the next hit of whatever it was they were using. I had paid for it, after all, and a junky never misses out on drugs they paid for. At that time Matt and I no longer even had sex – our relationship had disintegrated into a drug friendship. Antonio's friends followed me and Matt around to see if I was cheating on their friend.

At the end of the debauched festival while we packed out things, my heart was a drumbeat in my chest. I knew how much trouble I was in with Antonio. I had seen his friends spy on me. I lied when Antonio confronted me about hanging out with Matt. We had a shouting match in the middle of a road, with Antonio bellowing at me. I wanted to die. My heart pounded against my ribcage, louder and louder. Eventually it felt like it would make its way up into my throat. I wanted him to stop. When we finally managed to move the argument into my car, I thought to myself how easy the solution was to this problem. I broke up with him. This event happened in the first six months of our relationship.

After I had dropped him off, I went home to recover. I can't remember how or exactly when we decided to continue with the relationship, but we did.

The second major event in the relationship was when we decided to go to Graskop – a town far out in the wilderness. This was about two years into the relationship, but I stand corrected as my memory of that time is questionable. We would stay at a backpacker's inn and drove there in two cars. I left my car at home. I detested one of Antonio's friends. He was rude and obnoxious. I sensed an intangible darkness in him. Even with my intuition at a weak point, every inch of my being told me 'stay away!'. I was able to hear that insistent warning from my Higher Self. I did not heed it though …

We got there, chose our rooms, unpacked and began to party at a mile a minute. We had planned this party a couple of months in advance and by the time it arrived we were ready to send rockets into the sky. The alcohol flowed freely, and we had plenty of drugs. Eventually I found myself walking somewhere dreamily with Antonio's best friend. The one who made me feel uncomfortable. I had no idea how it happened. He took me into different rooms. I blacked in and out – I can't remember why he showed me the rooms.

I didn't know where Antonio or the rest of his friends were, but I was too spaced out to care. Finally, I blacked out completely.

When I became conscious again, Antonio was slapping me through the face. I was confused, I didn't know where I was or what I was doing. Why was he hurting me? I was horrified to find myself half-naked in somebody's bed with Antonio's wicked friend. Antonio and the rest of his friends stared at my body. They seemed perplexed and enraged in equal measures. I cried out and covered myself with my arms. How did this happen? I was virtually naked, and the whole group crowded around with their hostile stares and their demeaning questions.

I said I didn't know, because I didn't. It was one of the most humiliating and shameful moments of my life. Nobody asked the guy any harsh questions. In their eyes, I was the harlot and I was to blame. Someone gave me a shirt. I ran into a field behind the backpacker's property, but fence blocked my way. I wanted to get as far away as possible from those people, from that situation, from that horror. As I climbed the fence, it ripped into the underside of my wrist; I still have the scar. Eventually I felt Antonio pull at my legs, he tried to coax me to go back to the house of hell. He said I should stop making such a spectacle of myself. I stayed in the bedroom for the rest of the weekend, I refused to come out. I spoke to nobody.

The third experience connected to this relationship is the Tarot, Angel readings and magic I practised with Antonio's mother and her best friend. We made a set date on Saturdays where we'd smoke weed and read Tarot Cards for people who were not present and who did not request the readings. Antonio's mother's friend loved to gossip. She claimed the Angels spoke to her and said she had to help these people. I have yet to understand how she helped them by reading the Tarot behind their backs and discussing their business with us. She would constantly pry into my love life and my family story. Although it felt uncomfortable, I wanted to be a part of something and so I got sucked into her vortex. She was a part of my life until I met Victor. He detested her and I stopped seeing her.

After I broke up with Antonio, she still wanted me to visit her. She was broke and I often bought her weed. It was awkward. What made me even more uncomfortable and guilt-ridden was that her seven-year-old son would sit with us when we smoked weed. I must mention that these happenings opened me up to the idea of spirituality again. I often sat alone and thought about what I felt when I was with her and when we spoke about the Angels; I felt a peace, a relief of chaos from my chaotic life. I wanted more of that peace to infiltrate my being. Not all of it was bad. This woman tried to be good, although she was misguided. My boundaries were blurred. I had no idea when to say no or how to make good friends. I enjoyed the mysticism. I realised there is a whole lot about the world and how it works that I still do not understand. Antonio was esoteric himself, but his views were a little out there and I did not always understand his logic; or lack of it ... He believed that the lizard people controlled the world, that the greys regularly abducted his mother, and that he was a warrior in another life. This belief made it okay for him to wield his sword at mailmen.

When I finally broke up with Antonio, I felt free, but at the same time I still wanted his approval. The same old story ... My behaviour became unmanageable. I embarrassed myself with some of the things I did to retain his friendship. I felt insanely guilty and fucked-up by shame. Nightmares about Antonio and his friends haunted me throughout the first few years of my recovery. What I finally realised was that I did not know any better. I was damaged. Broken. My behaviour reflected my hurt and confusion. I injured myself the most in these situations. The guilt and shame I carried with me after the night at Graskop wasn't mine to carry. I wasn't sober, I wasn't of sound mind, I was taken advantage of. The man who claimed to love and care for me wasn't there to protect me. I chose the wrong people to be around. I wasn't in a safe place. I wasn't taking part in safe practices. I therefore released the guilt, shame, and embarrassment.

The repeated contact with my ex-boyfriends and the chaos it caused taught me about my bottomless need for affirmation and affection. It didn't matter how bad the other person was for me. I kept going back in an attempt to fill the gaping, leaking hole. I had a need for drama that required a certain amount of chaos in my life. With chaos there is less time to sit with the self and reflect.

There was a big change in me during 2014. Suddenly, I saw worth in myself. It was the result of a great deal of therapy and hard work. I examined my obsessive thoughts and where they originated. In the first book about The Law of Attraction I read, it was explained in such a way that I thought I had to feel amazingly joyful all the time. This is a dangerous perception. I laboured at feeling good. When I felt depressed, I judged myself. When I felt anxious, I became more anxious for not being able to shake the anxiety. In 2014 I grasped there was a process I had to work through to get to the emotional space I desired. They say those who have suffered have more compassion. I became interested in the concept of self-love. My uncle gave me a book and introduced me to Louise Hay's thoughts, this was the first time I read her book *You Can Heal Your Life*. I liked the concepts, but I didn't do the exercises until much later. I made loving myself a priority and it was much more challenging than I thought. The more determined I became, the harder I pushed against it. I repeated the affirmations to myself without believing them. With time, I began to believe some of them. I did mirror work too. It was embarrassing, but I pushed through. I used to look at myself in the shower mirror, smile bravely and say that I loved myself. It was appealing to get to delight in that. Sometimes I giggled and danced in front of the mirror. After a while, it became easier to be 'me' with myself. I recognised my smile, the way my eyes crinkle when I laugh. The way my teeth pop out of my mouth. I clearly saw the tooth for the first time. The tooth on the left side of my mouth that refuses to go back into my mouth and just sort of waves at everyone when I smile. Some days I wrote morning pages based on recommendations in *The Artists Way*. I spent a lot of time on my own. I enjoyed my own company and often got lost in my mind.

When I met my current sponsor, I finally began my Step Four. I examined my past and my enormous stockpile of resentments. I was infuriated with life. Many people told me I had anger issues, although

I wasn't aggressive or snappy. My Step Four was a minimalist three columns. The first was where I wrote the names of those people I resented or harmed. The second was why I resented them or how I harmed them. In the third column, I examined my part or role in the events – this was basically a list of my perceived character defects. I was fearful, enraged, hurt, expectant, jealous, insecure and so much more. As I did a timeline, I wrote down the resentment list from the earliest remembered event. I could see an overarching configuration. I grasped the onset of specific patterns and realised where they became default habits. I can say fear was one of my biggest problems. I resented myself the most, but I carried long-time ill will towards others as well. These pools of bitterness were not healthy or helpful in any way. There is an old saying about resentments being akin to swallowing poison and expecting the other person to die. Resentments made me sick and irrational. It was damn difficult to do this exercise. This Twelve-step Program was where I started. The more I delved into the Law of Attraction and the rest of this invaluable material, the stronger the song of Universal Truth sang throughout it. A common thread intertwined all these concepts. It involved love in one form or another. I had to learn to accept myself completely by removing my ego and believing in a power greater than myself. The steps taken to recover are based on spirituality. When I read Louise Hay's book, she mentioned self-love and self-acceptance, but spirituality was accentuated above all. I focused extensively that when I did that work, whereas when I did the Twelve-step work, it allowed me to concentrate more on the clearing of my past. The Twelve-step Program reintroduced me to my Higher Power; it taught me how to be accountable and to be sincerely honest with myself. I wanted to clear the past and make amends to those I harmed. Things began to shift, slowly. I did all the work at different times.

I knew that thoughts were based on belief systems, and that it created emotions. Thoughts are formed by a catalyst, by something that happens. I would be in a blissful mood early in the morning, and two hours later I might be in an abyss of depression. I would try and dissect which event I became reactive to. Gabriel would often question my reactiveness. Why I would let small things affect me in such a negative way? It might be trifling matters, such as not having enough money to put on my phone for data, or something my mom said, or any niggling, small issue that touched a nerve. When I finally became mindful of my mercurial thought processes, I managed to make sense of my reactive emotions.

It took heaps of energy, but I recognised how negative my thoughts were. Many of them came down to one simple thing: I felt I wasn't good enough. I tried to convince myself that I was, but I got stuck there for a while. I had to truly believe it, and it was hard to convince myself.

The relationship thing was a continuous struggle. I wrote many lists. To get to know myself I wrote lists of what I wanted. Those were incredibly difficult in the beginning, they got longer as I got to know myself better. I made several lists about my ideal man too.

2014/08/03

Why do I suddenly have fears around exercising? I used to enjoy it. It brought peace, energy and release into my life and physical well-being. In the last year and a half, I've done nothing for my body. I feel it in every cell of my being. Starting an exercise programme is an example of how unrealistic my self-expectation often turns out to be. When I begin a regime, I expect perfection, I expect fitness and I expect physical prowess. None of these things can come after only a few days of training. I also frequently catch myself drawing up unrealistic schedules. Making plans that could never work. I must deal with a lot of things now. I should balance everything equally. Another fear is a sense of inadequacy and not being able to keep up.

Isla Stone

2014/08/26

So much is going on. Work is going well, at the halfway house is going well and growing is going well. Then there is balancing the scales: Lily and I are annoyed with each other. Just thinking about it drains me. I desperately want to talk it out, but she avoids confrontation; I now see what it was like to deal with me back in the day ...

On Tuesday I confirmed with Samantha that I would work over the coming weekend. I told Lily. She said she would be home. Then on Wednesday afternoon she told me she would spend the weekend elsewhere; in fact, she would leave on Thursday already. This caught me off guard. She tends to leave all the house responsibilities up to me. I told her I felt stressed out. We needed an action plan. She used her impulsive nature as an excuse for dropping me.

I'm sick of taking most of the responsibility for our living arrangements. We both live here and should share responsibilities! She got her friend to come to look after the house, but that is it. She just asked her. The way she told me rather than asked me to convey to her friend what needed to be done pissed me off. She sent me a voice note. It seemed abusive. I had to leave my keys with her friend and collect them. I had to tell her friend what had to be done. When I work at the halfway house this kind of pressure is exactly what I don't need! Vindictive in return, I didn't tell Lily's friend to spray her plants seven times per day. Last month I spent money on myself and paid off debt. I didn't buy food, but then again, we never arranged to go food shopping either. Now I sit here.

*With even amounts of peace and frustration. I've been
sober for two-and-a-half years today. Knowing this is
immensely gratifying.*

At that time, I got stuck between two people who decided not to
work together as they used to. It was difficult for me as I had a loyalty
to both. Each of them helped me in my darkest times. They broke
away from each other and in an ugly way. I tried not to take sides,
but it became strenuous. I backed away from my recovery work to
avoid any involvement in their issues. I had respect for both of them
and their work. The hard thing for me was that I pedestalised them
and then both came crashing down. It was a good lesson for me to
realise no-one is infallible. I had to learn to accept people for who they
are, the good and the bad, as they do for me. Still, it was crushing to
see that sensational team split apart. I knew the best work they did
was when they did it together because they saved my life when they
worked together.

Lily and I had our struggles. She had difficulty with
communication, and my pet peeve was passive- aggressive people
who would not tell me what was wrong. I'm the first to say I'm sorry.
I guess the reason I got especially irritated was because I used to do
the same, before I found my voice. When people get passive-aggressive
continuously, I take big breaths. She would leave stuff on the floor
or slam her door. I was brought up in a home where everything was
done for us, the dishes were done for us, our clothes were washed for
us, our food was cooked for us. I didn't ever have to lift a finger. When
I lived on my own at the little cottage at the horse farm, I washed
dishes occasionally only. Then I patted myself on the back because
they didn't get mould on them like they did when I used drugs and
lived alone.

My mind has always been active, jumping from the mundane to
the magical in a beat. I've gotten a whole lot better at living down here
on the planet, but I'm less grounded in the here and now than most
people. It often felt as if I wasn't quite in my body. I would see my body

from the outside. I was here, but not quite here. This has improved a great deal too. When it came to dishes, washing, and cooking, I can't say I was an example of discipline. I preferred potting around in my head, time was better spent on thinking, reading, writing or daydreaming. Initially Lily cooked for us. It was lovely, I wasn't living on tinned food like I was used to. Then she asked me to cook, and I did. Her cooking was much better though because she was trained as a chef. We were broke, and poor little rich me enjoyed preparing lavish, interesting dishes from cook books. I thought that was how a good meal should be made. Besides, it was a good excuse not to cook too often.

I began to do a bit of baking again. My Grannie taught me how to bake when I was a little girl. It was unfortunate that Lily refused to eat anything with wheat in it. I couldn't bake for her and I didn't feel confident enough to cook for her or myself. It always ended up tasting crap, so I avoided cooking. We discussed it and I made an effort. I tried preparing meals when I wasn't exhausted from work and my mind didn't play tricks on me, or when we had food in the fridge. We lived on a shoestring budget in the beginning.

She convinced me to go to gym with her. I thought it a good idea, and it was. Once I was employed full time, I decided to get a gym instructor to help me because I had no idea what I was doing, and I would waste most of my time worrying about what to do instead of doing it. I was getting to know myself. I enjoyed gym. I was quite committed and went regularly in the mornings for a while. My body changed delightfully. People told me how good I looked. Compliments made me uncomfortable and awkward. I enjoyed the exercise and my healthy body, but I experienced such intense discomfort with the compliments that I eventually stopped going to gym.

At the halfway house Samantha was busy building on her business. She was adding an outpatient service and wanted me to help her. I was surprised that she would want me to be a part of it. She had roped in other people to assist as well. I was determined to become part of this, to follow through with it. I sat in on process groups, learning from the way the counsellors worked. Samantha wanted me to do an addictions counselling course. I was almost ready to do it, but I was broke and at the back of my mind I had a notion that I wanted to do a psychology degree instead. The changes, difficult vibes and split loyalties at the halfway house confused me. I didn't know who to be loyal to. I became more and more involved. My intuition said no.

2014/09/01

> *I'm worried and a little afraid that I might have pushed people away recently. I feel like a one-man island.*
>
> *Samantha has started working with all the other counsellors and I'm working with ... who knows? She has brought in two new people. Because I'm at work during the day, I can't be there all the time. I feel left out because when I go to the halfway house to catch up on happenings, I would realise I had missed most of the changes and discussions.*
>
> *Isla has a family of emptiness.*
>
> *I'm lonely. It's tough for me to be alone right now. It feels as if everyone is far away. My island is drifting further out to sea. I suppose not having a sponsor doesn't help. Not speaking to people doesn't help. Not working my Program properly doesn't help. I'm tired and unfocused right now. This new development with the one counsellor has taken me aback. It's scary and overwhelming. I must – just must – make the right choices now.*

Isla Stone

2014/10/27

It's funny how I can be in recovery for such a long time and yet still be oblivious about some feelings. It's still easier to supress my emotions, to turn a blind eye rather than to look them square in the eyes and face them. I don't work at the halfway house any longer. My heart is sore about it. I'm floating a bit in limbo. I'm empty and scared. For a long time, I used my involvement at the halfway house to fill me, to hold me and to keep me together. Working there made me feel a clarity of purpose again. Now, my sense of having a purpose is less significant. I'm also grappling with the loss of a close friend, a death, an end of an era. I'm desolate. I felt lonely there at times too, but I had distractions. Now I have no more diversions. I must face the loneliness. I don't have any friends or hobbies. I have no life. Although my life is fuller now than ever before, my activities only fill a tiny drop of my time. How must I live? How must I discover this consistently elusive thing called life? It almost comes within grasp, then frantically flutters away. I hear the people next door let their friends in and out of their home laughing and whooping for joy, where is mine?

2014/10/28

How do I fill up my life with good, positive things? I'm on Tinder now, where people ask me what I do in my spare time. I don't do anything specific in my spare time. I love diving, nature, rock-climbing, and yoga. I love travelling and adventurous things. But I haven't filled up my time with any of them. I've filled up my time with Angel Card readings, obsessive angst and desperate pleas for change. I've filled it up with rest, with step work and with sleep. I

love gym, but I go once a week only. Why don't I use my
time for things that make me happy? What am I afraid
of? Why do I constantly give my power away to others?
What can fill my days up? What will delight me and get
me one step closer to the contentment I seek?

Tinder, that curious app where we swipe left or right in the effort to get out there and meet someone. I decided to utilise this new technological advancement when Gabriel suggested it was time for me to date. I had no hobbies. I didn't hang out in bars and clubs any longer. I had gradually become a hermit.

I did meet a few people on Tinder, and it was an interesting experience although it wasn't the best place to meet one's soulmate. In reality, those were my first steps out into the world again because it forced me to meet new and different people. Considering I was the same girl who climbed on an aeroplane and flew halfway across the world to spend three months with strangers, I had become quite fearful of people during my years in recovery because I isolated so much.

I had to heal from the damage my drinking and drugging had caused. I always met the dates in public places. Most of them were solely that: first dates. I was disappointed. I wanted to meet the love of my life. I've always felt as if I'm in love with a man I've not met yet. I hugged my pillow at night with thoughts about how delicious it would be to have a partner with me through thick and thin. I still had trouble with the notion of intimacy and sex being separate things. I knew nobody else would complete me. I was a whole, complete being. No-one could give me the affirmation and love I required – I had to give it to myself. In part, this time held many tests. I had to choose what I really wanted for myself. In the past I always jumped into a relationship with the first man who showed the tiniest bit of interest in me. If a man approached me, I would attach myself to him because I didn't think I deserved more than him – at least he saw something in me, after all! This time around, I would – dare I say it – choose a man

I liked. I had to keep myself grounded to experience rejection without attaching myself to it. But I began to examine why I felt rejected rather than placidly accepting it. Once I became selective about the men I wanted to see, about who I felt would be a good fit for me without straight away accepting anyone who showed interest, I felt powerful. It was incredible.

Soon before I took ownership of my feelings about men something propelled me into change. This event is one of the deciding factors that helped me to move on from the halfway house.

I had an obsessive crush on one of the men who worked at the halfway house. Barbara told him how I felt about him. I was mortified. I worked with him and it was painfully awkward. After a week or two Samantha called a meeting with him, Barbara and me. It was hugely embarrassing to discuss this in a meeting. I was furious with Barbara. Friends don't do such things! I decided to leave. The Universe and I determined that my time there was over. I had to direct my energies elsewhere – possibly on myself.

During this time, I also met my new sponsor at a meeting. I asked for a new sponsor from the Universe and I asked for a meaningful connection. Women often struggle to find good sponsors. I thought it was unlikely to find one with whom I would share a profound, intimate trust. Once I got too close to someone, I closed off. She is still my sponsor, and for the first time in my life I allowed myself to gradually trust somebody besides Gabriel. It took a long time for me to get there. My sponsor is one of the most patient, compassionate people I've ever met. I've learnt so much from her, and she has been a source of immense wisdom and love.

I thought nothing of it at the time, but I made friends with people in the Fellowship. Timothy and his friend were the only men. When I first saw Tim from across the room in a meeting, my heart skipped a beat, my stomach tightened. I couldn't stop looking up across the table to catch his eyes. He had mesmerising green eyes and the meticulous hands of an artist. He wore his hair shaven – well, he was completely bald – and incredibly attractive.

Occasionally, the group would go for coffee after the meetings. Timothy invited me to go bowling with him and his friends a few times. I always got a thrill out of it; I had an liking in him, but it wasn't an obsessive crush. I always promised myself I would never date another alcoholic. I was told it's too dangerous, so I pushed the emotions to the back of my mind. I thought he was in a romantic relationship with a female friend who was always by his side. I couldn't quite identify what I felt, I just knew I loved being with him. He made me feel safe. He liked me for who I was. I knew I had to let go of any expectations and daydreams about him. I couldn't let my imagination run wild with me. I tried to avoid it; I didn't know if a relationship with another alcoholic could work. And I got involved with a guy I met on Tinder.

2014/11/27

It was a long day. I'll write more often from now on. I've been terrible at writing down my thoughts and impressions because I've become lazy. With me it's always extremes, all or nothing. Lately, I've gotten closer to a state of equilibrium. I did a lot of yoga during the last two weeks. I want to go again tomorrow morning. I've also gone to gym at least once a week for the last four months. I'm healthier, my body is happier. I'm more aware of myself, my movement. I searched for love for a long time. Not actively going into bars with desperation, but rather opening my heart, signalling my readiness to the Universe. And indeed, it worked. I met someone else on Tinder. He makes me laugh and feel woozy. My head goes into the clouds, my veins expand, the colour of the Universe is fed into every part of my being when I see him. Yet I carry a measure of fear. A subconscious monster of past experiences is slipping away little by little. Sometimes I have a sense of uncertainty. At other times I'm absolutely sure he is the perfect match for me. I should enable good communication and freedom from my side. Although I can't pinpoint it, I've learnt many things during the last few months. It's a real yet intangible transformation. There's been a change, but I'm not quite sure what it is. It's a good change, a growth spurt. Maybe I've managed to find a seldomly glimpsed piece within at last. Not as a result of anything other than having taken a few leaps of faith.

2014/12/06

It was Lara's birthday yesterday. Today, it's her housewarming and birthday party. I never had a housewarming with Lily. I feel obsessive, jealous, insecure, fearful, and envious about the I guy I met. If I send him a message and he doesn't respond, I worry about him not liking me anymore. Am I too crazy, obsessive, jealous, insecure, and fearful? It's amusing, actually. I must accept the facts around this because I can either choose to become self-destructive around this blossoming relationship or I can choose to cherish it.

Firstly, if this does not work out, I did not lose something I already had. Secondly, I'm happy and content with who I am. Thirdly, if it does not work out it's for the best because so far everything in my life has worked out that way. I may feel disappointed, upset or heartsick, but it will not be the end of the world for me. Fourthly, I'll then know I deserve more than what he could offer. In my insecurity I'm mulling about the possibility that he might have been pursuing someone who wasn't interested. Am I his second choice? Of course, I know I had many obsessions and pursuits before him. It's

*essentially my own insecurity double-backed on myself.
I fear the fire may disappear or be subdued because of my
fearful thoughts. Relatively speaking he is also facing a
difficult time. He's a bit paranoid, and possibly I might
be placing far too much emphasis on my behaviour here.
His ex-girlfriend lives in his backyard. For me it isn't a
problem, but I wonder what she looks like. Why has he
never spoken about her?*

*Just a special memory for the future: I woke up this
morning at 5.30 and I came for a smoke. There were
clouds in the sky, in my vision looking up to my left I
saw a straight slice of rainbow. It came out of a dark
cloud that extended down beyond the trees. The image
before me was as though someone might have opened a
bottle somewhere in the distance and from it, a rainbow
blasted toward the sky, where it curved perfectly into the
cloud. For about five minutes it was exquisite.*

2014/12/21

*Fear and worry debilitate me. I worry about him not
wanting to see me. I'm anxious to have lost something
that hasn't even started yet. Were my feelings about him
false and untrue? Have I lied to myself about how I feel
to avoid disappointment? There is a distance between
us. I've asked and prayed for a solid straight in my face
answer. Is he the one for me, or a lesson to carry on and
move on? Why do I worry about these things? Why do I
worry about rejection? Because my whole life was based
on a lie where I heard I'm only worthy of being rejected.
That is not true! I'm worthy of respect, understanding
and love. I'm worthy of sincere love. I'm worthy.*

The experience with dating this man was important. It showed me how insecure and fearful I still was. It gave me an opportunity to examine my sense of unworthiness. I pined after him but dug deep in my intuition. I ran after him while he wasn't as interested as I was. I gave more than I received.

I stopped, looked at my behaviour and recognised it belied a feeling of worthiness. When I was feeling bad about myself my life didn't work well. My intuition is always right. Why was I more interested than he was? It was simple, because I wanted the companionship, I was lonely, and I liked him more than he liked me. There is nothing wrong with that. Yes, I had a history of rejection. I was undoubtedly still attracted to someone who would reject me because I was still not as well-versed at this exercise. There wasn't anything wrong with me. I'm intensely rooted in my feminine energy; I'm emotional and that is okay. This was all a part of my journey. I would never have understood what I understand now If I didn't experience then what I did and if I didn't learn from it what I did. I used to be damn hard on myself for not getting it right. For being overly insecure, emotional, fearful or clingy. However, I learnt from those experiences. I understand my worthiness now. I do not have to feel any of those emotions any more. When I know my worth, truly understand it and broadly accept every little part of me, the good and the bad, then those feelings miraculously and automatically fall away.

This feeling of worthiness came after masses of work at understanding myself and rediscovery. It was a process, parts of it was painful and bits of it was excellent. The terrific parts mostly started after the pain got better. The pain got worse before it got better, but it was worth it. This applies to every aspect of my life. My love life, my work life, my family life, my friendships and physical health, as well as my spiritual well-being.

CHAPTER 8

A New Understanding and Saying Goodbye

At the beginning of every new year at the Pharma company I became cumulatively more depressed, especially after my holidays. We would hit the ground running in January. I enjoyed many aspects of my work, but things started to change. The company grew, and I was moved into a new team. I had communication glitches with my new manager. Previously, I reported to Maureen. I thought she was marvellous. Some people criticised the way she managed her team, but I got along with her swimmingly. Our relationship became overly co-dependent and familiar. It became unhealthy in some ways. The other members in the team noticed and suspected favouritism. The tension was palpable to me. Perhaps others didn't perceive it that way, but I often felt excluded from the office dealings. I was in the lower part of the tier. This was understandable. I was never partial to complaints, negativity or office gossip. I despised that kind of thing; I always kept my mouth shut as best as I could and tried my best not to give my two cents worth in those types of conversations. There were days when I got home and had to release the steam by speaking to Lily about it all. I still allowed it to affect me. I was learning about how people loved being unhappy. They would complain behind closed doors, but then still put on a smile to be friendly and seem helpful out in the open. They could say callous, nasty, harsh things about others, but then hug those same people, kiss them, and give them gifts. I did not understand any of it. It confused me. I judged them, but I probably do the same thing sometimes when I find something unbearable in someone else.

The office was a pleasant space; we often had engaging events during the week when we could eat ourselves sick for one promotion or another. We worked hard. I mainly worked late nights in the beginning when I still assisted with the planning. I enjoyed it immensely. We would work on weekends and our small team thoroughly connected during the times we were frustrated to tears. When I was moved into the new team, I did other work, mainly creditors and Systems, Applications and Products: Enterprise Resource Planning (SAP: ERP) procurement training for the rest of the procurement team. The affable evening work stopped, and I struggled with my new work. It was mind-numbing. I could not find any joy in the day-to-day and month-to-month drag of the accounting cycle. I did this for about two and a half years. My diary entries capture my increasing despondency despite trying with all my might to remain focused. In that time, there was considerable growth. This gave me the courage to make changes I had yearned for but had postponed for a long time.

These are the entries where I started on a new diary.

> *'Living in the moment, right here right now releases you from fear.'*

2015/01/02

> *I'm slightly depressed, probably because I had such a scintillating time away. I got to forget about work, the guy, Gabriel, and recovery for a while. I escaped from fear's cage momentarily. I went to Stellenbosch to visit my aunt. My Grannie and Uncle Marius were there too. Now I'm trapped in anguish again. I never wanted to work in the corporate world. It scares me that I allow my soul to darken slightly more every day. When I started working at the halfway house it wasn't ideal, but I uncovered a piece of my puzzle there.*

Every day I walk the stairs at the Pharma company thanking my Higher Power for my job. Yet, I question if it this is the only way to live. Should I sacrifice my skills and my passions for job security? It's hard to live with absolute faith, knowing God has a Higher Plan for me. Today I just feel like a bee, a minion, a zombie. Numb.

2015/02/01

I was utterly happy today. I still am. The day worked out delightfully. I'm not sure what made it so perfect, but it was lovely.

I bought this diary because I want to write down my thoughts again. I need to put stuff down. I must remind myself about my forgetfulness. This Sunday morning, in the meeting I attend regularly, I was prompted to remember something. I recalled how – not so long ago – I used to go through my days with a witheringly unworthiness.

I had an existential crisis in Standard Nine. This phrase is etched in my mind. It surprised me when they told me *that* was the problem. It made me sound smart when I always felt kind of stupid. I didn't recognise my worthiness and wit back then. I suddenly became aware of being coddled in this safe environment, living this comfortable life while others suffered from famine, war, and fear. I felt guilty for having this life. It was unfair for me to be here when others hurt. Looking back now I recognise that I had suffered in my way. But not to the extent of others, not for survival. I know I should find gratitude in every moment, every breath, every heartbeat.

I'll never understand God's reasoning or the Higher Plan. All I know is that here is not all there is.

I spoke about Universal Truth already. I encounter it when something touches me deeply, or someone says something that rings true in my heart. I intuitively know the truth. It is just that – Universal Truth.

2015/03/01

This weekend was incredible.

I turned thirty yesterday. On the 26th of February I celebrated my Three-Years sobriety and clean time. I've grown up. I've taken some responsibility for where I came from instead of blaming my past defects and actions entirely on others. Looking back, I guess, I accept that I've made enormous progress. On Friday I got lots of birthday wishes from everyone at work. We had cake for a colleague's farewell. For a while I had become quite obsessed with the fact that the one guy at work asked me about my birthday. I don't know if I should have invited him or not. I'm glad I didn't because I'm not desperate for that kind of companionship. Friday, I took a half day off. I came home and then I decided to go visit my mom. I felt ill and thought a nap at my mother's house would comfort me. I stayed there for a while and made arrangements for the coming weekend with my mom. She was somewhat ill herself. She seemed down, but the circumstances at home is of such a nature that I'm not surprised.

On Saturday I woke up to the smell of the most delicious breakfast but found no-one home. It felt like any other day. When Lily finally returned from her early morning escapades in a giggling, chirpy mood I quickly jumped in my car to buy cigarettes. When I got back the table was set. Breakfast was ready for me inclusive of Lily and dunked wings from KFC. The giggling was about Lily demanding dunked wings at 7.00 in her pyjamas. I'm really going to miss her. Her plane ticket is booked for the 2nd of July. My heart aches every time I think about it. I remind myself that all grand chapters must come to an end for new ones to open.

2015/03/09

I had a dream about a book the other night at the halfway house. I looked after the house this past weekend. I'm still surprised that I said yes. It wasn't too bad. I did get slightly irritable at times, but I tried to surrender those feelings.

I've met another interesting character on Tinder. He has a name. He has a vocation.

Yesterday I had an orgasm in a meeting without touching myself. I've no idea what that is about.

I like this guy, but I haven't met him yet. I must constantly remind myself that my brain is filling in the gaps.

Samantha paid me for the weekend that I worked. I didn't expect money from her. I have a sense of being strong. Tired but powerful.

In my therapy session with Gabriel in the week prior to my Third-Year thanksgiving and thirtieth birthday, we had an impactful, in-depth therapy session. My Higher Powers showed up with absolute gusto. There was no uncertainty – They were speaking to me. In the Epigraph to this book (and again in Chapter 1), I quote the poem

'Soaring'. A therapist gave me the poem and we discussed the concept of flying over the edge during one of my first days in treatment in 2012. It resonated with me so impactfully. This was one of the first things that changed the way I perceived life. In pre-thanksgiving therapy session with Gabriel in 2015, he pulled out a pack of cards and asked me to pick a card. They were all facing down. I took one and was astonished to see my card with *this* poem written in black and white. The synchronicity tickled me. I smiled at him and asked him if I was soaring yet. He let me keep the card.

Lily decided to move to Bangkok. I was so fearful for her. She asked me to go with her, but I didn't know what I would do there. I told myself that I had too much going for me here. She had studied over the last few years to become a teacher. I looked at her in awe. She followed her dreams and aspirations with unqualified faith and conviction. Lily may have seemed gentle, but she knew what she wanted. Before we moved in together, she lived with her boyfriend. Everyone thought they would get married. They met in high school and were together for many years. She enrolled for her B.Ed. through a well known correspondence university in South Africa when they were still together. She paid for it herself. When we lived together, she still studied while she worked as a student teacher. She also did au pair work in-between. On top of that she regularly attended church functions and played in the church bands. She loved playing her piano and singing. Her light shone brightly and I felt dim beside her. She kept shining brighter because she embraced her talents and her passions. Her life exploded with luminosity. I didn't know how she achieved this state of light and I refused to go to the church to find out! I became conscious later that she simply embraced life. Her walls of fear were much lower than my own. When she decided to move to Bangkok I wanted to go too. But I didn't know if I would be able to teach English, or what I would do or how my life would pan out. I didn't know what I wanted yet. I was still insecure on many levels. I told myself I was on a mission to find a vocation, to rediscover myself, and to find love. What

I mostly did, however, was to make excuses because I was afraid. I had no idea what I would do if I didn't find a job in Bangkok.

My heart was broken. Lily and I had an intimate bond. We enjoyed each other's company. We understood each other and spent hours talking at night, sipping cups of tea on our balcony in the home we created. I heard and understood her story and she heard and understood mine. We connected on countless levels. The close family connection astonished me. We are both free spirits. She found her spirituality through church, and that is her gift. She showed me how to look after myself; how to push myself into directions I intuitively knew I had to follow. Her magical glow lights the path for the people who connect with her. She is a child of light. That morning for my birthday was the best birthday celebration I ever had. She put so much effort into it, for me. I was incredibly touched by her affectionate gesture. What I appreciated most, was the joy. The giggling light-heartedness of the moment. A joyful life is created when we immerse ourselves in those special moments. The months leading up to her departure were difficult. I had to come to terms with the end of our time together. Her departure devastated me.

2015/03/16

> I must be straightforward with myself right now. I've been miserable the last few months. I don't know if it's a chemical depression, my circumstances, negative self-reflection or merely seasonal blues.

> I've been up and down. Sometimes I think God doesn't hear me, but I know it is self-indulgent. I have all the things I asked for – and more – but I feel stuck. My plan had to be faulty because I can't see a way forward. I'm not sure what I want any more. I've never known what I wanted. I'm holding on to something I think I'll be good at. That's all I've ever done.

Aptitude test results once indicated that I was capable of being absolutely anything. I always set my sights high. I set it beyond the stars, but mostly so I could impress other people. Now I know what I'm good at, but I'm still afraid to fail. I'm afraid to apply to a university. I'm scared. This fear holds me back now. It has kept me immobilised all my life. The unnatural fear of the alcoholic. I'm praying to God to remove it, but I don't know if I'm praying hard enough.

Today was difficult. I thought to myself why not me. Why can't I have good things? Why can't I do fun things? Why can't I do exciting things? Why is everyone living and I'm not? Is God holding me back or am I holding myself back?

I think it's me. I really want to change it. I deserve to live a life. I deserve to have fun, to do fun things, live my dreams. I deserve happiness. I'm a good woman with marvellous qualities. I truly deserve a splendid life. One day at a time. Sometimes one breath at a time. Last night I dreamt I relapsed on alcohol. I dreamt that I chose to drink. It was a terrible dream that depressed me the whole day.

I know the defect of character that came up today was jealousy. I'm jealous that everyone in the finance team went to Milan while I got left behind. I'm jealous about being less skilled than them. Loneliness and fear of being alone forever; expectations about the new guy I met on Tinder.

Today I truly wanted to give up, I wanted to crumple up into a microscopic corner, melt, and disappear. I'm exhausted and miserable.

2015/04/10

My Guardian Angel finally got through to me today. I've been overwhelmed. This whole week since the two senior managers resigned at work, I had dreams about the office. I can never recall dreams about work. I was initially employed by a woman General Manager, she left not long after that.

I'm also bugged by a sense of having taken on some of my mother's characteristics; I'm now focusing more on my analytical ability than my creative mind.

I'm preoccupied by the aptitude test I did recently. I want to consider what other jobs would suit me better. What's the use of working in accounts when I count down every second and have endless smokes to let time pass? My life is not supposed to be like this. I choose job satisfaction. I choose complete happiness. I don't know what will make me happy; all I know is that I'm bored. Theoretically, I know I'm truly blessed to have this job. I'm thankful for it, but I choose to believe life can be better for me on an emotional level. I deserve fulfilment. My balance is out of whack. I'm on my cell phone way too much. I'm too distracted at work, I'm too absentminded to concentrate on my emotions. It's been like this ever since John got sick. It became worse as Lily's departure approached. I've been going to less meetings. I've been offish towards my friends. It's probably because of all the stuff on my emotional plate.

Isla Stone

2015/04/14

> *I woke up dizzy, feeling light-headed. I felt ill and tired the whole day. One of the many challenges in recovery is to discern the reason for feeling out of sorts. Sometimes, it's confusing to distinguish whether I'm physically ill or merely emotionally down.*

> *I have two more sponsees. I was shocked that the one asked me to help her because she has more sober time than me. I saw an old friend of mine. We sat and talked for about three hours. He asked me if I wanted to sleep with him. I said no. Still no further news from the guy I met on Tinder. It seems like Lily was right about him. I hope she isn't, because I slept with him. I've been trying relentlessly to get in touch with God and the Angels, but there is a blockage. I messaged Barbara about the Third Step. It's about turning my will and my life over to the care of my Higher Power as I understand Him. To do that, I must let go of what I want. I must let go of what I think I want. I must let go of what I think is best for me. Only my Higher Power knows what is best for me. If I'm stressed, worried or anxious it's because I'm holding on to the outcomes of what I want. I must have faith that God will help me to get to where He wants me to be because ultimately God is in me. God wants me to be happy and to succeed. He wants me to live a peaceful, serene, and joyful life.*

This was a particularly dark time for me, I wrestled with my need for affirmation and somehow always ended up with one man or another. Afterwards I would feel terrible. I tried to simulate a sense of romance in these moments, but it was phony. I shared detail about my escapades with Tim and his friend when I saw them at meetings.

Tim became more detached. That was when I knew I felt more for him than I was willing to admit. I kept telling myself a relationship with him would be a disaster. Two addicts can't work.

Lily's departure was on the edge of my mind, but I tried to avoid the thought. I tried my best to stay positive for work.

Lily took me to do a formal aptitude test. She'd done hers there and it helped her with her decision to become a teacher. My aptitude test created more confusion than solutions. It also gave an indication of what I was experiencing emotionally in my current profession: 'minimal to no satisfaction and in danger of an overwhelming depression'.

The result indicated my aptitude was well-suited for the health care industry. It suggested I would thrive as a health care specialist. I could have become a psychologist, but the woman advised me to stay away from that profession since I would end up becoming too emotionally involved in the patient's stories. She recommended becoming a nutritionist or a doctor as a career path.

I wanted to jump off a bridge.

The test results didn't help me in the least. I couldn't see myself doing those things. I didn't have the courage to go back to formal science studies now, years after my huge 'failure' when I attempted attaining a B.Sc. at the beginning of my recovery. There was no hope for me there. I kept the report on the coffee table, so I could flip through it every now and then to remind myself how miserable I was. It frustrated me that I did not know what I wanted to do. I was still encapsulated in this fear of doing something I disliked and being miserable as a result. Oh, the irony. I was living a self-fulfilling prophecy. I still pined for a life where I would wake up in the morning with passion for my existence and excitement about the day ahead. Instead I woke up with a heavy weight in my stomach and a tight chest. I did not want that any more.

As every day passed, I fought harder against being consumed by these feelings. The daily monotony of sitting at my desk, looking at the computer screen and repeating the same useless things was soul-destroying. I didn't achieve anything for myself. I barely survived from one pay check to the next one. I could pay my bills; I appreciated that. I could pay Gabriel; I was self-sufficient for the first time in my life. I could buy my own food. I had no debt because I decided not to use credit cards to pay extra for unaffordable things. I paid cash for all big purchases. But something still eluded me. My work was all-consuming and extraordinarily demanding.

It sucked the energy right out of me. I still lived with an intense amount of fear. I couldn't get out of my situation. I was constantly fixed in this cycle of doing something I didn't want to do. I prayed for change, for an opportunity that would help me to leave that situation behind. My previous work was similar – I worked at my parents' company in the Finance Department. I was miserable there too. It felt like when people saw me, for some reason it said FINANCE on my forehead.

I had created this misery for myself. I regretted so much of my past. And I despised people who did what they loved. Many of those around me lived their passions. I was injured to the core for not being one of them. Then I turned it onto myself. Surely, it wasn't their fault that they were loving life! They worked hard to get where they wanted to be, I did not. I dived into the self-pity pool. I blamed it on my hard life, the hurt I've suffered and the debilitating abuse. I lived in this cycle for a while. This state of being stuck. I really hoped and prayed for something to change. I didn't understand the necessity of actioning then. Nothing would change if I kept doing the same things every day.

2015/05/24

> *So, it has been a while since I last wrote. My mind has lifted me off my feet and carried me to different dimensions I could only dream of. I've plenty on my mind, piles of stuff I'm holding on to, many fear-based thoughts. I did it again, made the same mistake again.*

I went to a man's house knowing full well what would
happen, but I was acting out. I required chaos to make
me feel worthy and whole. It was a lapse in judgement.
I'm angered at my stupidity and my inexplicable need
for self-destruction. Two steps forward three steps back.
I must forgive myself for my actions. I deserve better than
this. I must forgive my body and myself.

This is an important subject. Many women struggle with this. I did not value myself around men. I saw myself as an object. I didn't consider the possibility that there might be anything else of interest about me apart from my body and the sexual gratification I could give. To me sex was love. My character and my values lost their power. All that was left was my body because I could not see how else it could possibly work. It did not make much sense to me. I used sex to get what I wanted in my previous relationships and in my life. I wanted affirmation mainly, a sense of love and intimacy. I thought sex was just that. I hoped to feel warm and fuzzy after being touched. It didn't work that way; I felt used most of the time. Of course, I displayed the same behaviour repeatedly. My history taught me this was the only way to get affirmation and love from a man. This was how life worked. I never felt safe and loved when my stepfather snuggled up behind me in bed in the mornings. Whenever I showed unease about his 'snuggling', his surliness and anger intensified for extended periods. I broke the cycle by understanding and facing the reality of this behaviour.

I hated the feeling of guilt and shame, because I wasn't true to myself. I didn't give myself enough credit. I felt like a measly piece of flesh, when what I am is infinitely much more than that. I began to examine my being. What do I like in me, apart from my sexuality? I did a sexual inventory of my past behaviour, so I could identify patterns in my conduct. It wasn't easy, but as soon as I did it, my actions made sense.

Isla Stone

2015/06/28

I'm stressed. I really could use some quiet time. I want to get away from everyone and everything for a while. I want to close myself up in my space and cry and scream and shout and kick and sleep.

My insides are damp with sorrow. I'm angry, I'm tired. I'm frustrated and desolate. I'm done with shitty people and lost causes.

I'm lonely. Sometimes it seems to me that I'm incapable of having intimate relationships. I have difficulty to maintain friendships because I struggle with intimacy. Even after three years in sobriety I must still change many things. At times I'm stuck. Then I feel I haven't changed anything. I've made mere droplets of progress. I push too hard and lose track of the tangible progress I've made.

I mourn Lily's leaving. We have spent so many good times together. She was my pillar of strength and opened my mind to new ideas. She showed me the courage and determination I wished to find in myself. I'm going to miss her and her cheerful laugh. I cried today. I'll probably cry lots of other times in my silence. I didn't write enough about the fun we had together. I'll miss John when he is gone even though he complicates my mom and Alex's lives. I'm being self-centred around Lily. I'm focusing on my loss; not on her adventure. I obsess about my choice of staying behind, my cage at the Pharmaceutical company. I wish it was me who could escape. My life has so many notes of satisfaction, yet I focus on the negative aspects. I'm depressed. I'm anxious at work. I'm frustrated about not taking steps towards a better future for myself. My excuses lie in my idle idea that I'm waiting for doors to open. I don't see any, but I'm waiting for the miracle to fall into my lap.

How I wish I had a thought or an idea I could make my own! I want to be confident enough to follow through with something. I'm a scared, lonesome, selfish soul trying her utmost to find her place in this world. My world is small. I can't find anything to be or to hold on to that makes me feel worthy.

These are only my thoughts right now; they are not me. This is not my truth. They are negative and regressive. I can't allow them to consume me. I deserve goodness in my life.

In self-absorption, I made Lily's thrilling adventure about me and my despair. I often felt guilty about this. I didn't know how to process the loss. It was difficult; I burnt up inside. I wasn't sure how to approach the subject. In the days before she left, there were times where we simply sat together in silence. Then there were other times where we cried.

The night before she left, we had an agonising little farewell party. My sister and some other of Lily's friends were there and everyone pitched in to help her pack her bags, to roll her clothes up into bundles to fit as much as possible in her bag. I distantly watched from the doorway. I had a memory of my own enthusiastic packing-the-evening-before when I went to Malaysia, but I completely blocked it from my mind. I felt rejected. Was she leaving because of me?

And so, the end came. I had to go to the airport to say goodbye to Lily. I didn't write about saying goodbye to her in my diary. I was in complete denial. I did not want to face the actuality that I would live alone now.

I knew there would be a huge hole in my life from here onwards. Lily filled that void perfectly and comfortably. Our mutual support was incomparable to anything either of us had ever experienced before. We didn't know it while we were living it. We took it for granted. The days and weeks melted together, I killed some of her plants, she nurtured some of my maggots, I brought a cat home, she threw him in the shower, I hated washing dishes, she hated talking about her emotions. The list goes on. We lived together. It was some of the best times of our lives.

2015/06/29

> *Today I sent my CV to my mom. Any action is better than no action at all. I asked my friend about the project he had mentioned. He said he has heard nothing. I'm not sure he is telling me the truth. I've surrendered this situation to my Higher Power. My boss was made the financial director today. At least this is good news. Maybe things will start progressing rapidly now. I'm thankful for that.*
>
> *I saw a great grey egret and a white flock of birds this morning. I welcome these cosmic, positive signs. Later, I also saw two white egrets flying together. They were gorgeous. I didn't appreciate that sight as much because I had finished work by then and my mind was racing.*
>
> *I want to write Lily a goodbye letter, but I'm not sure if she will want to read it. She avoids emotion as much as I do. We are the same that way.*
>
> *I'm overwhelmed by every day. Sometimes I find it difficult to breathe. I'm thankful for my job, I'm doing*

my best, but I choose a healthier, happier, more mentally stimulating, and financially stable life.

2015/08/12

I haven't written in a while. Work has been challenging and emotionally draining. I'm stuck doing something I don't want to. I hate it. It has consumed me for the past few weeks. Even my Angel Cards held back. I had to change my thoughts and my vibrations, or I would be a captive in a perpetual cycle of stuckness. I don't want that. I'm more positive, clearer, focused. I should act on my dream. My first stages are ready, now I must break them into achievable smaller pieces. It will happen, it will be successful. I'll do the things I want to do. I can and am doing these things now.

Once I started doing morning pages everything shifted. The more I open myself up to the world, the more it opens itself up to me. I'm allowing the energy to flow. That was the missing ingredient. I blocked the Universal Energy by having low vibration. I never grasped how important it was to have a healthy diet or how important exercise is. Being in nature and breathing fresh air also contributes to a shift in my vibrational energy. The more I allow myself to open to the world, the more energy flows to and through me.

The better I feel the more fun I have. Then it's easier to relax and breathe. That's when it's easier to access higher vibrational energy. Then I have more abundance in my life, an abundance of money, love, fun, joy, freedom, and energy. When I flow through life, float through the stream to majestic places instead of staying and stagnating in infested waters in puddles filled with scum.

I've received many gifts this week. Above all, I got love and acceptance from Alex for which I'm completely grateful. I'm thankful for mending my relationship with my mom.

I was close, so close. My research had reached a summit. I nearly understood it all. Some of the fundamentals were still missing. I knew that when I vibrated on a higher level, I could get what I wanted. It was difficult still, because I wasn't sure what I wanted. I knew I wanted to be happy, to live life, and to enjoy my work. I wanted to have better friends and to become unstuck.

I got a little closer to what I wanted and further away from what I did not want. In retrospect, I appreciate how this contrast helped me to approach the space where I finally am today. I noticed my unhappiness with what I was doing. I began to experience an inner shift, although I didn't act yet. It took me much longer to get to that point. I was still finding the missing pieces. I had to fill in some bits before I could become fully aware of where I wanted to go. The concept of higher vibrational energy was new to me. I heard it somewhere.

I loved my Angel Cards. I read them every day. When I was still living with my parents – before the John debacle – there was a terrible day where I planned a quick exit again; I wouldn't even write letters or anything. I decided to read my Angel Cards just once more. When I spread the cards out on my bed, the bedside lamp flitted. That reading saved me. I heard what I needed to hear (or read what I needed to read). I was safe and at peace. Everything was okay in that moment. I survived another day. My Angel Cards have immense wisdom. Because I read them every day, I became obsessed about some cards. If they appeared, I would have a hard or volatile day. If the 'bad' cards popped up in a spread, I would have a knot in my stomach the whole day. I'd wait for the sudden clang of the axe. Sometimes the clang never happened, often it did. In retrospect, my obsession with these cards were harmful. I based my expectations for the day ahead on the cards that came up.

Some of the cards were positive. Once or twice incredible things happened when these encouraging cards came up, but I developed an expectation. When these cards came up, I would forcefully hope for something incredible to happen. Then nothing happened. I would come home, exhausted with disappointment and contemplate where I must have gone wrong in the day. The cards played a large part in my well-being when I wasn't overly expectant or obsessive. When I really needed them to tell me what I had to hear (not what I wanted to hear), they were good for me.

I stopped reading them every day after a while. I used them as a channel for connecting to my Spirit Guides and Higher Power. It was even more fluid and easy when I became adept at making that connection without the cards.

After recurrently reading about vibrational shifts and energy in my Angel Cards, these words started to stand out to me. I listened to the Hay House World Summit 2015, I listened to the 'Clarity' clip between Dr Wayne Dyer and Esther Hicks. This is where I discovered Abraham Hicks, via Esther Hicks. I still listen to her clips on YouTube. I loved it, although I did find the channelled ideas a bit strange. I had difficulty to fully absorb it. I still focused extensively on my Program and Louise Hay. I tried my best to love myself. It was still hard – I did many things that stood in contradiction to loving myself. I slept around; I disrespected my happiness and my body. I don't even want to think about what I ate. Despite that, I made some small steps in the direction of overall health. I recognised behaviours I wanted to stop and observed why I displayed those behaviours. I went to gym occasionally. I was satisfied with my overall health even though the food I ate wasn't of outstandingly high quality or vibration. The balancing of it all seemed impossible. Lily often gave me grief about my diet. I ate whatever I wanted. I have a weakness for sugar. I love baking and eating wheaty, caky, sugary treats. It felt good to drink milk and eat chocolates. I ate for the feeling, not the taste. I'd go to Woolies and buy a tray of cupcakes, a bag of malted chocolates, and some biscuits. I'd go home to pig out on my own. Lily would never have put that in her body. She often asked me if I didn't have a wheat intolerance, like her. Those foods lifted my spirit but would end with a self-loathing stomach ache. Then I would promise myself to never, ever do it again, until I justified it to myself the next time I binged.

After Lily moved to Bangkok, I stopped binge eating as often. A load of unhealthy snacks in one sitting made me ill. I had become more aware of my body and how it responded to what I put into it. A few days after a binge I would feel depressed and sickly. All the sugar changed my brain chemistry and made me miserable. I still ate sweet things, but not as much. I binge ate often before the emotional and spiritual shift I experienced at that time. The change was gradual, almost unnoticeable. I can't even say how it happened. I now know what changed it; I had taken one step closer to having a bit more love for myself.

Food was a touchy subject when I grew up. I couldn't eat whatever I wanted to because John would often claim ownership of some of the food in the house. These items would be the nice things, the tasty things I could not buy for myself. Things that would induce guilt for being eaten. Chocolates, chocolate spreads, biscuits and sweets were kept off limits in the refrigerator or pantry. I always had to ask if I could eat anything except the bread. If I wanted a glass of milk I would have to ask, if I wanted some cold drink I would have to ask. There would be fights and screaming in the house if I gobbled up something I wasn't supposed to eat. I didn't have much self-control either. If I ate some chocolate spread, I would eat the whole tub, if I ate the chocolate, I would eat the whole chocolate. If I ate the biscuits, I would eat all the biscuits. I was never one for half-measures. Sharing and having to be considerate restricted me. I would bake my own things at home. Then I could eat the whole cake, or the whole batch of flapjacks. That's how I got around the problem. This resulted in a weight problem in high school. The emotional eating kept me from going insane. I didn't fathom how dysfunctional it was. I thought there must be something wrong with me for being so greedy. I always got myself into trouble because of it. It was like that from the day I walked into the house with John. He had a problem with my weight, and often made me exercise. He would put me on diets too. He would not let me buy my own clothes. At the beginning of every new season, he would go with me to buy the clothes he wanted me to wear. I was never really allowed to choose clothes I wanted. He reared me into the shape he wanted me to be in. I've often spoken to Gabriel about this. It is terrifying, in retrospect. I'm immensely grateful that I found my voice and got out of the house. I'm thankful that I can see my own abilities, strengths, and power. That was by far my biggest blessing.

When Lily and I lived together, I was processing my emotions about John, the possibility of his imminent death, and the confusion this caused me. I had never hated someone I loved so much. The contradictory emotions were extreme. The feeling of when he dies it will be better, and then feeling horribly guilty for even thinking that. My anger towards him scared me at times.

Pushing and pulling, pushing and pulling ...

During 2014 John told us he would die soon. He said he was terminally ill. After a few years of fear, it dawned on me that he was lying, he may have been ill but he wasn't on his death bed. I was livid with myself. I had fallen for his lies again. It was yet another one more of his manipulative games. He was playing with all of us. I was furious with my mother because she stayed with him out of a sense of misplaced duty. I was angry. The more I tried to forgive him as my Program told me, the more he did to piss me off. My brother suffered because of the emotional abuse he experienced every day. My mother unravelled slowly. The woman I once respected for her strength and capabilities had turned into a crumpled heap of despair. I didn't know what to do or where to turn. There was absolutely nothing I could do about it. It wasn't my choice. It was my mother's. She was the only one who could change it.

CHAPTER 9

A Beautiful Twist

The thought of a meaningful relationship intimidated me. I considered myself to be damaged goods. I was apprehensive about potential problems that I would somehow fail to deal with. I also feared I would simply not get the opportunity to be my best in a loving relationship. I still displayed many problematic behaviours. I was still needy, confused, and angry. I had worked on these aspects of myself intensively, but also cried many tears of terrible self-pity about it sometimes. Then I came to a time where I began accepting that I was who I was. When I came to accept myself absolutely, sincerely, and unequivocally for *all* my traits, I would be ready for a loving relationship. I knew if I wanted to be in a sustainable long-term relationship, I had to love myself first. When I loved myself first, saw myself as a whole person and not as a half a human where someone else would complete me, then only would I be ready for a relationship. The self-love grew steadily. I still had difficulties, I didn't completely love and accept myself, but I treated myself with a bit more respect than what I used to in the past. I tried to see myself and talk to myself with compassion. The negative self-talk still happened, but I looked at those words. I changed them.

Then one day Timothy and I were ready to embark on this journey. Finally, we both saw our value enough to start our relationship. We've had some trials and tribulations, but we're still together, we still love and adore each other. We still respect each other. I'm still grateful every day for sharing this experience with him. We're at the start of an adventure. It gets better, more fulfilling, and exciting every day. We try not to forget where we came from. We appreciate each other. The core of our relationship is that I can do what I want to do, and he can do what he wants to do. We are two separate entities. We come together to share our experiences after each day.

One day Timothy arrived at the Sunday meeting after not having been there for a while. The day before, someone at a mutual friend's party told me Tim was in a new relationship. I was excited when he pitched up at the Sunday meeting. When we had a coffee break, he told me he had broken up with the woman. Of course I was pleased, although I tried my utmost not to show it. I was undeniably attracted to him and would do whatever I could to stand close to him at meetings. He came to me to say goodbye after the meeting. My face warmed up when he approached me. When he wrapped his arms around my shoulders, I pulled back from him a little and looked him in the eye. He nodded slightly. A knowing entered my being, I knew it was the right time. So did he. In that moment it was clear that I had known him since forever. I was home. When he let me go, he asked me if I wanted to go out for dinner. I said yes.

He is fourteen years older than me. He has two unique sons who call me 'stepmom'. I love them dearly. Although I'm not that much older than them, I think of them as my children. I'm a proud stepmom. It's weird, I know. I never thought I would feel this way, but I do. His eldest son is twenty-six and his younger son is twenty-three. They are intelligent and handsome men and they've embraced me as their father's partner. Tim is special. He is honourable, honest and loyal. He raised his sons to be same and I'm proud of the men they are. The quality of honour in a man has been scarce in my life. I'll always be thankful that I discovered this admirable human being. He will apologise if he is wrong, he will assist wherever he can, and he will never take advantage of anyone or any situation. He always, always does the right thing. He is principled, discerning, and strong. To me, he could have been a knight at the round table. He is an incredible father, and that to me is priceless. His children love and respect him.

There was a time when I was much too involved in the conditions of the other person's love to live my own life. I was afraid that if I did not do what my partner wanted me to do, they would leave me. I would sit and stare at my boyfriends while they were doing whatever it was that they were doing. Some of them played computer games or mended furniture. I had no interests of my own. My interests purely involved that of my partners before I worked on myself. I had an intense fear of losing the one I was with based on a false belief that I wasn't good enough. It was so intense that I felt it in every bone of my body. I was a hopeless co-dependent.

Seeking their approval, my partners' choices also affected my own preferred drugs and types of alcohol. Usually I would be happy to use whatever they were using. I developed a preference for some of these substances over time. I had no hobbies or passions. Of course, I tried at times. I made feeble attempts at pursuing my old passions. I didn't know for sure if these were still passions – I was out of touch with myself. I lost pieces of me, they crumbled away and disappeared into the chaos of my life.

I didn't experience any of this in my new relationship with Tim. I took the time to get to know myself again. I hadn't yet re-established all my passions, but I knew what I liked. During our relationship I've allowed myself to explore who I am even more.

2015/10/12

> So much change has embraced my life since Lily left. I'm swept up in a wave of remarkable transformation. It seems that Lily's departure held a gift – it granted me a greater opportunity for the restoration of happiness. I've been crazy busy. My life has been full. I've had the privilege of being in a relationship with another addict. His name is Timothy. I've known Tim for almost a year now. I met him at one of the meetings I attended on and off, but where he genuinely stuck with me was at my regular meeting. I started going to this meeting last year when I asked Dahlia to be my sponsor. I attend it consistently. I had a crush on him, but not an obsessive

one. I kept on reminding myself that I chose not to be with another addict. Our subtle flirting went on for almost a year. A month and a half ago his first (brief) relationship in recovery came to an end. I had not seen him for a while at the meeting. Two Sundays ago, he was there. We hugged after the meeting. He stood on the step, and I came and hugged him. I looked up into his eyes. His warmth filled me. I knew this was perfect; we both belonged in that place at that time. We knew it was the right time. When we went out for our first date, we didn't even kiss. We were such awkward addicts. We didn't kiss on the second date either. On the third date we played tennis with his friends. He suggested that we grab something to eat afterwards. We ended up at a burger place. At the table, after we paid the bill, he looked me in the eyes and kissed me. It felt completely natural, with his safe arm around my shoulders. We have virtually seen each other every day since. We had our first date on the 31st of August.

I can't believe how fast time has flown by. We have fallen into a profound love. It's been overwhelming and exciting. I still adore spending time on my own, but I also love spending time with him. I'm sincerely appreciative for this experience with him, for his care, his understanding, his love, and his attention to detail. I appreciate his soul, the man that he is. It has been huge adjustment for me. I'm used to being on my own, doing my own thing, throwing the ashes of my soul in the air to see where they land. I've started training for the warrior race with some new friends. My life is fuller than ever before.

2015/12/11

Today marks my second day at Port St. Johns. I have enjoyed it immensely. I was last here with Barbara back in 2013. Wow!

I can't believe how long ago that was. I have a history in recovery now. I've made new friends and immense progress. It's gratifying to reflect upon the innumerable changes in my life. Good, great, marvellous changes. Tim and I have been together for almost four months That is insane! We miss each other. I wish he could be here with me in Port St. Johns. He is at home working. But we'll get an opportunity to go away together soon enough.

I wanted to leave the Pharma company at the beginning of this year. I had heaps of hopes for ages. But if my plans had come to fruition already who knows where I'd be now? Most certainly not in this moment and most certainly not this happy. Even after everything, I still forget that I don't know what is best for me, but that God does. I must learn to let go more; to trust more. I must do my Steps Eight and Nine. This holiday is Step Eight and when I get back it's Step Nine. It's crucial to do both soon. I also want to write a letter to Francis; he is coming up quite often in my mind.

I'm grateful today.

2016/01/04

My day started off with a bit of anxiety. It was time to go back to work. It unfolded decently though. After work I went past the pharmacy to get some medicine. I waited for Timothy to respond to my messages. I wanted to swing by his place for a cup of coffee. This has become a bit of a routine and my irritation levels escalated because he didn't text me to let me know what was going on. I became anxious and nervous. What if he doesn't want to be with me any more? What if I'm annoying him? What if he feels I'm too clingy? What if he doesn't find me attractive because I gained weight during the holidays? I immediately became defensive. I decided that I wouldn't see him this afternoon. Then I stopped myself ... just breathe.

These are insane thoughts full of fear and insecurity. I'm me. I'm good enough. I'm lovable.

I must do things for myself, strictly for me. What Timothy does is none of my business. This is my life. I love Tim and Tim loves me.

I need to do some exercise; yoga, running or gym. I need some endorphins.

After I saw Tim, I went to my parents in a miff mood. I'm trapped, and I'm the one who built the cage. Today I wrote about it in the morning pages.

I herewith release these feelings.

In the first three months of our relationship, Tim went to Ballito for his cousin's wedding. The invitations were sent out a few months prior to us starting our relationship. He was single at that time, so there wasn't a space for me. Our relationship was new, fresh, and exciting. My mother went to Umhlanga on the same weekend for a work function and this coincided with my Grannie and Uncle Marius' holiday in Ballito. Everyone I knew was in KwaZulu-Natal and I was cemented in Centurion. Timothy suggested I should take the trip with him although I wouldn't be able to attend the wedding. I was fine with him going on his own. I would spend some time with myself in Centurion. On the Friday I was irritated and anxious. I decided to surprise him and called to let him know I would fly to Ballito that Friday evening. Tim was elated, but when he picked me up at the airport, he looked a bit ill. He complained of a terrible ache in his stomach. He said it was probably caused by some meat he had for dinner and told me he had to go the loo. He said everything would be fine.

Tim had lived with an untreated inguinal hernia for a couple of years. This is caused by a weak area in the stomach muscles and organs or tissue, such as the intestines, get pushed out of that space.

We got to Tim's uncle's beach house, where we were staying with Tim's sons and his brother. As the night progressed, so did his stomach ache. The pharmacies were all closed. We had no medication with us. He sweated feverishly and became incoherent. His brother went to a garage shop to buy some Epsom Salts. I fed Tim a whole teaspoon of this dissolved in water. I didn't know one is supposed to use only a tiny pinch. He groaned in anguish while coiled up in a damp ball in the middle of the bed. Every so often he would sprint to the bathroom, belching loudly into the toilet bowl. I've never seen anyone as ill. I was sick with worry. After a great deal of coaxing and bargaining he allowed us to call his mother, who rushed over. She said we should take him to the closest hospital. He didn't have medical aid, but fortunately, his uncle and mother paid for him to be admitted into a private hospital.

The doctor who examined him at the clinic told us sternly that Tim would die if he didn't get surgery immediately. His hernia had become incarcerated. They moved him to another facility for an emergency operation. I was distressed by the thought that I had barely found this honourable man and now he is on his deathbed. I spent a great deal of time with his mom, brother, and sons during and after his operation. It was slightly awkward since we didn't know each other well. But sitting there in the waiting room, we shared our mutual love for and worry about Tim. We were hugely relieved when they told us they'd managed to fix the hernia. He would survive. This experience brought us all much closer together. I was thankful to have been there, and to offer support to him and his family. At the same time, I appreciated the support I received from them.

During December 2015, I went to Port St. Johns with my mother and Alex. I experienced infinite gratitude. Where two years prior I wasn't allowed to see my brother, I was now on holiday with him and my mom. I still had unresolved emotions towards my mother. I still needed her affirmation with my whole being. My work with Gabriel was directed extensively towards not having any expectations of her and her behaviour. I always wanted her to be something that she wasn't. I wanted her to hug me; to love me. I wanted her to cuddle me, to pull the covers to my chin and say everything would be okay. I wanted my mother to come to my house to help me hang my curtains because I had no idea how to do it. I wanted her to say that what John did wasn't my fault. I wanted to hear her say that she loves me unconditionally, that she would always keep me safe and protected. I wanted her to tell me there were magical things in this world, that absolutely anything was possible if I put my mind to it. I wanted her to feel I could reach the stars; that I was her precious, fabulous, delightful child. None of those things happened when I was young or an adult. She did her best. She made sure there was food on our table, that we had a bed to sleep in and a roof over our heads. She made sure I went to school and got an education. I valued her opinion on non-emotional decisions. I would often get overly emotional, while she was logical, rational, and mostly right. She ensured that I had a car and could go to universities, even though I didn't achieve much. My mother did her best with the emotional and physical tools she had.

I set myself up for disappointment day after day, waiting for the fairy in the palm of her hand with the unrealistic expectations I placed upon her. She was the one who kept things real. She made mistakes, horrible mistakes, but we all do. I allowed my anger in. It was okay to feel. It was okay to allow myself the emotions that showed their hues in my body. The emotions flash viscerally inside my body. They occur in a range of colours and in different areas; every colour is different and is associated with an emotion. A flash of red anger, behind my eyes. A seize of dirty yellow clenching at my solar plexus when I'm consumed with anxiety. As I became more aware of where my emotions displayed themselves, it became easier to breathe into them to calm them. I did not understand why she kept me away from my brother, or why she was still with John after the secret spilled out. I did not understand why – in her shock – she blamed me. I was hurt and angry. I spent nights screaming into my pillow.

I had a choice, like I did with my father. Do I carry these angry emotions with me? Do I allow them to determine what I do or how I behave? Love is much more powerful than anger and hurt. On my life journey I've met many people who discarded their fathers because they felt their fathers discarded or abandoned them. I had faith in my father. As a result, now I have a relationship with him, and I'm grateful and enjoy our relationship. The same has happened over time with my mother. The joy and acceptance I experienced with my mother after the saga is beyond anything I can describe. It's probably because I stopped having expectations of her. Once I let go of expectations, the strangest thing happened. The Universe suddenly allowed blocked energy to flow. My mother suddenly listened to me. I felt accepted and heard. When I decided to let go, our relationship blossomed.

2016/02/14

> *So many eventful things have happened in the last three*
> *weeks or so. I've been taken up in a huge whirlwind.*
> *One with feathers and beauty. I'm thankful. Excited, but*
> *nervous and a bit anxious as well. A huge task lies ahead*
> *of me. I hope and pray that I'll be capable of pulling this*

off. Tonight, I'm going to pray. And tomorrow and the next day.

I haven't written down my true emotions in the longest time. I haven't been authentic in my writings for the longest time. Where do I begin?

Frida and I got in touch again recently. It was exciting to hear from her again. So, what happened is that she asked me to help her with one of her groups. I agreed. Most of her gatherings are process groups, but this was one of the Fellowship groups she ran from her centre. It has taken me long to get used to it, but I'll get the hang of it quickly. I believe in myself. Life unfolds with elegance if you allow it to. As it went on Frida asked me to help more, which I'm happy to do. We were starting a business called the Wellness Toolbox. It is an addictions auditing company. I'm sure it will take off like a shuttle and fly straight into the stratosphere!

2016/02/21

My mother's stubbornness turned this into a testing day. Recently I found out she allowed the psychiatrist to prescribe Xanor to Alex. I flipped. It's a benzodiazepine! John himself is a benzo addict. She allows the doctor to prescribe this to Alex, yet she constantly talks about her worry that he might have an addictive personality. I went to see her today to see how she was doing. She pissed me off thoroughly. She won't listen to anything I say. She is happy in her sick, narrow space; her chaos driven existence. I wanted to have my birthday there, but John is going to get hair implants done on Friday. Apparently, he is of the opinion that our relationship needs work. He does not deserve my energy or time of day. I wanted to have my birthday at Grannie's house, but she and Uncle Marius are going away.

I'm a little down. Just for today I feel this way. I'm hurt that my mother didn't ask me about my life or myself. Her self-centredness wounded me. At the end of it I should be okay. I know she will never be the mother I want her to be. I've accepted that, but I forget sometimes. I accept that John will always be there because she can't change. She chooses not to. I accept that she will never love me in the way I expect her to. Sometimes I feel cold towards her and the situation. I'm tired of it. No more. I'll not allow it to get me down any more. I let it go. I put this situation, my mom, Alex, John into a bubble and I ask God to take them into His capable hands and find the solutions that will benefit all concerned. I'm in gratitude.

I was surprised when my mother invited me along to Port St. Johns that December. For many years she only took Alex and his friend along. They boys would go fishing or riding their bikes. The friend's presence made it easier for my mother because she didn't have to entertain Alex all the time.

It was a year of awkward reconciliation and I appreciated it and accepted the invitation. Although we did not get her regular holiday unit, it was still at the bottom of the lodge that she frequented. She found herself a spot on the patio with a view of Port St. Johns' beauty. She would sit there for hours at a time on her cell phone and play games and smoke.

John always had some reason for not going along on holiday. He rarely spent a holiday with my mom and Alex. I saw my mom was depressed. It distressed me. It was the first time in my life I saw her staring mindlessly at her phone and smoking one cigarette after the other. I asked her if she would consider getting help for depression, but she said she was fine. She told me she was simply having a bad time, that it would pass after the holiday. We spoke about what happened in the past years in great depth. She was tormented and enraged. She blamed herself and called herself a bad mother. She said she had failed all three of her children.

The more I tried to convince her otherwise, the more she stuck to this self-directed guilt and anger.

CHAPTER 10

A True Lesson in Self-love

I exerted myself in the months that followed these entries. I worked at the Pharma company, then I went to the centre where Frida did the therapy groups in the evenings. I went three nights a week – sometimes even more – and ultimately, I burnt myself out.

The initial idea was that I work with Frida to assist her with the group on Wednesdays only. It was tough. I wasn't confident and thought I had to know lots more than I did. When I look back now, I can see how much wisdom I actually had. I had no belief in my ability to transfer my knowledge to the people in the group. It was just a meeting, not a process group, it was hardly a therapy session. I took it far too seriously. I took everything too seriously; I kept myself tightly wound up about everything I did. I wanted to show how well I did this because I saw it as my ticket out of the Pharma company. I wanted to create a place for myself there. I was fully dedicated. It was good to be a part of the team. I got keys to the house.

At the back of my mind I had a niggling sense of not pushing myself enough to get my own practice going. I envisioned my own touch-therapy business. However, what I honestly wanted was to be as good as Frida; I wanted to be a psychologist. I wanted to be someone who could do what she and Gabriel did. During these months I sat in her process groups and concentrated on what she said and how she said it. I loved process groups from the outset of my recovery, mostly when the attention wasn't focused on me. I loved how Frida ran them. She was expertly skilled and used her own experiences in the groups to help others to see their own torment and work through it with her guidance. She was a genius. I applied for a correspondence course to study counselling. I did not do my research properly and was horrified to find out in my first lecture that unfortunately it wasn't good for much. It was a basic course I couldn't do much with.

The Wellness Toolbox was Tim's idea and I was over the moon about it. It could help many people and reach them by planting a seed. Frida was initially happy to help, but she avoided the meetings we scheduled to discuss it. It fell flat after a while. I felt used. She was trying to further her practice. I didn't get any fee for my work, I gave my everything, yet I didn't get much in return. These were all choices I made.

2016/05/09

> *My insides are knotted. I can't breathe properly. I'm ensnared in a microscopic space at this Pharma place. It's engulfing me. My face, arms and legs don't fit here any more; I'm being squashed. Marks are left on my skin from this small space where I work. I hate it there, the mindless chatter. I'm exhausted from reconciling and asking and begging for help and then not receiving it. It saps my energy even to write about it. I'm tired of scraping through, of asking without receiving, of scarcely getting through each month. I'm tired of doing errands for people. I really want to get away. It's my impression that everyone there is vastly better than me, and entirely different from me. It's all about their food, their diets, how much work they have. How hard it is for them and how desperate they are to lose their weight while I struggle making it through the month.*
>
> *I love Tim. He makes me happy. But now work sucks the happiness out of me. It's horrid. Tim thinks it's him. It's not. I'm despondent at work. I fear I may be manipulating others out of desperation. I should change my perspective. I must get my mind right, or I won't*

get myself out of this situation. My heart breaks for Alex – he feels worthless. I know that feeling all too well. I don't experience it as often nowadays. I told him he is the smartest kid I know. His marks at school were bad because of everything he must deal with at home. I admire his courage. He is a warrior. I'm distressed about where he is in his life. I love him tremendously and I told him he would not have been spared if he wasn't meant for something greater.

One of my friends' parents was murdered. I can't imagine, I can't bring myself to understand the concept of murder. It makes me sick; no-one should be allowed to take something as valuable as a life. I can't even grasp that anyone feels they have the right to do that.

I don't know if I can trust the people at the centre. I feel funny about the place. Intuition is such a valuable gift; it would be unwise for me not to listen to something so important. Frida is a good friend. She truly believes in my capabilities despite my own reservations. Where does all this leave me?

I try my best to do the right things and to follow my intuition, but sometimes my heart and what I want to believe gets in the way. I'm a dreamer.

I'll never give up on that.

I'll never give up on people.

Please guide me Angels and God and Universe, please show me the right direction. Please help me to follow my intuition and guide me to what to do next.

Isla Stone

2016/05/24

> *Last night I cried myself to sleep; it was cathartic. Right now, I sense that a drifting piece of me has come back into me. Today I hope things will work out well. I've been hypersensitive and irritable with others; it has tired me out. I'm depressed, and I've been for a while now. I can't get myself to do anything that I must do. I'm adrift in lethargy.*

> *This depression has weighed me down for ages, even since before Lily left. It has been more than a year now. I was completely willing to give up last night – I was close. But I fought it. Today will be a better day. Some days I want to give up. On other days I want to keep fighting. I'm not the person who walked into recovery four years ago. I'm lost, but not as lost as I used to be.*

> *I'll break free from the places I don't want to be.*

2016/06/06

> *The past weeks were tough. I've not written much because I've been in a daze, a fuzz. I had a testing episode. I struggled, and I was petrified. I felt alone. I know it's an illusion; I'm not alone. Tim held my hand and guided me the whole time. So did all my friends. God showed me that I wasn't alone either. Even Ginja was with me. My boss was also supportive. All of this happened for a reason. I'll be okay; I found a quaint new place. I'm thankful for this cottage. It was effortless to find. I'm on new medication that seems to work well. I'm listening to metal again to help me wake up in the mornings. I'm less anxious and the weird smell in my*

*nose is gone. I still stare into space, but I like that and
it's not damaging.*

I'm feeling okay.

Life will continue.

I hope things will change for the better.

Inevitably, I woke up in terror one morning. The world caved in
without any reason. I experienced an extraordinary, abnormal sense
of fear. My heart raced; my palms sweated profusely. I knew logically
that the fear was unfounded. I had all these strange physiological
changes overnight, filling me with anxiety. I made an appointment
with my psychiatrist. She diagnosed me with temporal lobe epilepsy
and a bit of a break-down. She changed the medication I was on. It was
a drastic lifestyle adjustment. The medication knocked me out before
bed. It took me ages to wake up in the mornings. In the beginning
I listened to heavy metal and woke up an hour early to get myself
awake. The anxiety subsided. I tried to continue to go to the centre,
but the groups ended far too late in the evenings. By the time I got
home and took my medication it was so late that I couldn't function
when I woke up in the mornings. It was a vicious cycle. I did finally
adjust to the medication after about six months. I stopped going to
the groups and meetings with Frida at the centre and didn't attempt
to go back regularly. Later I realised I did not have the confidence
to run with the opportunity that the universe had provided to me.
I had a chance to do quite a lot and to make a living by doing what
I loved: working with people. But I wasn't ready yet. I held on to the
Pharma company because it gave me a steady income. Frida reckoned
I could simply leave my job. It seemed unrealistic. I didn't have to be
a psychologist. There were many other things that I could consider
at that centre; it was an esoteric healing centre. I was afraid of myself
and my capabilities. What if I succeeded?

At the same time, I worked myself into a coma because I avoided myself and my emotions. I accepted that I had not worked entirely as thoroughly on myself as I had thought. What I disliked the most about all this 'getting better' palaver was that I had to work on myself continuously. Then, the minute I thought I made progress, I saw something else I had to address and felt like I was still ten steps behind. I had extreme expectations of myself.

I signed a lease on the apartment Lily and I had shared for another year after she left. The rent increased and I didn't have a housemate. It was a big, expensive apartment and my finances were tight. Nevertheless, Tim and I had many romantic evenings there watching movies or listening to the night sounds by the river. I miss that place now. During that year it became evident that it would probably be more financially viable if I moved into a cheaper place. Tim helped to convince me of my own thoughts. I decided to move to a cottage on a distant road out in a quiet suburb. It was closer to work in a pretty area on a hill. Still, it somehow felt like a mistake to move there.

I experienced loads of changes. I was holding on to the old too tightly. I undoubtedly wanted the change, but I did not allow myself to embrace it.

2016/06/15

I hope I'll feel better today. I went to yoga yesterday and I managed to do all the postures. I want to go more often now. If I go every day, I'll feel a whole lot better. Yesterday I cried and cried and cried. I sobbed like I did when I was a girl weeping about her daddy. I adore my father. I have this huge space in my heart for him. I don't know if that was to my own detriment. His absence caused huge heartache, a pounding ache in my chest. Last night he called me. I missed three of his calls and then called him back. He said he was sick. I always hate when he is sick. The one time when I was younger, probably in my early teens, I saw him after many years. It was weird. He was ill at that point too. When I got home afterwards, I went into shock. My whole body trembled, and my Grannie had to give me some tea and put me on the couch. I said I was worried about him, but I was actually in shock about seeing him after so many years.

Last night we spoke for a while. It was a good conversation. Later, he called me again and we spoke some more. Then we said goodbye. My phone froze, and he said goodbye again and I said goodbye again, and he said goodbye again, and I said goodbye again. It went on and we giggled. My phone eventually died. The point is that my dad never put down the phone first, because it happened before, and I thought we were playing a game. I'm the one who must switch off the phone first every time. It's a symbol of his love for me, his need to connect with me, and not knowing how. After speaking to him last night I cried non-stop. He stayed on the phone with me because I thought something might have gone wrong with my wheel before we said goodbye. As if he could do something about it from Zimbabwe! I love him. For the first time now, I truly understand. I know he loves me too.

An epic moment, a life changing event happened right there in the car. I did not expect anything different on that day. Many people told me how much my father loved me, and he would reiterate this. The fears I had held on to suddenly vanished. I had to believe in his love. If I didn't make space for it to be believable, I might not recognise it when it was given to me. I was ready for this moment. A palm reader told me the same thing in a bar one night. It was part of my pilgrimage to discover that I was worthy of love. In this moment it all became clear to me. I had an awakening of sorts. Throughout the years we had made memories. He taught me how to drive on a dirt road on my grandfather's farm when I visited him again in my teens. The day before he was supposed to fetch me, I panicked. I was anxious, thinking he might not pitch up. But he did. That is where the change started happening. It was a slow process for me to acknowledge the love I was receiving. I went to visit him a few times on the farm, thereafter he bought a house in White River in Mpumalanga. I visited him there. One year when I was in my twenties and still an emotional wreck, I ran away to him. My father was there for me, even though he was somewhat petrified. When I was alienated from the family he was there. He was by no means perfect, but he has tried to rectify the mess that was created when I was younger. He had my back. He still does. The most important thing is his pride in me. He believes in my abilities, he stands there at the back of the stage with his pom poms and cheers me on, no matter what he thinks about the overall situation.

2016/07/04

> *I'm tired and irritable. I'm numb on the inside, angry, and disappointed. I'm lost and alone. I moved into a new place last weekend. I've scaled down and I've lost my motivation. Nothing that I wanted came to fruition. I can't leave the Pharma company, although I desperately want to. I'm trapped in a tiny house. Nothing is being done about the Toolbox. It's such a terrific tool for all of us! Why is nothing happening? I don't understand. I'm upset because I wanted to find a way to resign. I believed I would find a miracle. This new space is cosy, but it's a bit scary sometimes. I feel disjointed, confused, and uprooted. Timothy gets hung up on issues that do not have immediate solutions, while I try to stay focused on whatever is immediately resolvable. It frustrates me when we have conversations where topics go off on a*

tangent that have no relevance to the immediate fixes that can be found.

I don't like it, I'm tired of being stressed, of pain, of fighting. I don't want to do that any more. I don't want to hurt or care any longer. I want to be. I've had moments of simply being. Right now, the source of my unhappiness and discontentment is my weariness of hoping things will change at career level. The medication may have a role in my mood. The move was another big change. Every time I get a bit closer to my ideal, something hits me and gets me down again. I'm probably wasting my life. I've wasted it up to now. I've not experienced the life I want. I never will.

Or maybe I'm melodramatic and wallowing in an enormous puddle of self-pity. I did not hand in one of my assignments for the counselling course. It upsets me. Surely if work was a huge threat to my soul's well-being then God would make a miracle happen. Also, if I wasn't meant to be here in this new home it would never have worked out this way. On the same token maybe, I wasn't ready for the counselling thing with Frida.

When I'm ready – and the time is right – it will happen. I should merely change my thought processes. If I change the way I look at things, the things I look at change. I'm always safe and protected.

Tomorrow will be a better day.

Isla Stone

2016/07/05

I did not sleep well last night. I imagined I heard sounds. I probably just had many dreams. Perhaps if I can recall those dreams, they might provide answers? My answers must be there, beyond the exhaustion, fear, frustration, defeatism. The answers are within my grasp and the Angels want to tell me. I have this idea to leave a daily diary there at the centre and put up massage types and charge amounts. Then cross out the times that I'm not available. Then people can make appointments in the book as they please.

I'm waiting for the miracle. I'm am ready and open to receive. I'm staying positive and think of only good and happy things.

*Second entry in the evening

I'm depressed. I've worked late a second night in a row. I haven't gone to the centre nor have I attempted any physical activity. On the inside, I'm broken, hopeless, lost, and empty. Work hollows me out. It chips away at me every day. It's getting worse now. The country is in flames. I never like to admit or write about it. Tim says we have boiling frog syndrome. This morning I drove past a crime scene. I suppose in a way it's positive that there was a scene with police. Maybe things are taking a turn for the better. Even Ginja can sense my offishness. I fear this feeling might have to do with the new medication.

Not having any clarity makes me despondent. I must be abnormal. Maybe I should stay at the Pharma company.

Maybe that's all that God ever intended for me. Perhaps that's okay.

2016/07/06

Today I feel better because I choose my thoughts. Yesterday's gratitude list helped me. I'm going to focus on my thoughts and turn them around. Anything negative, I'll turn into a positive gratitude.

Plain and simple.

Focus on the small stuff.

Moment by moment.

Breath by breath.

I now understand that my stepfather was even sicker than I thought. The abuse was surreptitious. Insidious. No abuse is worse than any other. No one deserves to be misused. I always felt that the worst kind of cruelty can't be seen. The emotional, sexual, mental and verbal violence in our home was so intangible. I could never go to someone to show them broken bones or blue eyes. I lived with perpetual confusion and fear. Having said that, I do not think that if I had physical bruises it would have been any easier. My psychotherapy taught me that John is a narcissist. The healthier I became, the more I recognised the scary levels of dysfunction in my family. John's illness seemed to be degenerative. The abuse seemed to get worse over time. My mother lost much of her strength and determination. Lara and I felt she was progressively losing her soul. She had become a shell of a human being. John used gaslighting often, and I only understood this later.

I always thought there was something terribly wrong with me when I was a teen and in my early twenties. He often told me what a liar I was. When I tried to defend myself with facts, he would say that I was lying or twisting his words. It was often about simple things, like a permission to eat something or going out. He would agree to something, but later he would shout, scream, and claim it was done behind his back. I would break my head attempting to recall the initial conversation. Then I'd second-guess myself and assume I must have misunderstood his consent. A recent example is from a while ago when I helped out at their company. My mom and I went out to get lunch. I asked John if he wanted something to eat. He said no. When I came back, he made a 'joke' about 'it being okay'. He said he'll just starve and teased that he is used to this kind of treatment. He told me that he sent me an email stipulating what he wanted for lunch. Slight nuances, scant changes in words, to make me think I did something wrong or misunderstood on purpose.

The same went with the sexual abuse when I was a girl. He would climb into bed with me, and 'cuddle'. It was subtle. He would touch my breasts and my vagina with little flits of his hands. I froze. He told me to relax. He would smile and ask if I thought he was a pervert. I was afraid to answer him because I didn't know what the right answer might have been. I knew what I felt, but I didn't know what to say. I didn't want anyone to get into trouble. I was taught early in life that by being a martyr and a sacrificial lamb, I could make things pan out okay. I could keep things on an even keel and keep everyone safe if I did what I needed to do. This happened from so early on in my life. There was never any penetration. It was merely a continuous uncomfortable, fear inducing environment to grow up in. I blocked it out, as I previously mentioned. It was hard to forgive him. I struggled to accept that this happened and that I couldn't change anything. I now had to resign myself to his presence whenever I wanted to see my mother and brother. The Program taught me that forgiveness was important. I tried to pray, and did all kinds of things akin to praying, like attending full moon ceremonies. I hated myself the most for allowing it to happen to me, and then for not stopping it from happening to my sister. The forgiveness had to begin with me.

2016/07/10

> *So much is going through my mind. I can't seem to pinpoint a thought. Lately, I've been unusually neat. It does not bug me. Tim and I had such a sensational weekend together. It was delightful. Things have finally calmed down. Silence has come. My mind has stumbled on a sanctuary in this cosy place. I'm safe here. Right now, I want to purge and throw out all the tangled emotions of the last month and a half.*

> *John.*

> *As of late John has gotten sicker in his head. He has lied and lied and lied. His psychosis has gotten progressively worse. I assume his addiction to benzodiazepines, codeine and plastic surgery has become unmanageable. Why do I try to figure out what he is doing with his weird moves and behaviours? He is obviously not happy. He wants to leave my mom. He is moving clients away from his own company and he has taken a loan of R500 000.00 for a lifesaving treatment for his heart. This does not make sense to me. He hasn't allowed my mother to go with him when he sees a doctor or goes for his surgeries. He threatens to die and then he is miraculously cured. Next thing we hear, he is undergoing a lifesaving treatment. He speaks of assisted suicide with my mother, and constantly scares Alex about his imminent demise.*

None of it I can believe. He has abused my mother to such a degree that she is incapable of seeing her power to get away from him.

My mother.

When I see my mother, I get this pain in my chest, this aching. I wish beyond anything else in this world that she could find happiness and freedom from this situation that has gotten out of control. Her shoulders are always scrunched up defensively and her face tells stories of unknown hardship and loneliness.

Somehow, I've run out of words. My words are gone. I require nothing in this moment, I'm content. I do not want to think about where things are going or where things have been. I have no urge to move anything anywhere. Right now, in this moment I'm peaceful. Nothing can be better or should be any other way. This is how it's meant to be.

2016/08/14

This past week I struggled with keeping to my meal plan. The cravings had much to do with my period. Ginja is hurt and I'm worried about him. Tim and I had a lovely date night. I fall more in love with him every day. I saw my mother yesterday. She was in such a good space; I'm happy to see that she is feeling better. My issues with John are retreating into a sense of just having had a bad dream. The damage is still there, but it's less evident. Some days are better than others. I'm worried because I've not done my assignment. This is the second assignment now. I'm disappointing myself; I'm

*cross with myself for not having done it. Then again, I
look back at the happenings of the last while and realise
I've not been in a great space until recently. I had to build
myself back up again. It took me a while to learn that it
has been harder, rather than easier.*

After the medication change, I decided to exercise again. I stopped
all structured physical activity when Lily moved to Bangkok. Now I
went back to gym and got an instructor. I followed a prescribed eating
plan to the letter and was astonished by how much better I felt. This
wasn't a half-hearted attempt. You know by now that I struggle with
following through with new regimes. Even after my recovery, this
periodical lack of perseverance is a hurdle. Thankfully, the one thing
I *did* follow through with has been my recovery. I kept telling myself
to follow through with growth. If I followed through, I would learn
more about myself and my recovery. I stayed sober and I tried. My
recovery is a huge achievement for me.

With other things, however, it would often happen that I would
initiate something and then leave it unfinished. Completing things
was a difficult or impossible task. I had heaps of motivation at the
onset. Then I thought about how I couldn't genuinely do it, or how
these other people were much better at it than I. I would tell myself
there was no real point in me trying because they could do it much
better. I wanted to be the best, I wanted perfection, I wanted the
first prize. I often placed obstacles in front of myself. I could never
live up to my own standards, and then I would give up because I did
not do as well as I expected myself to do. I was hard on myself. The
sense of disappointment was so familiar that I did not change that
behaviour until much later. I was used to disappointment and anger
with myself. Feeling incapable because that was all I ever knew. The
training was excellent. I looked healthy. People commented on how
stunning I looked. I hated it. My reaction surprised me. I couldn't take
a compliment – it scared me. The reason I went to gym had nothing to
do with how I looked; it had to do with my health. I wanted to remove

the excess medication out of my body. I didn't want to gain weight. I kept going to gym and felt good. In addition to the adjustment in my medication, the exercise improved my mood. I did it for myself and forgot about the compliments. This reaction still irked me. These realisations came seeping in slowly. I had some time to live on my own again and to take some time for self-discovery. When I stopped going to the centre, I stopped focusing on others. I began to focus on myself. I had to get to know myself without distractions. Timothy was still in the foreground, but he was stable and strong and healthy.

2016/08/30

> *I realise now that I've written in two diaries without thinking about it. Today I'm home with a stomach bug. I have noticed how much my life has changed in a year. I'm beyond grateful. Today is the first anniversary of being with Tim. I'm thankful beyond words for the honour to be in such a loving relationship.*

> *Last night I had a bad moment, where I read Tarot Cards. The future was supposed to hold changes and the Tower Card. I didn't like that. I'm speaking to the Universe every day asking for positive outcomes. I believe I deserve them. All I can do is to live one day at a time. I'm going to the doctor now. When I come back, I'll listen to some shares and do some step work. Frida texted me this morning to ask if I'm coping. I believe I'm okay, but I do feel tired. It might be the medication.*

> **Second entry of the day*

> *I got back from my Doctor now. I have an enterovirus. I've been doing well of late with my health. It does get me down when I get ill, but I must accept it. I ate way too*

much over the weekend. Eating badly affects my health.
I feel utterly miserable. This too shall pass. I must be
patient with myself, I mustn't push myself too hard. I
know I get frustrated when things don't go the way I
want or change the way I want them to. I've avoided
loads of things. I've been angry that I tried and failed.
However, if I don't attempt new things I'll never know.

I tried to talk myself into a positive place. My frame of mind was terrible. I blamed all my unhappiness on my job. I had finally gotten into the most devoted relationship, and I was still not happy. All my unhappiness and pessimism were now aimed at my job. It made me miserable. Please do not misunderstand me, it was hardly roses and violets, but working there wasn't all that bad either. I got money once a month, I worked with cool people and if I had placed my positive energies into the work instead of wasting it all on negativity on misery, I may have had different things to say. I may have been in a much better frame of mind. It was all about my attitude at the end.

It had nothing to do with my circumstances. Once I comprehended that I had to change my attitude towards everything in my life – even my work circumstances – change happened. One of the many secrets of life is that it doesn't get better once your circumstances improve, your circumstances improve once your attitude changes. The attitude I speak of here is how I perceived things. When I focused on things to be miserable about and held on to them, I lived in that cycle. I perpetuated it, and nothing changed. Nothing changes if nothing changes. I knew this in my heart and at the end of every journal entry I wrote a gratitude list. Although I often did not truly feel that gratitude, these lists did help me to feel a bit better about the things I wrote about. I first felt an incredible wave of gratitude shortly after going into recovery on the day when I drove along and suddenly saw colour again. Like I said, it was a day like any other until that gratitude flooded me. It was the most incredible thing I had ever experienced. All my life I intentionally attempted to numb my emotions, and that day I experienced something exquisite. I was convinced I would never allow numbing of my emotions again. I was staggered when I recognised how much good I've withheld from myself. When I numbed the difficult emotions, I deprived myself of the good ones too.

Once I zoned my attention on things I liked at work, rather than those I dislike, it became easier to work there. I was less exhausted when I got home. The obsession finally left me. The honesty of that moment hurt. I had to admit that God might not have much else planned for me. I hurt myself by saying that, and it confirmed how much work I still had to do on myself. The way I wrote about my days, the way I felt about myself. I was practicing self-love, but the key word here was practicing. I still hadn't come to accept myself.

I was entangled in a feeling that I had worked bloody hard but had gotten nowhere. I still had to do extensive work to be something or to be recognised as someone. I didn't know what this something was, but I thought when I reached that point, I would finally be acceptable. I wanted everyone around me to accept me. If I had a better career or made more money maybe my mom would find me more acceptable, maybe John would find me more acceptable, maybe my father would find me more acceptable. I pushed in the wrong directions to grow for the wrong reasons. The biggest lesson I learnt from this time in my life is that you can't force growth. It happens naturally. I did grow during this time. As a matter of fact, I experienced a growth spurt, but I did not grow in the way I expected to

2016/08/31

> *Thoughts become things. This is truer than I ever imagined. I spent the last two days at home on sick leave and I did some research. Beyond anything I believe this now. Feelings, thoughts, the way I perceive my reality becomes reality. I have learnt that all of this is attached to spiritual practices. My Higher Self knows what I'm here to do and every day I'm more in tune with my Her.*

I'm here to absorb every bit of the physical experience. To live, to love, to be. I'm an extremist; I want these experiences so intensely. I want to travel, to enjoy my work, and be my own boss, I want to sow love all over the world and teach people what I have learnt, and what I'm still going to learn. Life is full to the brim. I want to absorb it, feel it, breathe it!

The shackles of fear are behind me now, there is nothing to fear. Fear is nothing. The self creates it. I overcome fear now, it's no longer an attachment to me, I allow it no power over me. I release fear and replace it with faith and love.

Love is the ultimate power of this Universe. If I have love, then fear can't find me. Fear is a projection of the future. Love and faith are living in the now. I choose life, passion and understanding of my fellow man.

Today I'm thankful that I had this moment. It taught me about my ability to love.

2016/09/06

I dreamt about Mr Chambers. I walked up to him and I could not see clearly. He could not see me when I walked up behind him. He said, 'Hello Isla'. I said, 'Hello Mr Chambers. I miss art'. He responded with, 'I miss art too, especially the primary and secondary colours'.

Art is something I truly love. I've lost that part of me.

There was a sudden change, a good one. I could finally think again. The all-consuming dark hole of despair I often found myself in for the better part of two years finally and slowly dissolved. I was caught in a recurring depression, but I only realised it when I started to get better. Anxiety and incorrect medication might have caused it. The modest granny flat I had moved into to save some money was cosy, but it took a some getting used to. It sat in front of the main house up on a hill. There was no wall in front of the entrance. It was directly accessible from the street. It was a quiet neighbourhood with a vigilant neighbourhood watch. I had a sense of safety, but there were times at night when I sat in my dinky lounge and felt that someone was watching my silhouette through the curtains. I thought nothing of it and ascribed it to normal new home paranoia. I didn't watch TV when I lived on my own. I would often sit and watch YouTube videos on my laptop.

One evening Tim and I were relaxing at my cottage. I had not been living there for long. We watched a movie and then went to bed. I left a narrow kitchen window with burglar bars open for my cat. I was puzzled and disoriented when Tim woke me up the next morning to ask why I had left the door open. I had not. Anxiously, he wanted to know why I left the gate open. I said I hadn't. He ran to the lounge and asked where my laptop was. It confused me. I suddenly had a horrid realisation that someone had broken into my home. The bile in my stomach fell all the way to my feet. I stayed calm and looked outside. My car was still there. I looked inside the house and saw that our cell phones were missing. They were charging in my bedroom right next to the bed. I felt violated. I didn't care about my belongings. Gratitude flooded me. We were safe. Horrible crimes happen in South Africa. I worried about Timothy's cell phone. I hated knowing someone had come into my home without my permission. They came into my safe place. The place where I made my nest. It disturbed me.

I had worked hard to create a shelter for myself. I had no other safe places before, and my home had to be a secure place where I could relax out of harm's way. It had to be comfortable to climb into the bath when I wanted to, to read when I wanted to or to meditate as much or as deeply as I wanted to.

I went through all the necessary motions. I called the police and logged a case. Nothing came of it; they suspected the culprits could have been spying on us from a hill on the other side of the valley. There was another break-in the weekend after that. Luckily, I was visiting Tim at the time. I made immediate plans to move in with Tim. We would get a new place. We'd been dating for a year by then. Moving in together felt right. And safer. The Universe conspired with us. It was strange and stressful, but it was how it was supposed to be. One of Tim's friends had mentioned the availability of a complex stand-alone house a few times. It was the perfect place for us.

2016/09/13

> *I meditated twice a day for about a week and a half now. I'm calmer; more connected to my Higher Self. I do a chakra meditation, a love meditation, a letting go meditation. Sometimes I do a quiet meditation. I concentrated on this situation at work. I've released and surrendered it to God and the Angels. I guess I've been somewhat obsessive about this spiritual growth spurt, but I've learnt a huge amount.*

> *I'm acting out in rebellion and in the process cutting off my nose to spite my face. I've embarked on this exploration of health for myself. My well-being, mind body and soul. My mood episode made me decide I had to take drastic action to make a lifestyle change; hence, the meal plans and exercise. Many people remarked about how much weight I lost, how much better I look, how much happier I seem to be. This is true, but when I want to eat a chocolate or ice cream, I get a look from my mother, Tim or my sister and that upsets me. I don't like being told what I can and can't eat. I had enough of that when I lived at home with my stepfather. When Tim goes*

on a diet, he is pedantic and can stick to it forever. I know that these people love me and are seeking to support me, however I'm defiant and have a deep-seated anger around food. This is where I take it overboard. I eat badly because I get mad – which is sort of pointless. It's not for anyone else but me. This I do purely for me because I care about myself. I care about health and mental stability. So, I can stop this rebellion now, it's silly and futile. John is far away, he tried to control me through what I ate and how I looked. It's not his fault. He is sick and filled with anguish.

Sitting here in silence for two weeks I hoped my meditations would manifest a message from the Angels for some guidance. However, it seems only my ego is talking.

I've read many books and I've been in a process of getting to know myself better for years now, yet over the last few weeks I mulled over what makes me happy. What fills me with passion and with life?

2016/10/20

I'm confused but also collected, alone but whole, angry yet peaceful. Torn but as one. I see this in all my writings about my misery at work. I know there is another reason, a buried reason for this unhappiness, this obstacle, this broken part of my life. There's a part of myself I haven't examined. I've actively avoided it. I'm not sure which part of my life it is. Louise Hay writes that people with a sense of not being good enough often experience difficulties in parts of their life. I know I still carry limiting belief systems. I guess I did not want to accept the necessity to do more work on myself because – holy shit! – I've done a crapload of work! At times I feel the progress is minimal …

First Louise says to write down a list of things I believe I'm 'supposed' to do. The operative phrase being 'supposed to'.

I'm supposed to work for a salary.
I'm supposed to be less than my parents are.
I'm supposed to be unhappy.
I'm supposed to struggle.
I'm supposed to sit with difficulty.
I'm supposed to be stuck.
What the fuck Louise?

My parents did it that way and my mom insist that I do it this way.

It is John's expectation.

It seems that I want to sabotage something in my life because my template is that I should have instability or unhappiness somewhere in my life.

John and my mother don't take me seriously and think that I'm incompetent.

My mother has been stuck in the same cycle her whole life and I'm taking on her stuckness.

2016/11/16

I was in a terrible emotional space these last few weeks. I'm angry and frustrated and irritable. I'm also physically drained and exhausted. I don't know how things will pan out. It makes me feel lost and confused. I don't know where to turn. It clouds my soul's landscape. I want to leave The Pharma company. I yearn for something else to do; something I'll love and where I can be free to make my own decisions.

Gabriel upset me today, he said I should do the course they are offering at work. Fuck them and their degrees! Fuck them for treating me like this continuously. I'm fed up with their shit. My motives are dual. I want to do something I love. I want to get away from the corporate fuck-up that this place is. It represents a society that is unacceptable to me. I live it day in and day out, shovelling shit. I'm bored and frustrated and exhausted. I'm thoroughly sick of this job. I'm tired of seeing my potential without accessing it. I want to study next year, but that won't happen. We can't afford it. I'm tired of being placed on the side, not being involved and being second-rate. I'm tired of worrying about money. I'm tired of not having friends I can trust; I'm tired of worrying about my family. I'm tired of being tired. I'm exhausted trying to find this fucking middle ground between recovery, mental health and healthy relationships and all the other shit that goes with it. I'm tired of being used and feeling like a victim. I'm tired of wanting John to accept me. I'm tired of not living. Life evades me.

I'm tired of finding things to be tired of and I'm tired of misery. I'm not made for this; this is how I feel today. Despite these emotions, hope still burns in my chest. It can't be extinguished. I hope to have a holiday in December, I hope to leave this wretched company behind forever and ever. Then I might get to find my path. Hope forever burns in my belly, but today it glows faintly, like the embers of a dying flame. I know these thoughts are unhelpful for me. I'll purge some more. I'm weary of being understanding, of saying yes, it's okay, when it's not. When that lady said she would follow up about me going to go to Paris, but didn't, I kept quiet. I've been making masses of excuses. No more.

When I set a boundary – no excuse.

When I'm upset – speak my mind.

When I feel hard done by – say it.

No more of this keeping quiet it's God's will crap. God without works is dead. I have a voice, I have a mind, I have a mouth and a tongue. I've had enough.

It was an adjustment for us to live together. Timothy was – apart from a brief fling with another woman shortly before we started dating – single for eleven years. I had no long-term relationships for three years until I fell in love with him. We were used to doing our own thing and being busy with our own activities. He loves his television. I lived without a TV for three years. I had to get used to the incessant noise, and compromise was on our cards. I was and am still bad with doing housework. I grew up spoilt that way, I hardly even made my bed when I was a child. Timothy was particular about the cleanliness of the house. Everything needs to be a certain way. He is painstakingly pedantic when it comes to things like the dishes, and food. I on the other hand, didn't bother much with dishes, nor cooking. The poor man starved the first few times he came to visit me, and I realised I had to feed him more than once a day. Living together was tough, but we both tried to make it work. I'm still not a perfect dish washer, nor am I the perfect cook. He often does the bulk of the housework.

I try though. Where I used to just eat a tin of tuna or a readymade salad from the grocery store, I now proudly switch on the stove. I've rediscovered my ability and passion for cooking and baking. I've made progress but am still far from perfecting it. What did help me to start looking at cooking my own meals even before Tim and I moved in together was strangely enough, the diet plan the gym instructor gave me. It was quite simple, and I had to make things to eat in advance. It was the first time in my adult life that I ate properly, and I felt strong and driven. This was more motivation to eat well. Unfortunately, when the break-in happened and I moved, I stopped going to the instructor and cancelled my gym subscription because I was moving to a completely different part of town. I had to begin all over again. I got increasingly tired of work and the corporate industry.

The more I thought about where I was, the more I understood how I had enabled the people to treat me the way they did at the company. I had to leave. Something more intuitive than mere dislike and misery was driving me. In retrospect, I understand many of the reasons I felt such discomfort. My behaviour contributed greatly to how people treated me. I wanted to allow myself to explore my full potential, to allow myself to grow where I was more suited to grow. There were not many opportunities there for me because I had lower qualifications than my colleagues. At the end of that year they suggested I should do a course in bookkeeping; this was my worst fear. The last thing I wanted to do was for the company to pay for my studies when I seriously contemplated a swift exit.

I felt obligated to do the course as they had given me the position I needed so desperately those years ago. I applied for the course and completed it the following year. It dumbfounds me how I could complete a course I had no interest in, but when it came to something that I actually enjoyed I hardly ever got beyond the first assignment. There was a discussion about a possibility that I could go to Paris. I would have loved that! I think they never let me go because I wasn't qualified enough. I got frustrated and thought they dangled a carrot in front of my nose, knowing they wouldn't send me. That was one of the last straws. I kept reasoning that if I did more work, if I was agreeable, if I worked for longer hours, if I said yes, if I did whatever I needed to do, I would be rewarded somehow. I wasn't, and the affirmation never came. I wasn't satisfied. I was miserable, and I was always going to be miserable. I didn't want to fail, and I wanted to show my mom she could take me seriously even though I knew this job wasn't for me. But I didn't know what the alternative should be and I was afraid of trying something else. I was caught in a belief system that this was the only way I could survive, and that my job determined my value as a human being.

I finally got going with the work set out in Louise Hay's *You Can Heal Your Life*. The exercise in the above journal entry was done from her book. I was horrified to find the belief systems I was aware of and spoke about, were still solidified in my behaviour and my choices. I was still downright despondent and feeling unworthy. I had much more work to do. I was far more interested in getting to the end of the rainbow than the actual adventure towards it. I wanted to eat all the cake at once. I know better now. When I wrote down the answers to her questions, I wrote them without really thinking about them, they flowed out of my pen. The truth of my subconscious came out loud and clear, I made a firm decision that this would be part of my next journey. I had to follow through and complete the exercises in the Louise Hay book that I had put off for such a long time.

One of the worst things I did was to not speak up for myself. I would often say, it's okay, don't worry, it happens, I don't mind. When instead, I felt a huge injustice was done or I that my boundaries were overstepped. I had several bones to pick with my boss. He could have honed his management skills – he was quite boorish at times. But I kept my mouth shut most of the time. I didn't respect myself enough to speak up. I kept myself hopeless by not saying I was unhappy with what went on around me. It aggravated my despondency. It was easier said than done. I had enabled this behaviour in others since forever. I allowed them to treat me in this way from the beginning and to change that would have been an enormous and exhausting task which wouldn't have been in my interest because this wasn't the career I wanted to pursue. This had a lot to do with my inability to see the worth within myself and the rooted insecurities I carried.

2016/12/24

> *I'm in Port St. Johns with my mom again. We've been here for five days, since the 19th. So far, I've gone swimming, went to the ocean once, eaten out, gone on a boat trip, seen thunder and lighting, listened to Christmas Carols and ate dinner with Ally and his friend.*

> *I saw a fish eagle sweep low over the water to grab a fish straight out of the water with its large talons. I bonded with my mom, relaxed, read, made a fire and cooked meat! I went shopping, watered a panting black Labrador that came running out of nowhere and then acquainted myself with a neighbour and her daughter in the pool.*

> *On my to-do list: I want to still go to the beach and see the sunrise, go on a hike, do some mountain biking, walk through the forest, sit on the beach and see the waterfall.*

> *Tonight, we'll braai a fish and a chicken flatty for Christmas Eve.*

2016/12/27

> *Two more full days in Port St. Johns. I'm sort of excited and at the same time dreading my return to Centurion. I don't look forward to what is next. I do not know what is next. Well, my distant hope of hopes is that there will be a change. I dream about bright and intriguing*

undertakings with Tim next year. I want to resign from the Pharma company and establish myself as a successful entrepreneur. Those are my wishes for the coming year. That those blocks, those tangible fears will dissipate and all I'll be left with is this the strength of faith and manifestation.

The last few days here were quiet and peaceful, at times a bit boring, and other times eventful. I feel relaxed. The sense of impending doom and the urge to take action has slowly melted away. All that is left is the feeling that I want to have fun. Therein lies the difference.

I meditated today. It seems a quiet and a still mind makes for better progress.

Every now and then a butterfly vibrates in my solar plexus, especially now that it's coming close to the end of the holiday. I should breathe deeply and take it one day at a time. I've really bonded magnificently with my mom and Ally. My mom appears to have calmed down considerably. She was more relaxed this holiday, I'm grateful for this.

Today I'm also grateful for the wind on my cheeks and the warmth of the air. I'm grateful for the stickiness on my skin and the humidity of every breath I inhale. I'm grateful for my sun kissed skin and my beach blonde hair. I'm grateful for being here in Port St. Johns. I'm grateful for the birds, the hornbills, and the geckos on the ceiling. I'm grateful for the large herons and the tree that proudly shows off her green flowers in the morning. They transform into a pigment of peach in the afternoon, fall off at night, and then she blooms in green all over again

in the morning. I'm grateful for the brown frogs and the
sandy beaches.

I had an excellent holiday with my mom and Alex. The tension between us had by now completely melted away. I had the most marvellous time with her especially. Alex was older. He was preoccupied with the teenage stuff he did with his best friend. They would wander out at twilight and come home late at night after playing around on their skateboards and doing who knows what. The town is small and safe, so they couldn't get into too much trouble. My mom said she caught them once holding on to the back of a driving car to catch extra speed with their skateboards. This holiday was a special one, my mom and I were alone again, and she had opened to me and who I really am. She started accepting me for me. It was incredible to connect with her without any pretending. The one day she took me to the fairy forest. We spoke and walked through the forest and I made jokes about seeing real fairies. I saw a root growing in a circle out of the ground. I told my mom it was a fairy circle and said we should stand inside it to see the fairies. She humoured me and stood with me in the circle. We giggled and with our arms wrapped around each other I saw the young girl that was hidden in my mother. I had never seen her before. This was such a special moment for me.

CHAPTER 11

A Year of Positive Affirmations

In 2017 I woke up. Something big shifted in me. I went back to work to kick off the new year yet again at the Pharma company. I felt the familiar despondency of a new year at the company, but something more powerful rumbled in the pit of my stomach. I would call this self-respect and self-belief. These were still embers, not a huge fire. Yet, it was there. That year my superiors wanted me to study a bookkeeping to trial balance course. I applied the year before, and everything was set to go in the new year. After my holiday I mentally prepared myself to go back. The week started like any other, but on the second day my neck had gone into a terrible spasm and I went to the hospital emergency room to get an injection for the agony. What I got instead was a huge scare. The doctors were concerned about the stiffness in my neck and did all kinds of tests. Their biggest concern was that I might have had a blood clot in my lungs. They diagnosed me with pneumonia and sent me home with a huge dosage of anti-biotics. I was off from work for a couple of days, and then I went back to my house doctor because something did not seem right. Things were not getting any better. I went to work when I could, but the problem was getting progressively worse. My doctor diagnosed me with tick bite fever and gave me another course of anti-biotics. I decided to go for second opinion. One night, at dinner with Timothy and his son I felt particularly ill. My stomach went into a terrible spasm. I've had tummy problems since I can remember.

In 2011 I started passing gall stones, my gall bladder went septic and was removed. After that I struggled immensely with certain foods, especially vegetables high in fibre that were not cooked well. That night the suspect vegetable was a piece of broccoli. I was in agony, and I couldn't sit in one place. For the first time in my life, I fainted. I had a sense of losing my ability to hold on to life. I fainted in the bedroom and Tim and his son did not hear me fall. It was a strange experience; I was awake, but I could not move.

I've known many people who have fainting spells. Anna passed out incredibly often, particularly when she bumped her funny bone. It was different for me. I had never experienced this before. I got up from the floor once I gained control of all my bodily functions and went to Tim. I had to hold on for dear life as I felt I could slip out of consciousness at any moment. My main thought was that I had to keep myself alive. I hollered instructions, and we were all in the car in five minutes. I calmed down after a while, and I felt better. I told Tim to turn around and that I was okay. What that moment did for me was push me. A thousand thoughts sped through my mind. I thought it was okay to die; I'm not afraid of death. I know there is something better after this. But I didn't want to die. I haven't done half of the things I was meant to do here. I just knew this. I haven't lived enough on this plane and I needed to do more, release this fear and leap into life to get soaked in the delight, the love and the enjoyment of it.

Life was always so close yet so far. What was life to me? I kept asking myself that question. I love many things. A list of them would fill a book. I love people, even though I can't stand them at times. I revel in new experiences and the memories they provide. I absorb the beauty and magnificence of life. I'm invigorated by meaningful interactions with people; conversations that give me goose bumps. I enjoy travelling, opening myself up to the excitement and possibilities it has to offer. I care about the natural world and appreciate the incredible luminosity and life mother nature freely gives with no expectation in return, apart from respect. I have a passion for art; I look at it and read it as though the images were a book. I find second-hand books irresistible. I fancy the idea of someone else, somewhere holding that book in their hands, experiencing those same pages with their own imagination. I love music and classical compositions. I'm crazy about diving and breathing underwater while gazing into the deep blue gardens of fish and coral. I admire different cultures and the beauty of every individual.

There is immeasurably much to love, although I couldn't feel that love any more. The passion was gone. I knew I loved those things, but I focused my energy on healing from the hurt. It was a lot of difficulty to process. My passion for life was reignited on the day that I fainted, when I thought I might be losing my grip on life. I wanted to immerse myself into life after that day.

I finally got to the root of the problem of my physical dis-ease. I had the Epstein Barr virus. I was booked off for three weeks, and the company accommodated that. I took the time to look at where I was going wrong. The first thing I did was to go through all the exercises in Louise Hay's *You Can Heal Your Life*. I wrote it all down and practised mirror work every day.

I did positive affirmations and wrote a whole list on coloured pieces of paper. I said them out loud and looked myself in the eyes whilst I said them to see my facial expressions. There were many hard questions and I had to really consider the answers I gave. It was interesting to see where I was and how far I had come too. I looked at forgiveness. I hurt myself the most and had to extend the greater portion of forgiveness towards myself.

In the process I started with a project. I've always loved books, and one day when Tim and I went bowling we passed an old, seemingly run-down bookshop. The friendly owner showed me around the bookshelves. To my greatest surprise these old books were in an impeccable condition. Most of them were collector's items, worth thousands of Rands. I fell in love with the shop at once. The decorations on the end papers of some books fascinated me. These beautiful old books were decorated with marbled paper. I was delighted to find out that these were all printed one at a time, and that there was an incredibly fascinating process involved.

I began doing research about it in 2016 for the first time, and then during 2017 when I was ill, I really put my back into it. I wanted to learn how to marble paper. It enthralled me. It took a while to get the right items together to start doing my own marbling projects. When I received my box of supplies at last, it was like opening a magic kit. Whilst discovering how to marble paper, I discovered how to cleanse the inner waters of my soul. It helped me to hear more clearly and to see lucidly. I had held on to heaps of resentment even though I thought I'd let it go through my step work. The process itself was a spiritual cleansing. I wanted to rediscover the artist in me and followed a course of action stipulated in Julia Cameron's *The Artist's Way*. This was some of the most difficult self-work I've ever done. Now that I was rediscovering my inner artist again by doing the paper marbling, I had to find the creative mind I had avoided for years.

Historically, I was always told that being creative was less important than being analytical. When I was analytical, I was taken more seriously. When I was creative and artistic, I was told I would never understand life, and that I was doomed to live a mediocre life as an artist. I've always been creative; my sponsor gave me the nickname Feather because my head always seems to be in the clouds. I love imagining the impossible and living in creativity and colour. This has always been the space where I'm the happiest, the place where I'm safest, where no-one can harm me. I know this is not the best way to live and it has inhibited me from experiencing life the way I've always wanted to. I wanted to get out of my head. I wanted to learn how to communicate with others, to have conversations, to tell people what I was thinking instead of keeping everything locked up in the fairyland prison I had constructed for myself. I wanted to learn how to live life and be grounded. It was a transformational growth process. The year of positive affirmations changed my life. I continued with it as the year progressed and I healed from the glandular fever.

One of my colleagues retired in February and most of her work was dished out to me. I was snowed under and I became even more miserable. There were no prospects of a promotion in my near future and by that time I had so much work to do I didn't know where to turn. Cracks were beginning to show. I refused to nullify all my resilient personal growth and to start a cycle of mental ailments and desolation again. It was work or my mental health. I had to make a choice.

2017/01/10

Say yes to opportunities.

Yesterday I sat with Tim's son and a movie came up. The Yes Man. The man in the movie has to say yes to everything. If someone asks you if you want to do something you say yes. Obviously, it's a bit extreme. Last night I realised the levels of my discontent.

Firstly, I only live life half. I don't ever fully commit myself to anything. I keep holding back. I fear good things will be taken away from me. This is what my past experiences have taught me.

Secondly, I've not forgiven as I thought I have. I forgave, holding back slightly or even a lot because I made those past experiences a part of my identity.

Thirdly, I've not trusted myself for a long time, especially when it comes to making the right decisions or to live life the way I want to live it.

Those things and thoughts are all changing now. I choose to change them; I'm willing to change. I approve of myself. I've held back on life for thirty-two years of my existence on this planet. That is not gratitude. Fear is simply a figment of the imagination. A strange, intangible, untouchable thing that does not exist. Fear is gone.

Isla Stone

2017/01/12

I dreamt I could not walk. I had to crawl for an immeasurable distance. It was excruciating. I tried to stand, but because I had crawled so far it was too painful to stand up. I can stand up; nothing is ever too burdensome. I'm worthy. I let go of the need to crawl through life. I now stand up with strength from the Universe. I stretch myself out and it's superb.

In another dream I was back at the halfway house. It was covered in a hazy fog. Then I decided to open the door and the haze evaporated. I tried to light a cigarette. The lighter didn't work, and I found another one. There was something about that place. It reminded me of the house in Olievenhoutbosch.

2017/01/14

Today I had a lively day. Last night I went to bowling with Tim and a group of friends and my sister. First, I showed Lara the fantastic gem of a bookshop. My fascination and slight obsession with marbled paper was sparked again. Then we played bowls. Tim won this time, but I'll win next time. Ha ha! Today I want to get stuff for marbled paper. I still need turps and alum powder. Then I can start!

I spoke to Barbara again. She has relapsed again. I cried.

Today I did my affirmations, it's getting easier.

I get a bit restless to get going and to do everything fast. I remind myself often that there is no need for urgency.

Everything happens in good time. One small step at a time. I'll get there quickly. I do not know what the Universe's plan is, but I'm acting, I feel amazing and I know it will last. I'm excited about life.

2017/01/26

I saw Gabriel today. We spoke about some heavy stuff and I'm scraped raw. The month was a roller-coaster. When I faced my mortality and felt as if I was slipping away, I confronted two things.

One of them was that while I was fainting – during and on the floor – the thought that kept going through my mind was, 'nobody cares, nobody cares, nobody cares'. I felt that I'm the only one who can look after me and ensure my survival. My mortal, physical survival rests completely in my own hands. When I managed to get up, I went to Tim, slipping in and out of consciousness and holding on tightly to my physicality. I hated putting my survival in his hands.

The second thought that whirled through my mind while I tried to hold on was, 'I'm ready to go, it's okay'. And then the next thought, 'I'm not ready to go!'. There were so many important things I still wanted to do. I'm ready to do those things now. I'm willing to change. I approve of myself.

2017/01/31

I'm filled with hope. There is light at the end of the tunnel. I'm striving, aiming to reach it before the darkness closes in. As I take the next step into the light, behind me the darkness closes behind me forever. I should let go of some of my past that still clutches desperately at my ankles, grabbing, snatching, ripping – but I've removed myself from the bear hold it had on me. There was a huge amount of disappointment and fear and trauma. But it's over. It is done now.

I'm learning to trust myself again, to trust the Universe again. I'm getting it right. I'm making these changes and it is easy for me to do so. The feeling of being alone on a boat is not true, I'm surrounded with love. From people I can trust; people who love me.

Throughout my journey I've learnt various valuable lessons based on spiritual principles. The first is honesty. I learnt there were varying degrees in which I could be authentic with myself and others. The most important thing was being truthful with myself. Honesty with myself was the key to accomplish many precious things on a spiritual level. I wasn't frank with myself up to a certain stage of my growth. I wanted to pretend I was okay; that nothing terrible happened in my past. I wanted to profess that those experiences did not shape me. I did not want to be quite straightforward about who I was, and what I was capable of. I had many unique qualities that I did not acknowledge. I hid these traits from myself and others. The same went with the qualities on the other end of the scale. In life as a human being there is no such thing as good or bad. One balances out the other. Every light throws a shadow. I can't know my goodness if I don't know my darkness. I'm fallible, but this is the purpose of life. I constantly work to understand myself and why I react the way I do in certain situations. I then attempt to work on responding differently. That is where my growth is. The more I learn about my shadow, the more I explore my light. I was conditioned to believe there was good and bad, however without one end of the scale one would never know the other and there would never be anything to measure it by.

When I was a child, I would get terribly angry at times. A red-hot irritability and fury rose up into the tips of my fingers and down to the ends of my toes, and I would explode with rage. One day my mother got frustrated with me and told me that anger was a bad thing. After she gave me the talking to, I supressed my fury. I was taught that anger (and especially displaying anger) was a bad thing. This always made me suppress my rage, resulting in anxiety and depression. Later in my life people like Gabriel told me I was a remarkably angry person. It surprised me initially, until I allowed myself to feel the anger I had supressed for years. He was right, the people who knew me were right. When I got angry previously – before I allowed myself to express it – I saw red and walked away because when I lost my temper, I said things I could not retract.

As I've grown, I've learnt to accept my whole self, not only the bits I see and accept as good. I get jealous, I get angry. That is okay, if I know how to manage those emotions, to allow myself to get in touch with them and then to let them go. Holding on to them does not serve me. It's okay to acknowledge my mistakes; I'm human and within this realm I'm fallible. It's okay to make mistakes. How I deal with them and how I change my behaviour going forward is important. I try to change and to grow. I acknowledge my faults in the same way that I acknowledge my talents. It's not always easy, but I do it. Another important aspect within this realm of knowledge is that of denial. In the past – and even now, sometimes – I'm confronted with certain emotions or thoughts that I do not want to work with. I'll acknowledge them, but I have difficulty with accepting them. When the thoughts or emotions recur often, they continue to be an affliction. Ultimately, the pain of staying the same becomes more cumbersome than the pain of changing, and sooner or later I must change. I can only deal with denial-driven emotions or thoughts when I acknowledge and accept them. Then – and then only – can I change them.

Open-mindedness is another invaluable spiritual principle. It has assisted me in many areas of growth. In the beginning, when I concentrated on the Twelve-step Program to facilitate my growth,

I learnt about open-mindedness. So, I opened my mind further. I studied Taoism and Buddhism. My mind required a bit of stretching. My ego became a stumbling block after a few years. I did not want to listen to people new in the Program, or to people with what I perceived as less knowledge than my own. I didn't want to read more or grow more. I would get irritable with people in meetings because my understanding, I felt, had expanded far beyond theirs. I wasn't getting anything out of the meetings any more. I had outgrown certain people and I couldn't relate to them any longer. My ego needed a bit of a deflation. I'd left the open-mindedness I held so dear in a corner, forgotten.

I can learn something from anyone, I can take something from a meeting, or from someone who speaks to me. When I let go of my ego, I become open-minded and teachable. When I'm teachable, I'm malleable, and then I know that things are as they are meant to be. Source/God/The Universe speaks to me through others. When I'm closed off, I do not get the messages I need to hear. I enjoy my silence, the eternal space where I can explore endless, untouchable possibilities. I've explored those places for hours and I love being there. The only thing is that I'm not an island, nor am I on a ship alone on this ocean floating around by myself without love from others. There are others who care about me. Although I pushed against it for an inordinate length of time, a moment came where I grasped the urge to embrace my humanity and the humanity of others. I must allow myself to connect to the other and let myself enjoy the experience of being in joy with another. Not just a partner and not just family, but everyone I meet.

Life is good when I allow it to happen and let go of seeking control.

2017/02/07

How to love the self? This is how we conquer evil in this world.

I got my marbling stuff yesterday and opening it was like unwrapping an enchanted gift from the Universe. I fell in love with these few items. I appreciate the love, beauty, care and charm that went into its packaging. I can't wait to start marbling! The art of Ebru has a mystical quality. I want to find out what that magic is.

Last night I went to an intense meeting. People were upset about something. I met a gentleman there and we discussed self-respect. He asked me if I do teachings and that took me aback. Maybe the Universe is telling me that I should start doing self-love workshops. I'll wait for a second confirmation; I've been fantasising about doing such workshops.

My mom looks tired. I'm worried about her. I smelt her in my car yesterday. I got caught up in a rain storm on my way to the car. When I got in, my drenched clothes held a whiff of my mother's perfume. I called her and spoke to her for a few moments.

2017/02/21

Good morning World! I'm writing morning pages. Today I'm thankful for one more day of being clean and sober, experiencing life one day at a time. There has been many 'just for todays' and it is close to my Five-Year celebration. I'm grateful for this journey. I've had the honour of getting so far. I slept well last night, and I feel uplifted. It's rainy with dark clouds hanging in the sky. I enjoy this weather. I saw Gabriel yesterday. He has been pushed to make a huge life choice. I'm proud of him for making such a huge change. I'm excited about the changes in my life. I'm trying new and exciting fun exercises. I want to make more marbled paper and try new techniques. I have an idea about marbling silk scarves; I think those will be pretty.

2017/03/03

I slept badly last night. All I dreamt about was sublime paint and art. The dirty pour, the cell effect. I'm experiencing a bizarre and ethereal change. Everything I used to think now seems downright wrong. All I want to do is to spend all my time on my art. It feels right. The colours are overpowering. Something is happening, and I love it. The Artists Way is showing me some things about me. I'm an artist. I love art. I've always loved it. When I allow myself to be open to my Higher Self nothing else seems to matter. This moment screams 'Paint, paint paint! Create, create, create!'.

I've been people-pleasing again this week. I should focus on growing as an artist instead. I'll go to a gallery for my weekly artist's date with myself. I'm worried about the bookkeeping course I missed last week, but I'll be okay if I go this week. Last night I sent my mom a message about her disconnectedness to everything. Lara asked me if she is too harsh with my mom. I said she is. On Wednesday I was profoundly down and depressed. I've been meaning to resign from the Pharma company and to start my own business for yonks. I suppose I only recently really started forming some sort of plan. If I put happy and joyful work into it this month then I create the possibility of doing it again the next month, or the month after. I want an art studio. I want to get a pouring medium for the paint to make it pour better, so I can get the cell effect. I need some more canvasses. I also finished my combs today.

The woman who assisted me with gathering the equipment and other consumables for my marbling project was so helpful. She sent me messages on how to create certain effects and patterns and helped me to troubleshoot some of the problems I could possibly encounter with the media of my choice. She really lit up my passion for marbling. I was even more entranced. Marbling is a demanding art technique and it fulfilled me greatly. It's quite ritualistic and had a peculiar calming effect on me. I became obsessed with discovering its details, its complexities and attempted to perfect it in too short a time. I became impatient and thought to myself that if it is not perfect now, it never will be. I decided to try another technique. It would delight me to get these elusive images onto canvas, and I learnt about acrylic pouring. This technique created cells due to the various densities of the different colours of the paints. It was the most magical thing I had ever seen. It took some perfecting, but that was the joy of it. The more I explored this the more the ideas of giving classes came up in the back of my mind. But I doubted my right to call myself an artist; giving classes would be a waste of people's time. I then considered that art therapy could be a lovely endeavour. That was another altogether onerous story.

The acrylic pouring technique moved me to using canvasses. I enjoyed the effects and gained more confidence in myself and my abilities. As I mentioned in my last diary entry, something suddenly happened, a transformation, maybe an artistic spiritual awakening. I dreamt in liquid flowing colours, moving, running, changing, glowing. My dreams were taken over by colours, paints, and effects. I became more desperate to leave the Pharma company. There was no creativity there, while this creative expansion happened in my other world. It was exploding, and I did not know what it meant. I carried on painting and marbling.

I continued with the bookkeeping to trial balance course at the college although I missed one or two classes. Magically, incredibly, I handed in all my assignments and I wrote all my tests. I then finished the course and passed the exam. I was gobsmacked. Grateful that I had finally managed to overcome my tendency to drop out of things halfway through.

Finally, I resigned from the Pharma company.

The work had become too much, I was exhausted. I decided my well-being was more important than what I thought I *must* do for the sake of financial security. My whole life I've been told that this was the only way to make money: go to work in the corporate sector every day and get a salary every month. I worked through several of my belief systems and the lies I had been living. I handed in my resignation in March of 2017 and I left that May. I was recklessly desperate to leave the company and I hadn't thought it through as well as I should have. Timothy and I fought often about this move. He was disappointed with my decision. I was damn angry with him for not hearing how I felt. When I look back today, I can see that it happened perfectly and in good time. It just did not work out the way I had planned.

I cashed in my provident fund and started looking for ideas of what to do next. I decided to support myself through being a SAP trainer. I had some idea of what I wanted to do in most of my other time. I wanted to paint.

The following entries reveal what I felt throughout these changes.

2017/03/09

> *I slept well. I'm pleased that I went to bed early. Complaining about work won't change anything. I worked out that it costs R30.00 to make a sheet of marbled paper. That excludes the three litres of water, the droppers, the flick brushes, and the combs. Gabriel wants some of my paintings; he wants four small ones.*
>
> *My family is fucked up, my mom is crumbling under the pressure, my sister rescuing her, John is a liar. I'm sick and tired of being worried about it all. I want to take Alex away from there. I'll talk to him.*

2017/03/11

*This morning my bed was warm and cosy and Tim held
me snugly in his arms. The clouds are surrealistically
hypnotic today. They look like paintings. I'm a bit groggy,
although I slept well. I'm filled with new energy for the
week. I studied yesterday. I should do it more often. I'm
calm and relieved that I studied. The sun has come up
for another day. I'm excited about my new adventure,
everything is changing because I'm willing to change.
I see that now. The paintings I made are beautiful. My
coffee is delicious. I meditated under the moon last night.
I appreciate all these blessings.*

*I ate less chocolate yesterday and my sinuses feel much
better this morning. I want my body to be happy. It is not
a difficult task. It's easy to eat healthily and to fill my
body with the essential nutrients to work at its optimal
level. This helps my body to vibrate with positive energy
at a higher level. The more I follow my intuition and
listen to the needs of my body the easier this gets.*

2017/03/13

*I slept well last night. I had a terrible day at work
yesterday. That heaviness overwhelmed and infiltrated
my whole being. I do two people's jobs. I'm trying my
best to not crumble under the pressure. I've prayed for
a miracle. I've hoped for a miracle. I do not want to
lose sight of my reality. My authenticity lies in my art,
my passion, my fire. I'm afraid it will engulf my art
and passion. I'm excited to meet with the artist Aunt
Marietta suggested. I hope she will help to give me the
answers that I need. This week I want to stand back from*

everything I want to achieve with my business. I want to relax and let the flow of the Universe take me to where I want to be. I have a fear that this will be taken away from me as quickly as it was given to me. I know I should change it. Work reflects that. Everything is in perfect order. I release my fears to the Universe. This is my time. I'm free from my past and from my past behaviours.

I spoke to one of my sponsees. She is doing well. The other one is much slower and less willing to change. Recovery is hard for her. I've gotten back into contact with three of my trusted friends. I know I should stop isolating. I feel somewhat distant from everything today. Distant from the world, almost as though I didn't want to be a part of it. I must speak to my boss's boss about the workload and my ability to cope with it all. I must stand up for myself. This is a lesson. Yesterday, my mom got me a present for my birthday after Lara gave her a hard time about it. If Lara had not said anything my mom would not have gotten me anything. Lara made my mom feel guilty because of 2013, and the fall out we had. It confuses me. I'm angry with Lara. It wasn't her place. I had a memorable holiday with my mom, and I didn't expect anything more from her. This was Lara's stuff not mine. My creative space in the backyard has become my little haven, it feels like God resides there.

We lived in three houses during my childhood with John. The first house was in an estate. It was a dark and ominous place. This is where my mom and John had the fight about the revolver. Then we moved to a house in Olievenhoutbosch, in a larger house. The garden was full of cacti, the previous owners had a fascination with these plants. The whole garden was decorated with different species of weird and wonderful decorative cacti.

Our housekeeper, Rose had a son, Tshepo, whom she left to live with her family in Limpopo. She sent them money for his care and schooling every month. One day Rose came to my mother in a frantic state. She had discovered Tshepo was being sent out to the fields to herd cattle instead of going to school. Her family were not keeping their end of the bargain. My mother, the attentive woman and rescuer that she was, grabbed John and Rose and drove all the way to Limpopo that night to fetch Tshepo from her family and to bring him to our home. He was horribly malnourished when he came to us. He could not speak English. My mom struggled to find a school for him in Centurion. She tried many schools, and eventually found one that specialised in children whose first language wasn't English. Initially the principal of the school did not want to take him in because it wasn't the start of the school year and he was too old start Grade One. My mother fought tooth and nail for his enrolment. In the end the school took him in. He became part of our family and grew close to Lara especially. He is also part of the family business now.

The house in the estate was where I experienced my early teens and the first years of the fear I've had to unlearn. I befriended a compassionate, gentle boy. He was my best friend. We spent hours together. We spoke about everything and would often sit in the park at the end of the dead-end road where we stayed. He always listened to me, and I enjoyed spending time with someone I trusted. Our friendship was precious to me. I experienced so much instability and trauma in the other areas of my life; time with this boy was one of my few comforts. Our parents knew each other, and we'd often go to each other's houses for sleep overs and children's parties.

One day things changed, and puberty struck. He liked me as a girl now, no longer only as a friend. I felt uncomfortable with this new facet of our relationship. My stepfather molested me in the mornings – it was hard to play 'almost kiss' in the afternoon. I was confused and avoided the subject. I dodged his kisses. I liked him. I wanted to hang out with him, but I didn't understand or want to be with him in that way. It was all still so innocent, he just wanted to kiss me, but I was afraid. I didn't know what to expect because deep inside I knew what happened with John was of a sexual nature. This was the beginning of the end of our friendship.

2017/03/14

> *It's a tranquil day. I woke up knowing I do not have to go to work. I'm staying at home to study for my test. Ginja tried to kill a spotted mouse bird yesterday. We managed to save it. It eats fruit.*

> *Something weird is bubbling up. I can't quite establish what it is. Memories of our old house in Olievenhoutbosch keep surfacing. It seems clearer now than ever. The hard-stuck grit under my feet, the dying birds I tried to save. Nights of staying up late, doing my art whilst listening to The Phantom of the Opera. The echo of the music playing once the CD stopped for hours afterwards. Princess Diana dying in a car accident. Listening to music on the CD player with my best friend. Pepi my parrot. Listening to Lord of the Dance while I studied. The Russian rodents, and Sammy – our dalmatian – licking them with such love and vigour, drowning them with her saliva. The natural encyclopaedias. The bar where we thought we'd entertain people. We rarely did ... My yellow bedroom, my fish named Lucky. The piano, the cacti. My friends coming over and the bunch of us making flapjacks. That one friend with her lie. The other with his truth. The one friend with his crush on me. My childhood friend. Sitting on the wall waiting for my dad. The budgies dying. Running around the house, and then running in Olievenhoutbosch in the afternoons. The guy across the road, the huskies that kept escaping. Waiting for the bus. John reading my diary. Playing*

Barbies. Feeling lost. John getting shot at, Alex being born. My mother throwing the bag on the bed, screaming that we'd move back to my Grannie. Feeling insecure about my body and my weight, daydreaming about being thin. Never being content, except once. Looking in the mirror and saying this is good. I like this. You are pretty. I don't know what that all means. What I do know is that I based it on how I looked not on who I was. I wasn't taught how to love myself. How to approve of myself. I was an elfin girl. She was and is amazing. She is filled with love and cleverness. She is creative. She is compassionate and wise beyond her years, but I need her to free herself from being an adult. She needs to be a carefree child. She is safe now. She is looked after. Nothing will harm her. I'll make sure of that. She can have adventures and fulfil her carefree spirit with everything she has in her imagination that is good and nurturing for her. Isla child, you're free.

I pressurised myself to get things to happen. It was challenging to keep up with the demands at work. Emotionally there was a change within me. I went through a transformation. I had this firm belief that I had to start doing what was in my heart. Every day at work became problematic to me. I had to somehow change it and change it quickly. I wrote morning pages every day. I did all the exercises set out in *The Artist's Way*. I continued to go to meetings and did the things required for my recovery. I was growing.

Old, stale emotions I had avoided for years came creeping up. The exercises genuinely extricated old belief patterns. I believe it helped me to come to grips with the trauma I had experienced as a young girl. I knew what I experienced as a child with John was traumatic; being gaslighted and lied to every day was horrifically abusive to the core. However, I had never truly acknowledged the gravity of the situation. The abusive, dysfunctional home where the three of us grew up had lasting effects in our behaviours and lives. The true nature of my experience dawned on me after I started working on these aspects in that year. It was difficult. I faced some darkness, but I'm grateful about it. My outrage grew, not towards John, but towards my mother. She was the gatekeeper after all. I allowed myself to be angry. I allowed myself to feel.

I didn't have a solid plan to leave my job, but I tried desperately to find a way – any way – to leave. I grabbed at air. I decided I would do art classes with acrylic pouring and paper marbling. I did costings for the materials required. The idea was that I would make marbled paper and sell it. I would also sell acrylic pours on canvas. I placed pressure on myself to perform for my art, and suddenly the joy in it was lost. I could not find the ease with which I started. My ideas faded with the twine of fear that began twisting itself around my neck. The passion dissipated.

Fear after fear seeped into my thinking. I wasn't really an artist. My art wasn't good enough to sell. I didn't have enough experience. I thought, 'who do you think you are?'. I had a dilemma with space too, I couldn't paint in the house. It was too cramped, and I had to do all my painting and marbling outside. In winter I would wear warm clothes and when there were no clouds in the sky and the wind was calm, I would paint. It frustrated me to wait for the weather before I could create. There was a nit-picking woman in our complex who constantly checked up on everyone to ensure they abided by the rules. Nothing was to be left anywhere, not even in the open carport. After every painting stint, I had to pack up my materials and haul them back into the house. My canvasses could dry outside for a short while only.

It was problematic, and as the stresses increased it became easier to use challenges as an excuse not to paint often. I couldn't make large pieces of marbled paper because it required temperate, calm and clean conditions. Everyone who knows Centurion also knows about our violent and glorious thunder storms all through summer, and our nippy winter temperatures. I experienced a creative block. The fear grew to such an extent that I made many paintings, but I could not find the courage within myself to sell them. I experienced these mental processes as part of finding a solution – I had to leave the industry that confined me. The more I attempted to set up something before I resigned, the more it was pushing back. It wasn't working. I was getting in my own way.

During this time, it occurred to me the first requirement for change was that I had to be willing to change. I had wished for change for years, but I did not practically implement it. When I began making the effort to convince myself I was ready, the change slowly started manifesting.

The transformation was enchanting. I was thankful that something was happening. There was a vast shift. I didn't know what was coming, but I knew it was on its way. I was upbeat and positive. I had an idea of what I wanted. I was still afraid and to a degree still held on to the familiar. I was taught there was only one way to make money and be safe. That was the security I always knew. Going to work every day from 8.00 to 5.00 and getting a monthly salary with golden handcuffs. I held on to many expectations at that company. I wanted them to see my worth. I wanted them to see I gave it my all; that I tried to be the best I could be with the available resources. I was lying to myself because I had no passion. Where there is no passion there is only action. Where there is only action – and not inspired action – the best of the self is not given in any regard. I put in an effort, but I did not try my best because I did not love what I was busy with. I had lost any desire to be good at what I did. I tried to survive emotionally on a day-to-day basis. By then I felt no need to serve the company. I experienced too many hurtful disappointments, carried too many resentments. It was my own faltered expectations I had to deal with. It was my choice. I could have chosen to be happy where I was and with what I did, but I wasn't. I knew my personality and disposition were not well-suited for the place that I ended up in. There was no fault there. My prior choices where I had allowed myself to end up there created the situation. The experience served its purpose. I was grateful for that and will be forever.

Isla Stone

2017/03/29

Good morning world! I dreamt many dreams last night.
I'm sure I took instruction. I said yes. I saw grey, purple,
and green splattered across a canvas. It was sublime,
and I'm grateful to sit here today. My period has been
continuing for the last two weeks. I don't know why. I'm
not worried about it though. Maybe my body is cleansing
itself.

Timothy is getting ready to go to work. I'm sitting
writing in my journal. Last night I received a message.
'Stop trying so hard.' I smiled. I do that. I try too hard
sometimes. I have many paintings. They are all waiting
for new homes. That dream is there, and I'm trying to
recall it. It's at my fingertips. I'm listening to the piano
guys while I write this. Lily is coming over; she'll be
here in June. I'm thrilled! I'll visit Aunt Elizabeth and
Willem in Plettenberg Bay to see Lily there when she
comes back from Thailand. I'm a bit anxious. There
are a few things I want to act on. I want to go to the
bookshop. I must do it today.

2017/03/30

I'm irritable and out of sorts. Yesterday I sent an email to
Maureen and Walter. I'm angry that I've been driven to
this. But it constitutes growth. This is the juncture where
I'll tell them I'm done. I'm at a crossroads. I must make
a silent, earth-shattering decision. I don't know if I have
the courage to do so. Right now, I'm unsure, uncertain.
I'm praying for signs of what actions to take next. I know
that asking doesn't mean I can get it without action,
but that is my own limitation. I can't keep placing my

limitations on the Universe, I should have faith. I believe I'm worthy. I'm worthy. I'm willing to change. Today is Thursday. I've been emotionally wrestling with work. It has changed. I'm grateful for my art. I appreciate the opportunity it gives me to get out of my head. My two sponsees are doing okay. They are still fledglings. Last night my sponsor and I went to a meeting to listen to an old acquaintance's share. She had a stab at my sponsor as she has not yet let go of the past, and the hair on my neck raised in fury. I must remind myself we are all sick. We all experience this sickness in various degrees. I know when I judge I'm looking at a reflection of myself, I see something I do not like within myself.

2017/03/31

Timothy slept in the other room last night. I don't know if he was mad at me. Maybe he is. I was really depressed yesterday. Last night I didn't really eat. This is probably an indication of how bad it can get. I felt depressed because of the many emotions. I felt Timothy's rage. I felt upset because I didn't get to my sponsees enough. Gabriel is annoyed with me. I felt it, not getting to gym, not doing art, not studying, my mother, work! The insatiable desire to resign. Waiting for a miracle. Doing affirmations. God grant me the serenity to accept the things I can't change the courage to change the things I can, and the wisdom to know the difference. I asked Timothy for his friend's number, I think he is pissed off with me for that, or that I'm pushing to resign. That is not my intention.

CHAPTER 12

Stepping Out of the Cage

It's easier asking for forgiveness than asking for permission.

That is what I kept thinking to myself. I couldn't explain how I felt about the push; something told me I should move. The end had come. All I needed was a plan to help me get away from the suffocating squeeze of the Pharma company. I had to walk away because breathing was important. I had cheated myself out of freedom for an eon. I resigned a month after the last entry. I felt that my whole world was about to end when I sent my letter to my boss. I was afraid. Tim knew I would resign. He could do nothing to stop me. He was worried about my plans and our future. I knew I would be okay. Both of us would be okay. I knew.

My mother didn't want me to do it, Timothy didn't want me to do it. Everyone stood against this decision. I stood with me. I knew the Powers That Be supported me in this decision. The leap forward into the next phase of my life was full of freedom. I still had some emotions, old stale energies that I had to get rid of to see things more clearly. The last month at the company was tiring. They asked me to stay until the end of May 2017. I agreed, because I didn't really have a solid plan. I decided to focus on SAP. I was talented in understanding the system and picked it up quite quickly. During the last two months I thought about how liberating the new freedom would be. I worked hard and tried to finish as much as I could. I completed the course I embarked on at the beginning of the year. I did quite well and was proud of my achievement. The last day at the company was dreamlike. I left and didn't want to look back. There were still attachments there. I spent four months painting and putting ideas together for my next plan. I applied for admission to a SAP course.

In a joyous twist of events during July of that year Lily came back for a visit in Plettenberg Bay and I decided to spend a month there to reconnect with her. I missed her and could not wait to see her again after two years.

Our holiday was filled with both stress and joy. I was still afraid and would often find myself wondering about whether I had done the right thing or not. The freedom, the sensation of being alive and breathing was well worth it. I took myself seriously. I focused and tried too hard. I held on too tightly to everything, all my thoughts, all the things I wanted and to every emotion I felt.

Holding on tightly to these thoughts and fears and wants did not serve me, but this was a process I had to go through to understand the difference between letting them go or allowing and suppressing them. Previously, I thought I was letting these thoughts go. Nevertheless, my emotions told me a different story. It was a struggle to keep myself motivated during these months. I worried about Timothy and his disapproval. I fretted about whether I had made the right decision. But the decision was a relief as well. I cared too much about what the people around me wanted me to do instead of being at peace with what I knew in my heart. This was a tough lesson to learn. I had to trust my own judgement and intuition.

2017/04/01

April fools!

I wish.

Timothy is angry with me. I've decided to resign from the company. My art classes and art selling are not good or solid enough for him. I understand. I'm exhausted right now. I couldn't stop crying last night. I sobbed. I haven't wept like that in years. I still have faith. I went to my parent's house to pick up an infant bird for rescue and to drop off the painting my mom had bought. I couldn't stop crying. Timothy is fuming and I don't know if he is irritated with me or with the situation in general. I don't know where this will lead to. I'm really exhausted right now. I've thought about some of the options I can take going forward.

2017/04/10

I'm apprehensive about work and the next two months. It's difficult to deal with the resistance from both of my bosses. I'm under pressure at the office, and things at home are tough and edgy. Nobody hears me. I had to change my life and I know I'll do well. I'm strong and capable, and I'll be successful. I'll follow up with SAP for the course. I'll sell my art and I'll give art classes. I've allowed the stress to get to me. I can release all of this to God. I release my fears and the fears of the unknown to God. I'll take one step at a time, one tiny bite at a time. My stomach is in knots, so I'll do breathing exercises.

2017/04/11

I feel a bit shaky but okay today. I managed to get a few things done yesterday. Balboa Press contacted me and I know I must write a book. I'll work at the Pharma company for the next two months. I must finish studying for my bookkeeping to trial balance course. That is important. I'm also applying for the SAP course soon. Today I can sit and study after work. If I can, I want to make time for gym too. Last night my mother told me to retract my resignation. I was outraged. There is no way I could do that to myself now. She will never understand.

Isla Stone

2017/04/14

I'm thankful for this coming long-weekend. It's exhilarating to know I have four days to pull myself towards myself. The last three weeks were difficult, filled with emotions and stress. There's a lot of tension at the house and I've seen some of my character defects coming out. I don't quite know how to deal with them. My art seems to have taken a back seat while I'm trying to keep my head above water, paddling and gasping for air. I try desperately to hold on to my serenity while Tim's fear rips it from me every day. I'm stuck between this rock and a hard place. I try my best to stay amicable, to understand his side and where he is coming from. I simply do not feel supported; there's no positive hand holding mine saying, 'you can do this, like so many others'. I try my best to support him, I wish he could support me despite his fears. The pain of staying the same was greater than the pain of changing. I've reached this point and he doesn't understand that. I must change. I can't keep doing the same thing repeatedly expecting a different result. Universally this has coincided with economic instability, but then when would have been a good time to make this change? Bombs are being dropped in Afghanistan; Syria is full of chemicals. And South Africa? Well, South Africa fights a positive fight.

I had a satisfying breakfast of Maltabella. I'm hurting now, and tired. I should take a step back and look at myself. Tim isn't always wrong, but he is not always right.

Lily is coming to South Africa. I'm proud of her; she is doing exceptionally well. Maybe I do not understand

Step Three properly, although I'm sure that I do. Turning my life over to the care of God as I understand Him. It's like riding a bicycle, I've done it many times before. Once I let go, miracles happen. Maybe I'm causing this tension. Timothy does not have to agree with me or understand my actions. I don't need his approval. I will make sure I can carry my financial responsibility. I don't want to become a burden and will align my actions with that in mind. I'm used to not having support from those closest to me. I can handle this. I must do a Step Four on all of this and adjust my resentment levels. Timothy and I must have a formal 'communication session'.

It seemed to me that I had no support for my decision. I felt alone again. I resigned myself to the fact that I had to leave others behind if I wanted to live the life I deserved. I was adept at being alone. It was hard to know that my loved ones condemned my decisions. I fought against the world, alone and afraid. The ocean beat against the empty hull of my boat. The echoes of my loved ones' voices told me to forget about happiness. I was used to being alone on this ocean, in quiet waters and during the worst storms that I had ever faced. I could do this alone too.

Loneliness is a strange thing, you get used to the dim sound of your mind speaking to you, comforting you, telling you that you can do this. One day, the voice becomes a bit louder; it starts steering you, it says there is hope. If you teach that well-known internal voice to love you, it becomes your biggest ally. I know it doesn't scream at me any more, it doesn't tell me how terrible I'm at living life. It tells me to get back up when I'm down. It directs me to stay sane in the crazy times.

I often remind myself that I'll live with *me* for the rest of my life. No-one else. I'm the only one who need to live with my decisions. I'm responsible for them. Not my mother, not my sister, not my brother or my partner, they might die, they may live. I live with myself all the time, twenty-four hours a day and seven days a week. I have no break from myself. My opinion of myself matters the most. How I love myself matters the most. No-one else can help me like I can help myself, and no-one understands me the way I understand myself. That's it. Simple.

Once I took the time to get to know and understand myself – when I broke through the difficult task of being candid with myself and learning to love myself again – I started acting in a way that served my ultimate well-being.

2017/04/15

> *My feet are cold. I've not done my affirmations today. I'll make new ones. The old ones are messy and crumpled up. I haven't looked at The Artist's Way for a while. I started doing some of the answers yesterday. I'm angry and frustrated after the last few weeks. I sit with a sense of utter disappointment. Yesterday I swept up my art area and cleaned the space with love. I would really like to buy this house. Tim said the only way he could see me leave my job is if I did recruitment. So, I'll do it, that was the original plan. We had a good talk yesterday. I was stiff with frustration on Thursday. I screamed with all my might in my car. I went to SARS and thought I had everything sorted out. But I didn't. Everything happens in good time. Impatience is one of my character defects. This is an opportunity for me to work on my impatience. There is this sense of urgency, as if something is chasing me. Things I must do rather than the things I want to do. I really need a laptop. I've asked the Universe to provide me with what I need and what would be good for me; I'm open to receiving graciously. I feel okay today. This weekend I want to reconnect with myself. I want to love myself, and that is what I'm doing today.*

2017/04/16

I just brushed my teeth and hung out the washing. If you know me, you'll realise the washing part is a miracle and something to write home about. I had a shower earlier and then studied – arduously – for most of the day. I went past my mom to apologise. I spoke to her in a disrespectful way this week. I took her some bread that I baked with cream and sugar. It was too sweet for her, and admittedly fairly burnt around the edges. We spoke about Mauritius, about Alex, about Tim. She told me about problems with her car and about her dilemma in not being able to leave John. It's such a sensitive subject for me. I wish my mom could find happiness, she deserves happiness and serenity. I love her endlessly. I adore her, I respect her.

I want to exercise and eat healthy. I've done it before! I want to feel splendid and healthy and confident. I want to respect myself. My mom said my sugar problem stems from my great-grandmother from my dad's side. She used to comfort me with sweet things. She would often give me a teaspoon of crystallized honey, or a teaspoon of sugar. We had an endless supply of biscuits and milk or sweet rooibos tea and fruit. I remember the tangy smell of granadillas. Apart from the comfort foods, there were daily back rubs with baby powder after lunch time and the dainty music box she had on her dressing table. It would softly suss me to sleep with Für Elise. She doted on me.

One of the gentlemen at the Sunday meeting really touched a nerve when he spoke to me. I had a lump in my throat and my eyes burnt. I hate that feeling. He asked me what I saw in my picture, he asked me if I knew how it worked. I said I saw a moronic bird. He told me I see myself as a broken bird, unable to fly. He asked me why I saw myself like that. I said it could be a lack of confidence or a fear of failure. He said I valued myself by what I do and not by who I am, and in turn others will only value me for what I offer or become, rather than who I am. This is a vast truth, and something I've been trying to work on. It has been difficult. As a child I felt I wasn't valued for who I was, I threw temper tantrums to get attention. My father did not visit or see me and thus I believed I had to be something exceptional other than myself to be loved and accepted. John valued himself by how much money he made and by his success in business. He ingrained those values onto us from the word go. You must be something, you must achieve, you should be superbly intelligent to be accepted. You are not good enough as you are now. We were never going to be good enough by John's standards. The carrot of satisfying his requirements dangled in front of all our faces perpetually. When I thought I had it in my hands, he moved the carrot. John had an issue with my weight too and would tell me I was fat or overweight from the moment I hit puberty. Self-acceptance wasn't acceptable. Achieve the best body, achieve the highest grades, achieve the best of everything and only then will you be acceptable or lovable. I know this not to be true now, I'm changing this and telling myself I'm lovable as I am; I'm acceptable as I am. Right now, as I am, I'm enough.

My mother was changing. It was elusive at first, although I noticed it. As the years passed, she had developed a rasping smoker's cough. The years of living with an abusive narcissist took its toll on her. Many would suggest I should have been livid with her given the historic events. I was, but I don't easily keep grudges. I love without difficulty. I adore effortlessly. I appreciate readily. My mom was my mom. I loved her to the ends of the earth. She could drive anyone up the wall with her stubbornness. She could make you want to jump off a cliff if you dared to argue with her. She was always right, in her eyes, and that was the most frustrating thing about her. But she was the kindest, warmest human being. She loved easily too, and she was a sucker when it came to her belief that there was some good in others. I still try my best to find little glimpses of a soul in John; I try hard. I search every time I speak to him. He is ill, he knows no better. When I saw my mother and her suffering, I thought this kind of evil can only exist in hell. Then I realised she had chosen her path, and I had to step back. I understood she felt stuck; she felt like a prisoner. Many years of abuse undoubtedly will do that to the strongest human being. So, I stepped back, and I did what was right for me, and tried my utmost to let it go, to release it. It worked most of the time, and often I would go about my business and spread hope and have hope infiltrate my life at the same time. It had its challenging moments; it ebbed and flowed. Some days I wanted to do something about it. What could I do? How could I fix something utterly broken and unreasonable?

It was never up to me to fix.

My mom took strain in the years after the family secret came out. The knowledge that her husband had sexually abused her daughters fractured something in her soul. She was devastated when my brother was admitted into the psychiatric hospital. During that time, John – who had nothing to do with Alex's upbringing – had the psychiatrists and psychologists wrapped tightly around his manipulative finger. My mom wasn't allowed to see her son despite dedicating her whole life to his well-being and needs since the day he was born. She took her insomniac, difficult baby to countless doctors to find out what exactly ailed him. She made up for all the mothering time she missed with me and Lara because she was in her late thirties when Alex arrived, and had more time and financial security. As he grew up, my mother desperately spoke about Alex to anyone who would listen. She was on an endless quest to find out why he struggled at school, why he was uncommonly anxious, why he did not sleep. John made hardly any effort to help. He sat in front of the TV, high on his benzodiazepines and grinning at his Twitter followers on a cell phone.

Later, Alex was diagnosed with sensory integratory problems and low muscle tone. Soon after this palaver my mother took him to a sleep specialist. Restless leg syndrome was detected, and the specialist gave him medication for sleep and adjusted some of the other medications that he was on. It was successful. Alex finally slept after all the years of frantic research and agonising; my mother was successful. The damage, however, was done.

2017/05/10

> *This morning I feel warm and loved. Tim and I had a lovely, comforting cuddle. This weekend we'll meet up with the extended family at a riverside campsite in Vanderbijlpark. It'll be fascinating to see them all together again. I'll need a quiet place to do my writing. I've been sitting here getting distracted watching TV. It annoys me. I bought snacks this morning for our trip.*
>
> *I had my last cigarette last night. I've used work as an excuse for smoking. I remember my mom's cough and how my grandfather died …*

2017/05/29

> *I'm counting down the days before I leave the company. Two more days to go then I'll be out of here!*
>
> *This morning I'm elated and grateful. I bought my plane ticket to George airport to visit Plettenberg Bay for the 1ˢᵗ of June, and I can't wait to see Lily. She has already*

arrived. Over the last few days I've increased my clarity and my vibrational energy. Yesterday my mom told me and Lara on the family group that Alex has a stash of weed. She was horrified; so was I.

I listened to the Hay House audio clips and remember hearing that when you are on a higher vibrational plane and something troubling happens, you find an opportunity within it. When I got home from work my mom asked me to fetch her. She had to pick Alex up and she'd had too much to drink. She didn't want to drive. I fetched her and we discussed how we would approach the situation with him. Because I had walked this journey previously, I could give advice on possible evasive strategies he might use. My mom and I bonded. We fetched Alex; he had a look of concern on his face. He probably knew someone would find his weed. He was tense, although he pretended not to be. Once we were on the open road my mother turned around and said, 'So, Ally, we discovered your stash'. He tried to play dumb. We pulled it out of him, bit by bit. He is a bad liar. He said he had only tried it once or twice and that it made him ill.

I made an amends with him that night. I apologised to him. I told him that I know I was selfish during my using days. I also said I'm sorry about the year I had to stay away. I told him it wasn't his fault in any way, although I could not give him detail about it. He would figure it out in time. I apologised to him. The first day I saw him after that year was the happiest day of my life. I still have that picture of us. He had tears in his eyes, and I hope he understands. The opportunity and time were right for me to make the amends to him. I love Alex with all my heart. It was agonising not to see him for a year. Today my life is magnificent, incredible. I'm privileged to live in this light.

2017/06/01

I'm overjoyed. Today my heart is whole and full. I'm in Plettenberg Bay.

The last few days were filled with incredible emotion. I was in shock when I saw Lily at the airport. Willem, her father, took a video of us hugging each other. I'm feeling these emotions even now as I sit and write this, and every now and then I let the tears fall over my cheeks. I was tired after the flight.

Today I'm content although I miss Tim a bit; but absence makes the heart grow fonder. Lily and I are still connected and still talk as if nothing has changed. It's brilliant. We are closer now than before she left. I love her like my soul sister – unconditionally. This visit is the best thing and the most perfect gift I could ever have asked for or given myself. I'm extremely proud of my inner child for allowing herself to be free this way. Life is wonderful.

2017/06/04

I'm healing again after a spell where my focus on myself expanded and my physical being became incoherent and disjointed. I'm contracting back into my physical body and mental mind, my spirit and my soul. I'm emotional but at peace. Undulations of emotions, high tide and low tide. My emotions are unreachable, intangible. I *feel solid but numb. Lonely but with Source. So much of the work that I've done on myself to become who I know I want to be feels left in dribs and drabs trailing behind me. I'm not grounded, but seeing Lily is good for me. Listening to her talking about her growth makes me smile. I'm thrilled she has truly found herself. She has experienced life. Perhaps I could have made that move myself? Although, at that time I felt unworthy and unwilling to embrace my gifts of art and love. Maybe I could have grown too. I did grow! At the same time, I admit that I stole from myself at that point. But I had to. It brought me to this understanding, and this growth. It was necessary.*

It's no longer necessary for me to live in smallness, to experience on a small-scale only. It's time for me to live. I choose passion. I choose connection and enchantment, I choose fearlessness, I choose release to be in tune with life. I choose life.

2017/06/05

The day is nice and warm, the hot wind has come from inland and is spreading itself onto the coast with its warm love. I'm at peace, creative and joyful. Everything I feel here is enveloped in ease. It's easy to move here, to live here, everything happens perfectly, peacefully, yet energetically. Living here is adventurous, connected, clean, delightful, easy, perfect, creative, enchanting, fun, loving, homely, safe, alive.

Right now, I'm in my vortex creating my own reality, manifesting my truth and needs. Art is my outlet. I'm imbued in utter serenity now that my life is in its next renewed chapter. Walking in this beauty, knowing it's my truth. Starting to see the things I was too busy to see, life is full of sweetness, art, and creativity. Opening myself up to this makes me fall in love with life.

2017/06/09

A huge fire swept the area in the last days. There is smoke everywhere, it's cold, the wind is slow. I slept well last night. Yesterday we went to help at the community hall. It was a bit chaotic. I hope today will be easier. People lost their homes in the blaze. Knysna burnt badly. From what I heard, two-hundred-and-fifty-nine homes burnt down. We drove through some of the destruction, it was horrific. The fires ravaged everything people held dear. Years of beauty swept away in a day of chaos. I suppose nature sometimes cleans the old to make room for the new, the fresh and the exquisite. I already saw new fresh green grass grow amongst the blackened charred death. Life is forever renewing, forever rebuilding and revitalising everything. It grows continually without thinking about whether it should be here or there. It just is where it intuitively knows it must be. The journey is as enjoyable as the destination. Overthinking takes away from knowing. It removes me from my natural well-being. I'm in an effortless state of clarity.

The day after I finally stepped out of the Pharma company for what I thought would be the last time, I left to visit Lily in Plettenberg Bay. She came to visit from Bangkok. The moment I saw her I sobbed. I became conscious of how much I truly missed her. We held on to each other for a long time at the airport greeting spot. Once we started chatting, we couldn't stop. It was amazing to see her after almost two years.

After being apart for all that time and not really being in contact much we had even more to talk about than when she left. We were like two children, giggling and laughing, joyous to see each other again.

It was a fairy tale time. I needed that break desperately after leaving the company, I was drained. The strain of the previous few months had taken its toll on me. I was giddy with excitement, dizzy with the fresh ocean air and the charming community. I wanted to move there immediately. I loved the inventive freedom people allowed themselves to experience daily in the small town. The novel experience of such an artistic hamlet inspired me. I felt right at home. I loved the friendliness and the sense of kinship.

About a week into my stay a fire broke out in Knysna. It was an horrific event that continued for days. Relief efforts and aid was sent from all over South Africa to assist the communities in the affected areas. The devastation grew. Initially, I heard about only a few hundred houses, but in actuality one-thousand-one-hundred-and-sixty-eight residences had burnt down a few days after Lily and I had gone on a road trip to the Knysna area. It was unrecognisable when we went to look at the damage. As we drove on the road that linked Plettenberg Bay and Knysna, it felt like the apocalypse. The previously luscious green landscape was now a grey, ashen graveyard. We drove there to help friends of my aunt and uncle. The fire ravished the trees and vegetation around their friend's golf estate. When they arrived at my aunt and uncle's home the night before, they said the only thing they took was a bottle of wine. There was no time to think, so they reckoned wine was a good option. The fire moved inexplicably fast. I met some of the victims while I assisted at the community centre in Knysna. A forlorn elderly couple walked in on one of those days. The gentleman had only his shoes on his feet. It was burnt from the fire, and the only possessions they had left were the scorched clothes on their backs. They were too embarrassed to ask for assistance because they felt there were others who needed the help more than them. I tried to convince them otherwise. The fire was selective. One house would be burnt down, with the neighbouring one being unscathed. It was terrible to see.

People's willingness to help astonished me. Everyone able-bodied person jumped in to assist those in need. It was a community helping each other. I had never known anything like that. I come from a big city where it's every man for himself. Centurion is a hard place, with fast-living people, deadlines, ambitions and – often – an apparent lack of altruism.

I spent time catching up with my Grannie and Elizabeth. The breakfasts were delicious, and coffee was plentiful. Lily and I went hiking, we went to the little market on Saturdays, we walked the labyrinth. We would often go for walks. I spent lots of my time alone too.

One afternoon the two of us decided to go for a walk to a well-known cliff on the beach. Aunt Elizabeth dropped us off close to the spot, to give us more time to explore. We saw starfish and penguins. We climbed to the apex and sat for an hour chatting. Lily asked me a question, and while I explained my answer to her, we had a spiritual moment. A huge wave crashed beneath us, and the rock we sat on resounded with the power of the ocean.

As we climbed down from the point, we noticed something in the water. A pod of dolphins swam alongside the coast where we walked. They seemed to get more excited at our laughter and romping. They jumped out of the water to get closer to us. We edged closer to the water to be near them. It was one of the greatest afternoons ever. I've never felt this close to the Creator, nature and another human being as I did then.

While I spent time with Lily, I noticed how my heart had hardened over time. I tried to find the reason for this. My ability to enjoy people and to be guided by joy had dissipated. I had no gladness or passion for the longest time. I tried to simulate that feeling in vein. I tried to force my emotions. I tried too hard and wanted to control things too much. I was still too fearful. Fear was an eternal captor holding me hostage.

The main cause of my cynicism was that I did not allow myself to step into my power.

There was a way in which I had to learn to let go. That holiday taught me to dream again, to allow myself to let go of self-judgement. I still condemned myself harshly. Although I practiced self-love, I could still be ruthless with myself. I wanted to allow myself to absorb life. I was far from actively doing it. I berated myself for not wanting to do certain things, like staying up late with my cousin and her brother and his girlfriend. I judged myself for not wanting to go out and do things. I started experiencing self-doubt. Finally, I gave in one night and went along, it wasn't that bad, I felt a bit uncomfortable. They were strange and different. I still experienced a challenge with one huge component. I'm not a ship alone on an open ocean. I'm a human being; interaction with others, speaking with others, allowing others into my space is part of living. I don't have to jump in and do everything for everyone, I don't have to be self-sacrificing for everyone I meet. I don't even have to rescue everyone I meet. I can simply be willing to communicate and attempt to connect with others. That evening a woman sat with me. She is an artist, and she said we should play a game. She would start drawing something, then I should add something to what she drew. Then she would add something onto what I drew, and so on. I was apprehensive because I was only really beginning to rediscover my artistic abilities. I was insecure. I didn't want her to pass judgement on my inadequate artwork. I decided to go with it. I learnt something from that experience. There is no judgement in the artist. The artist allows. The artist simply expresses what is at that moment, there is no good or bad. I felt accepted in that moment.

I didn't want the holiday to end but the time came when I had to return to Centurion. I packed my bags, and waved a sad goodbye to the rocking ocean, to the magical people, to Lily.

On my return, I would have to confront my decision to walk away from the Pharma company without another job.

CHAPTER 13

The Death and Rebirth

I tried a few things. I had many ambitious ideas of what I wanted to do. I wanted to leave the corporate company and do something I loved. I wanted to enjoy my job. Behind the scenes I practiced manifestation. I had only manifested a few things in the past, and at that these were never significant. I hadn't manifested things of major importance, nor had I done any manifesting under pressure.

Having said that, I hadn't done extensive research on the definite workings of manifestation, or the science of the whole practice either. What is manifestation? It's the practice of creating your own reality. It is the act of thinking about what you want, and then it appears. There are many things that come with this though. I previously mentioned reading and testing Rhonda Byrne's *The Secret*. I watched the movie several times. What fascinated me the most was how I felt when I watched it. It rang the bells of Universal Truth within me. I wanted to understand where it all fit in. I tried manifesting money, my perfect job, lottery winnings. None of those came to fruition. There was much more to this than merely asking, believing, and receiving.

I came across a woman called Esther Hicks. She channels blocks of thought from the energy she calls Abraham. My understanding of the Powers That Be is that I'll never truly understand what lies beyond this physical reality. Nevertheless, it's fun trying to figure it out. The best thing that comes with it is the emotions it can evoke. When my head floats, when I have goose bumps during a conversation or listening to music, when I meditate and hear something, or see something so inexplicable my heart wants to expand, I know that this is Source.

I began listening to Esther Hicks channelling Abraham. It was valuable, wise information. I recognised how much I still had to learn about practical manifestation exercises.

The odyssey of the last six years has taught me many things in peculiar ways. I've always been interested in holistic healing. My manifestation practice and research have taught me more about self-love and self-acceptance than I could ever have dreamt of.

2017/07/06

> *At the end of May, I finally walked out of the Pharma company. I was done with the politics, the waste of time, the energy sapping, the fighting, and the feeling of not being good enough every day. I was finished with not enjoying what I did. I liked the people; I hated the job. I truly disliked where I was and chose to change it. I'm especially anxious today. The sense of smallness grabbed me after the holiday. It's difficult to be my authentic self again. I suspect I'm putting too much pressure on myself. If I look at everything I attempted to do in the last three weeks, I can see the stress I'm creating. Of course I'll feel this way! I'm squeezing myself into a tiny claustrophobic hole again.*

> *I'm trying to focus on one thing at a time. One action at a time, one breath at a time, one unique aspect at a time. I've been painting, planning paintings, writing a book, doing a SAP course, going to the centre, being open to connecting with people, massaging, getting art classes up and running. I've been putting unrealistic expectations on myself, absurd expectations. I can let God take over instead and lead me. Release and surrender. I know my art had led me here. That is what I should concentrate on. That and SAP.*

My alignment with myself is out of whack. Something bugs me. Lily went back to Bangkok. I buried my heartache about it deeply though.

2017/07/11

I'm still drowsy this morning, but I had masses of energy yesterday. It will bubble up again today. I'm waking up once more. Yesterday was interesting, I went to see Maureen. I'm contracting in at the Pharma company again for three days a week. I'm not sure what to expect. Today I'm going to see the SAP instructor at 10.00. I must still complete a few things he sent me.

2017/07/12

Yesterday I unpacked my negative self-talk. John has crawled back into my head. I'm steeped in the overall feeling of not being good enough because I insist that I should be way further in my life by now. After the argument with Tim two weeks ago where I froze and then hid under the blanket it became evident to me that there was something else at play. I was afraid and nervous, and shut down during the argument. It has taken me a week and a half to process what happened. I turned five years old again whenever I experienced an unpredictable situation that reminded me of being a child with no control over my environment. Potentially volatile confrontation scares me. I was afraid of a shouting match. It took me right back to John's one-sided shouting matches with me. I froze. I regressed and climbed under the covers, refusing to face it. I spoke to Tim after this happened. We discussed it and I told him it wasn't him. I understood my behaviour and tried to explain it to him.

Years of recovery and still there were more behaviours and facets of myself I had to understand and work on. I was peeling away layers from myself. It was never-ending and frustrating that something so debilitating in my behaviour could still surface. When I resigned from the Pharma company, Timothy was concerned about how we would afford to pay rent. I had money in the bank after paying out a policy, but it wouldn't last forever. One day the tension became too much. Tim snapped, his temper flared, and he fought with me. I didn't respond much during the argument. I sat quietly. I was scared stiff. I could not move for fear of cracking a muscle. My whole body tightened, and when he calmed down, I excused myself and walked to the bedroom. I closed the door and pulled the duvet covers over my head. I began to cry, overwhelmed by the feeling that I was right back in front of my stepfather. I knew this wasn't the reality, but it did not change the experience. I understood why Tim was angry; we hardly ever fight. If we have a disagreement, we discuss it over a cup of coffee, or we have a debate. This was the first time we ever had a fight. I had to learn how to respond in this type of argument. My reaction was more upsetting to me than the actual argument. This reactive regression was completely based on my past experiences with abuse. I had to learn that a disagreement doesn't mean I must engage in a heated screaming match. These days, I just say that I would rather have a conversation when everyone has calmed down; I leave the room and go on with something else.

Even then, it took less time for me to process what was happening and what my thought processes were than at the beginning of my journey. The fantastic thing about having a sponsor is that when you speak to them and they relate to you, you recognise you are not the only one who has or ever will experience whatever it is you're going through. My sponsor experienced something remarkably similar and explained to me that she also froze. We worked on our behaviour together and overcame it together.

I did a SAP course. I thought I could become a consultant. It would allow me time to paint and be creative, whilst also earning money. I was uncertain about what I wanted to do or how I would go about it. I learnt a lot during the SAP course. I enjoyed it tremendously, however there was still something in my heart that shouted I was heading in the wrong direction. I had barely left the corporate industry and here I was, working towards building a career in a corporate environment again. The SAP trainer was a jolly gentleman full of innovative ideas. I asked him to help me find a job in the industry and he was happy to oblige. We met for coffee. He suggested that we start a business together. Since I had nothing else to do, I jumped at the opportunity. At the same time the Pharma company called me back and asked that I contract in for a couple of months until they could find a suitable replacement for my position. I agreed. My financial situation was precarious, and it suited me to go back for the time they suggested. My SAP-partner and I wanted to start a service business. Our ideas varied slightly. I thought that over time our ideas would align. Yet again, this was a corporate business, mainly focused upon corporate businesses and offering a service to them. I wasn't completely aligned with the project.

2017/07/17

Today is a great day. I feel fantastic. It's a bit cold outside. Yesterday we went to see my mom, Alex and Lara. Alex's hair has grown into a thick mop and his shapely eyebrows are so gorgeous – it looks as though he gets them waxed. They are perfect.

My mom told me about John's latest ailment: an enlarged prostate; I don't have much sympathy for him any more. I don't feel animosity, just not sympathy.

Yesterday Tim and I made love. Lying in each other's arms afterwards, we listened to a significant song that reminded me of days gone by. I could still picture our broken family when we had joyful moments listening to music on the hi-fi, dancing to the tunes and singing our lungs out.

Tim is getting ready to go out to a business meeting and I'm planning my day. It's a bit cold to do art today. I've made a promise to myself that I would complete some of the tasks I've put off repeatedly for a while. Making the marbling combs are a whole lot more difficult than I suspected they would be. I'll ask Tim to help me. Today is Alex's birthday. He is sixteen years old. I can't believe it. His voice has broken, and his facial hair is growing. I still picture him as a little boy. I've had sixteen years of a different kind of life, a different kind of existence with Alex as part of it. A child so extraordinary, so gentle, so different. His suffering so palpable and evident, since birth.

Ginja is sitting on my lap, I love him dearly.

2017/07/28

I'm grateful today. I managed to get up early this morning again to go running. My back and bum are a bit stiff. My running trainer wasn't there this morning. He had overslept but caught up with me in his car after a while. I told him his body probably needed the rest. I'm impressed with myself for being so strong. I didn't know I was capable of this. The other night I dreamt my body was muscled, lean, healthy, and super fit, without a single bit of fat on it. I had a six-pack! However, I had pain. I suffered and prayed for the addiction to be taken away.

I reflected at length about this dream. I suppose there is a healthy well-balanced person within my body or my mind. A holistic, fit, lively being who has found a subtle balance of self-love and acceptance. She has released all fears and lives to serve others by sharing the knowledge and wisdom she has gained. She is not afraid of herself. She can walk to the edge of all her darkness and insanity and come back unscathed whenever she wants. This woman is strong. She has no hang ups about who she is. This woman is frantically trying to clamber out of the soft marshmallow sanatorium I've created for her. The bit at my mouth that I've placed there to hide words, thoughts and feelings is pulled taught. The only one who can remove that bit is me. Speaking true words, singing the siren song of life is my next chapter. Communication is key. I must tell people openly where they stand with me. I've had this thought: John has been my greatest teacher.

2017/08/21

I'm despondent today. I ate heaps of sugar yesterday, although I know this is wrong for my body. I also failed my SAP exam. It brings up feelings of failure from the past where I perceived myself as incapable and stupid. I know this is a lie. I'm angry about not getting past the blocks I've experienced around my art. My self-destructive actions have hijacked me again. I could sleep for a whole day. My vortex feels far away right now. I want to write a book, be an artist, give art therapy classes, and I want to study psychology. What I'm currently doing is studying for SAP, working at the Pharma company (again) and not progressing significantly with anything else. Why do I not allow myself to do the things I say I want to do? Won't those things fulfil me? No, I'm fulfilled and contented. I have a sense of peace. It will however bring me closer to my life's purpose. That is what I must do. I want to write a book, at first, I wanted to write about my life, my history where I was, what happened and what it's like now. Then I thought that I would just let it flow, and it did.

It's time for me to go to proper art classes. I've lost my art fever and creativity. I must learn again. I've been miles away from my Higher Self. I concentrated on SAP and studied like crazy during the past weeks. I'm trying to allow people in; I'm making progress slowly. This disconnection from my Higher Self started when I loaded sugar back into my diet. I'm powerless over this addiction and my life has become unmanageable. Sugar is an addiction for me, along with cigarettes and coffee. All these substances are things I lean on to feel better. I rely on in it to change my perspective and my experience. I've lingered in my denial for years. I know my stomach requires special care and attention. Things improved somewhat when I was on a specific diet for my gut. My inner child screamed in protest. Change is difficult, awkward, scary. I must believe it's safe to change. The physical exhaustion will leave me once I change the way I eat. My enthusiasm for life will increase exponentially. The running has made such a huge impact in my life. I feel terrible for not running this weekend. I've disappointed myself. I know I'm too hard on myself. I look forward to seeing Gabriel today. I haven't seen him in about a month!

There is a reason that I stopped doing the emotional digging and writing. My sponsor said something that touched a nerve two weeks ago. I still haven't been able to take my attention back to the subject. She said that she had met me almost three years ago but that she still doesn't know me. Even after many years of recovery I do not easily allow people into my emotional space, and I still do not trust people enough to make friends with them. After three years, I still haven't even allowed my sponsor to get too close. This worries me. I did not realise the extent of my guardedness. When I asked her why she thought I was this way, she said she suspected it was because of the trauma I went through in my family life. It is time, however, to allow people in now.

I started writing a letter to John. I'm hurt, disappointed, fearful, disgusted, and enraged. I'm not showing these emotions, they are inside of those thick, solid walls around myself. Allowing others inside is difficult, nearly impossible. It is dangerous. I'm fearful of what might happen if I were to let anyone in or if I were to let any of this anger out. I don't know where to find this anger, it is inaccessible. What would happen if I were to access it? Would I go crazy? The reason I'm glued here, blocked here, is because of this damage that this man, my greatest teacher, has created. I feel despondent.

I'm concerned about Alex, my mother, my dad. I'm angry with John, despondent about my path, angry with myself for not getting where I want to be, disturbed. I wonder what it would be like if I could steadfastly keep on track with what I said I would do (like pass my SAP exam). What would it have been like if I did what I said previously? I could have had my honours degree by now. Beating myself up about the past is useless and destructive. The only way forward is to live today.

During this transition I had much time to think about what I was moving toward. I decided I wanted to increase my creativity. In *The Artist's Way*, Julie Cameron suggests that running is a good exercise for the creative mind. I joined a running group close to our home and started running early in the mornings. I loved waking up at 4.00 in the mornings and to run into the dawn. The fresh air rushing into my lungs, the coolness of the breeze caressing my face, my feet rhythmically slapping the tar was cathartic. It was difficult in the beginning because I was unfit, but as my fitness increased, so did my enjoyment. I gradually began running longer distances. I impressed myself mightily when I completed my first 10 km run. I never even considered being able to run such a far distance.

Unfortunately, the fear overcame me. I worried that I wasn't skillful. During a 10 km run with my group there was an older woman running along with me one day. She had a knee injury and wasn't really supposed to be running. She had been running most of her adult life. I compared myself to her and guessed I wouldn't keep up with her. When she overtook me and became smaller in the distance ahead of me, resentment also overtook me. Why am I always left behind? That thought paralysed me. I started hyperventilating. I had to walk the remainder of the distance.

My business partner suggested I should write one of the SAP exams. I could only afford to attend one of the module courses, and the exam was based on a variety of different modules, or one large one that was exceptionally pricey. I decided to attempt the exam. I had previously worked on the application, I had the experience, and knew it quite well. I underestimated the difficulty of the exam and failed it quite miserably on my first attempt. I wrote the exam three times. It was a fiasco. I failed every time. My misplaced confidence was yet again a mere farce in the face of my maladjusted life.

In the second half of 2017 and early 2018 I experienced many awakenings. Moments where I had realisations and paradigm shifts when my mind was silent enough and I was calm enough to make the connections. Over the years, especially after getting into the relationship with Tim, and leaving the Pharma company, my internal chatter calmed down significantly. One of these insights was that after knowing my sponsor for more than three years and doing extensive step work with her, she still did not know me intimately. During a conversation one afternoon she mentioned to me in passing that I acted like a feather. She named me Feather-head, Feather for short and then Feath, because I lost the 'er' somewhere along the line when I didn't do what she told me to do. She said my defence mechanism of acting childlike and thoughtless was a barrier. She called it a wall that kept others at bay. I did it with everyone, including her. I recognised that this was how I acted within my family to protect myself. I played the happy go lucky clown; I made everyone laugh. It gave me enormous pleasure when I got my mom to crack a smile. It was safe for me to pretend I did not know what was going on, or to act stupid. This got me out of trouble and kept me out of many battles I did not want to fight. The stereotype of being blonde was my favourite. I played it well. This was dishonest and manipulative. I was untrue to myself. I avoided using my intelligence and power. This realisation was a major breakthrough. When I understood it was safe for me to be myself instead of hiding behind the mask that was a survival mechanism, I flourished.

I wrote an emotional letter to John. It touched on weighty and traumatic issues around our story. I pointed out experiences that scarred me and how they contributed to the behaviours I had to reverse with so much hard work. It was a cathartic process, and it was difficult to write it all down. As I put my pen to paper, memories flooded into my consciousness. Emotions filled me in the hues of a dirty rainbow. I intended to give that letter to him. A profound fury had risen within me. I was adamant to let him know how I felt.

Isla Stone

2017/08/26

I'm angry today! The rage sits in my muscles like it used to when I was a small child. I did not pass the exam on Friday. I feel embarrassed at work. Sentiments from years ago are coming back to me. They are unravelling in fury and wretchedness. We went to visit Grannie and Uncle Marius for the long-weekend. We drove past my grandfather's old farm. I was excited and nostalgic. So many memories. This weekend filled me with a myriad of different emotions. I can't put it into words. It's frustrating. All I know is that I'm irritable. I shouted at my mother. I lost my temper with her. She had too much to drink the one night. She repeatedly said there is something wrong with Alex, that he is mentally ill. I told her that emotional problems do not signify mental illness. He was damaged during his upbringing and by the psychopath who is his father. John is an abusive, bad man. I wrote the other day about the gravity of the situation, the extent of the abuse we experienced. He induced unending fear and used manipulation to get his way. I didn't blame Alex for being where he is mentally and emotionally. It also doesn't help that my mother keeps him in a glass box. I told her all of that. Well, I screamed at her while we sat at the fire. Then I walked off.

Yesterday I thought about how much I love my Grannie, I saw the sorrow in her eyes when we were about to leave, I felt it in my heart and my body. I wished she wouldn't leave me with my mother when we climbed into the car to go home. Now I had to look after my mom again.

2017/10/09

Some days I feel too old to be passionate about anything. I had a thought during one of my meditations the other night: 'A prisoner is only a man with limitations'.

I went through all my limitations and contemplated the thought. I've written about them and what they mean and why I feel that way. All of it is linked to how I perceive the Universe. The way I look through my mind and eyes. How do I change this? I know how. I decide to.

So, I made the decision to let go of all my fears and limitations. I'm cutting out some of my unhealthy habits too. I want the fire of passion to burn in my heart again. I made the decision to enjoy life; to break free from my prison. Today is the first day of the rest of my life.

I thought about enthusiasm yesterday. What subjects spark the fire of passion within me? Nature, the brilliance and perfection of it. My heart expands when I think of the natural beauty we're fortunate enough to experience on this planet. I love people, conversing with them and guiding them. Assisting them to see what they can do to better their lives. I adore art, it's awe-inspiring. It makes my heart chant in a mantra of joy. It is a medium through which the Universe speaks to us. Something is shifting and changing inside me.

When I woke up this morning, my decision to pursue life with zeal solidified. I feel changed.

Isla Stone

2017/10/19

My neck is stiff. I had strange dreams again. I only recently grasped the significance of the fight I had with my mom over the long-weekend. I also saw in retrospect how my Grannie and I reconnected that weekend. It healed our relationship. We communicate better now. I chatted to her and told her how thankful I am for everything she did for me. I wouldn't be who I am today if it wasn't for her. I imagine this conversation salved a fractured part of her.

During the fight with my mom, I had I walked away from her. I told her I couldn't argue with a sick person. After ten minutes, I went back and apologised for losing my temper. I dislike losing my temper because I don't like hurting the people that I love with my words. I know I can't control what I say when I'm angry. I have a sharp tongue. When I went into my mom's room to apologise, she said that I was right. I was flabbergasted. My mother never concedes. I wasn't aware of how important this moment was for my healing until yesterday. Tim kept telling me how proud he was of me. My sponsor said it was excellent that I finally had my say and spoke my truth. It was an important moment for me because I finally got angry and showed it.

2017/10/22

I feel restless. I have enormous amounts of pent up energy. My mind is occupied with exercise and the perfect body. The part of my body I wish I could see differently in the mirror. My stomach, my arms, my legs and my neck. I picture lean, strong muscles in my arms that have strength enough to climb walls and do pull-ups. I picture a strong and defined stomach; a powerful core. I want to feel good about my strength. I picture my legs having definition, especially my thighs. I picture my back muscles being firm and lean. I picture myself running marathons, climbing mountains, cycling in the dirt, swimming. I imagine going out to see the world and being less preoccupied with the taste of coffee and cigarettes. I visualise not craving sugar. I dream about being on top of the world and enjoying life, not fearing it. Ironically, there's a cup of coffee next to me on the table now, and I'm shoving biscuits in my mouth without tasting them. I'm swallowing them in gulps. I picture myself getting past this fear, this fear of life. Yesterday I saw my mom, she wasn't well. She walks like a rickety, broken old woman. I cried a lot this week, it's something I've not done for a while.

I had a dream that something would happen on the 4th of November. There is nothing I can do about it, my dream said I would be going back somewhere without saying goodbye to my mom. It did not seem final, but it was kind of ominous. I don't know what the dream meant. I've had three psychic visions recently. I've changed my medication. Maybe it's that? I'm not certain if they were all psychic visions or perhaps just glitches in the in the time frames of my mind.

The final healing of my past was taking place. The last remnants of the hidden pain were being scraped away. I had no choice. I had to unearth these issues that I was still skirting around. My co-dependent and self-destructive behaviours were caused by the festering pains just below the surface. I constantly had to push myself to grow, to get myself to a place where I could see from a higher perspective instead of gazing at my navel. It became easier to peel away the layers of the onion. I got closer to the core issues at hand. The behaviours and resulting fears that were holding me back from living the life I truly wanted to live started to have less of a hold over me even though it seemed worse before it got better.

In the last months of 2017, I asked my mother if I could work for her and John's company. I needed the income. The work I'd been doing wasn't paying enough to make ends meet. The business I planned with the SAP instructor took much longer to get off the ground than expected. I still hadn't managed to pass the SAP exam. I ran out of money – the exams were expensive. My mother wrote up a mini contract for me. She needed help with administrative work, and she was stressed due to the yearly renewal exercises. She was pleased to have me assist her at the company. In hindsight I comprehend that everything happens for a reason. I had to be there for me to go through the healing process.

I would fix me and my mom a cup of coffee every morning at the office and we'd take it downstairs and smoke a cigarette. She would tell me about the insanity of the workplace and her biggest challenges. It gave me more insight than before and, for the first time, I understood her daily life and the impact she made in other people's lives. I often thought she cared more for others than for me and Lara. I sometimes felt jealous that she made much more of an effort with my brother. Over time, I understood how – just like me – she had learnt from her past mistakes and adjusted how she handled situations in the best way that she could. She also did not receive a book on how to live life.

When I lost my temper with my mom during the weekend at my Grannie, I spoke my truth. But I felt terrible. I did not want to hurt her feelings. I knew she struggled with the same historic experiences we all had. She was still experiencing it every day, living with John. After being reassured that my anger was a healthy reaction, I felt much better and empowered. However, I still have a soft heart. The people I love completely can get away with murder. After the weekend I wrote a letter to my mother. I never gave it to her. It was the same healing exercise that I had done with John. I had a tremendous amount of anger towards her. I wrote about it in that letter.

I was still in the process of getting to know myself. I'm still in that process – it's a lifelong journey. I came to realise that when I'm distressed, I like to bake. It's an endearing and quirky trait that reminds me of my Grannie. I'm smiling as I write this. Tim knows that when I'm emotionally turmoiled, I bake to let off steam. My Grannie taught me how to bake with unvarying precision when I was a girl. We often stood in her large kitchen and rolled out cookies for the family during Christmas time. She baked in large quantities. She taught me how to bake cake and stick to a recipe just so. I loved the comfort and safety of baking with her. The smells of the biscuits baking in the oven comforted me. The dough we ate – giggling because we knew we weren't supposed to – tasted like heaven. My Grannie lives the absolute inner part of my heart. This is why I love baking; it brings those nostalgic moments to the fore. After I have baked a cake or biscuits, all is right in my world again.

2017/10/27

> It's time to wake up. The last three months were rough. I've been avoiding many things and healing has been taking place. I feel bruised, tired, and jaded. A couple of weeks ago I felt good and spiritually connected. Something was changing within. Then it abruptly stopped. I had a thought to contemplate. 'A prisoner is only a man with limitations.' I experienced an awakening. Every aspect of what I wrote down as limitations over the last few weeks has bound and gagged me thoroughly. I've allowed them to do so. I know fear is only a projection of my own mind. It's a memory of uncomfortable or hurtful past experiences or ideas that I want to avoid in future. Fear is self-destructive in nature. It does not serve

a purpose. It's a limitation. Fear makes my heart beat faster, puts nervous energy through my muscles, brings ringing to my ears, changes my mind about the things I actually want to do. The opposite of fear is faith. I forget this sometimes, especially when I'm scared. Even writing this word speeds up my heart. Fear is nothing. I remove the power of fear over me.

2017/12/23

Turmoil. Sadness. Worry.

I don't know what to do or say. I worry about my mother. I take her misery and sickness on. I choose to, I do not have to. I can choose to do this differently. She did not heed my warnings. Now it seems the inevitable time has come; the pressure has pushed her to the edge. I saw a crumbling woman in Port St. Johns. Her life is shattering. The foundation of her life is disintegrating. I don't know how to help her. I've learnt this is her lesson, not mine. I can't attempt to intervene. She has planned this meticulously before she came here, as did I. She is also stubborn. We all planned our journeys here. We are all one in the ocean of energy of Great Love. My mind has been accepting thoughts from different frequencies. Or blocks of thought. I can't understand them yet, they happen so quickly. I should stop and listen. The ocean is edging forward and back, sending waves up to the beach, then sucking it in again, rhythmically calling my name. I'm sitting on the beach listening and writing at the same time. My skin is sun-kissed more than it has ever been in my adult life. I feel energised. I'm eating healthier, even though it has been a challenge with this new gluten allergy I've developed. It's difficult not to get *resentful about this condition. I remind myself that I'm eating healthier; it's good for my body and my overall well-being.*

2017/12/26

This morning I'm grateful and at peace. On Christmas day Tim and I went for a walk. Along the way, an emotional wave overpowered me. I hyperventilated, my neck stiffened, my heart rate sped up. I felt debilitated. When we stopped to take a break, I told him I did not know where to place my family in my life and heart. They mean a lot to me, but they are nowhere to be found, they are all broken and distant. I know, and I understand, I accept nothing will change. I won't ever feel what I want to feel when I see them or spend time with them, but I really don't know how to get this right in my head and in my heart. Then I started crying; it was that sobbing with the pain right above the surface in my chest. It's painful. Alex started a family group on WhatsApp. I know he feels the same way.

Yesterday's Christmas was one of the best in the last three years. I felt loved and I enjoyed it. I had fun, laughed, ate ice-cream and wore a funny hat. I felt family. I appreciate this holiday. I'm grateful for all the blessings and experiences it brought me. The food, the sun the different beaches, the people. It was a splendid holiday. My heart is glowing. My skin is glowing, my face is glowing, my energy is replenished. Thank you, Universe, thank you for always looking out for me, for always making sure I'm okay. I love you with my whole being. I wish I could give you a hug and talk to you and say thank you. You always, always come through.

What I love about my quest is the recognition that the purpose of my pain is more evident after time has passed. I always try to determine the meaning of my suffering whilst I'm awash in the sordid waters of agony. I always hope a glimpse of the purpose will help me to lighten the darkness with a flame. But the real comprehension only comes afterwards.

Around the end of the year, I developed a severe allergy to gluten. My stomach clenched and I became nauseous every time I ate anything that contained it. At first, I was diagnosed with salmonella. When it became evident that it wasn't salmonella, I had blood tests done. The allergy was severe, and I had no other choice but to completely change my diet. This was a terrible time for me. I had to give up my beloved sugary baked goods and carbohydrates. My underlying depression flourished.

During that December Tim and I went on our first holiday together. His eldest son came with us and brought his girlfriend to join in the festivities. In 2017 we had been together for two years. During those years, we faced many trials and tribulations. Our relationship had stood the test of time. It felt as if we had been together forever by then. Tim was born in Ballito. Most of his extended family lives in the humid coastal city. He knows the east coast well and he can take you anywhere in that region. He wanted to show me his neck of the woods and share his childhood experiences.

I never thought I would be selective or difficult over my accommodation and living arrangements when I was on a holiday, but during this holiday I was surprised to discover I had become a bit of a snob. I took on my mother's tastes and preferred comfort over adventure. Our accommodation was dark and slightly uncomfortable. It wasn't the extravagance I was used to when I went on holiday with my mom in Port St. Johns. It was dusty and humid in the modest, squashed up space. It was claustrophobic. Our bedroom door could not close. I behaved like a spoilt child. I could not eat what I wanted to because I was on a strict diet. I was completely out of my comfort zone and it seemed as if all my control was taken away. I tried my best not to fight with Tim, just because I wasn't in control of all the decisions. He was simply excited to be on holiday. He wanted to show me how he grew up and what it was like for him. My personality defects surfaced one after the other. I was a royal pain.

We planned to drive through to Port St. Johnson a two-day road trip to visit my mom who was on holiday there. She asked me to go with her, but I had already arranged with Tim to go with him and his family. I could not forever continue to look after my mother. I wanted to make sure she was okay, and it was a relief that my Grannie and Lara went with her. I was shocked by the state she was in when we arrived in Port St. Johns. She was fragile and a ghost of her former self. I knew she wasn't well before she left for her holiday, but something must have happened during the last couple of weeks after I had seen her in Centurion.

Just before I left for holiday from their company, bedlam erupted at work again. She had to sort it out. It also came out that John was cheating on my mother again. This time his affair was with someone I used to be friends with. Over the years and after I got into recovery our friendship dissolved. She still liked the chaos, I had removed it from my life. She is young – far younger than me – and previously worked at their company. John had developed a fascination with her even before she worked for him. She had a slight build and childlike features. This revolted me. It disgusted me that someone who claimed to even be an acquaintance or friend would do such a thing. It nauseated me that John had a sexual relationship with someone he had known since her late teens.

My Grannie was upset and concerned about my mother while on holiday. She took me aside to discuss this; we went for a walk on the bustling main road of Port St. Johns. She asked if there wasn't anything we could do while we strolled amongst the street artists' stalls. I told my Grannie about my attempts to help my mom. I asked my mother multiple times to get help, to see a psychologist, to book herself into a psychiatric hospital. Her drinking had gotten out of hand. By this time the smell of beer was always rancid on her breath.

I did not have the heart to tell her that her drinking was a problem. Tim did though, and so did my Grannie. But my stubborn, obstinate mother always knew best for her and others. Grannie looked more worried than ever as we walked back to the holiday unit.

2018/01/01

> Today is the first day of the year. The dawn of a new era of our lives. I have a deep-seated awareness of newness, freshness, beauty, and joy. I'm content today. I'm ready to take this year on with gusto and enthusiasm. A weight has lifted off my shoulders. There will never be true perfection with regards to my personality. I must consistently push myself to grow. However, I've promised myself to take myself less seriously this year. It is time to lighten up, this year I'm changing my perspectives to the lighter side. I'm turning my face to the light. Happy, cheerful, peaceful, energetic, fun. This year I'm going to soar!

2018/01/15

> It's Monday. The weekend was filled with yoga, family and Tim. It was lovely. I'm a bit anxious about the week ahead. It's silly. Why worry? I've not yet heard anything from the Pharma company with regards to the proposal, I sent to them for the SAP training. I don't know what I'm going to do about an income this year. I've started off on a good foot with my business partner. I know when I put a 100 % into the business it will explode. Something is holding me back, mainly myself. I'm strong enough and energised to push through with our plan now. I really don't need to, nor want to worry about

what anyone else tells me at this moment. Everything happens for a reason.

2018/01/17

The meeting last night was nice. This year has started off drearily. I asked for quietness and now I'm complaining! I don't know why I can't find peace or a space within me where I'm okay with life. I allow anything and everything to worry me. I look back and see that I'm doing much better than before. The steps I've taken and the courage I've received has not been in vain. I've been anxious about leaving the Pharma company and being unemployed. This is where I am now. I wanted to pursue SAP to be a trainer. It sounded like a good idea and still does. I'll continue to pursue this. Insecure thoughts keep crossing my mind. I'm kidding myself; I'm not qualified enough; I have no idea what I'm doing. It's okay to have these thoughts, it's the only way I'll learn not to have them. There is a proposal lying on Maureen's desk. She hasn't said no. I've also sent my CV to another company that uses SAP. One of my friends is helping me. I'll send positive vibrations into the Universe. I'll always be looked after. All I can do this week is play, take it easy, release, and surrender. My stomach is giving me problems again. I mentioned in the meeting that I've been putting off going to the doctor. I said my imagination was playing outlandish tricks on me again.

2018/01/19

This morning I woke up with swollen eyelids, feeling the weight of a ten-ton truck on my chest. Tim was tense and quarrelsome at dinner last night. It was my perception that he aimed all his frustrations and bitterness at me. I became irate, but subtly so. The air was filled with a muffled tension; an unspoken vexation. He blames me for our situation. Or what he perceives to be 'a situation'. I know I don't have a job or an income, but I have enough money for two months of rent. This is wearisome, but it won't kill us. I stand by my choice to break free.

Last night I delved into remorse. I meandered into my memories. What if I could have my life over again? I would have done what I loved and stuck with it. I would have completed my studies in Ecology. I blamed it all on John in a fit of rage in my heart. Why, God? Why did I have all my experiences, just to end up here? In my youth I believed emphatically that anything was possible for anyone. That one could become or achieve anything. This was one of my core beliefs. I wanted to be an adventurer, an ecologist, a Darwinist, an Artist. I craved to see and touch and be a part of the world. I yearned to experience different cultures, meet new and intriguing people, smell different smells. I aspired to learn about the world. I hankered after a new adventure every day. I was thirsty for life. I wanted to be wholly a part of this world without a drop of fear. I longed to embrace every exciting experience this world has to offer in her magnificent beauty. I ached to dive in the oceans amongst the fish that dwell in the reefs. To fly in the skies. I hungered to touch and tickle and explore this world.

Instead I'm here on my bed crying again. Clueless about what I might do in my shrinking, shrivelling world. I'm tired of fighting, of hoping, of keeping face. Of walking through the depths of darkness that my soul has encountered amongst men. My soul is torn, fighting

to get in touch with God, frantic to feel God's love. I'm
lost again. I basically want to reset my life. Hit Control,
Alt, Delete. Restart. Hope for the best. Thus far this life
has been nothing but pain and disappointment and hurt
and fear. I'm fed up with it now.

As time moved on and we came into the next year I became increasingly worried about discovering my life's purpose. I didn't know what I truly wanted to pursue. I did not want to apply for another job in the industry I had left a short time ago. I wanted to become a consultant because I craved freedom and flexibility. That made sense to me, I wanted to have freedom to do what I chose, but also to make enough money to be comfortable. I practiced the Law of Attraction on a regular basis and began to understand the intricacies of how it works. I felt less anxious when I listened to Esther Hicks (Abraham Hicks) and practiced the Law of Attraction every day. There was far more in the Law of Attraction than getting what you ask for. It is an all-encompassing practice of the spiritual.

There were days where I wished my life was different. I wanted to live, but all my effort went into merely surviving. I was tired of fighting, of working on trauma. I wanted to enjoy my life. To let go of all the history and pain and just live. I thought I did it already with all my work, but I wasn't doing it effectively. I tortured myself by revisiting it all over again. I had to confront John to dispel the cycle of rumination and retraumatising myself in the process. The reason the subject kept creeping up was that I wanted to somehow find the ability within me to forgive him fully, wholly, but also to walk away. I did not want to feel any emotion about what happened. I wanted to move on with my life and soar across all the many stumbling blocks. My mom was still married to him, I saw him often, and he is my brothers' father. It is messy and complicated.

Towards the end of 2017 I still worked at the Pharma company on a temp basis. By the end of that year they found a replacement for my position. The financial director asked me to put a proposal together for SAP training. I compiled the document and sent it to her. Unfortunately, I had not passed the SAP exam. They rejected my proposal. I gave up after failing the exam the third time. I was despondent. After the holiday in December, I attempted to get myself fired up for the new year. Because I was used to hit the ground running at the Pharma company, it was unusual not being busy at the beginning of the year. I waited for things to happen. I worked hard with my partner. We met up at least once a week to work on our business plan. But it wasn't really moving forward. We were both ideas people, we were just not very good getting-things-done people.

There was severe tension between Tim and me. The situation made him angry. I tried to placate him unsuccessfully. I knew that I had created this. I had no confidence in myself to do the things I thought I could do. The more the tension piled up, the more my confidence faltered. It was a vicious cycle. I did fight it inside my mind. I knew I had to adjust my thoughts. My continuous fear finally lifted. I was worried, but I wasn't fearful.

2018/02/13

> *Contrast.*
>
> *What I want versus what I do not want. It shows me what I want when I see and experience what I do not want. Thus, contrast is such a magnificent thing, it pushes me into the direction of where I want to go. I'm sitting in the morning sun eating some breakfast. Eggs, ham, and fried banana. I love fried banana. In Malaysia I bought deep fried banana in batter. What can be better than a fried banana with some honey, butter, and ginger tea? Since my diet has changed dramatically, I've found other joys in healthier, fresh food. I'm not sure about the healthiness of fried banana, but I know it pleases me.*

Today I'm more at peace. Tim and I have gone to yoga quite frequently since the beginning of the year. Last night I meditated; I managed to calm my mind. My mom has been telling me about John's various ailments. She said he can't complete a whole day's work sometimes, because he is too ill. I'm not terribly sorry for him, he didn't heed anyone's warnings when he was popping the many pills without eating first. I don't know how I'm supposed to feel about it. Should I be sorry for him? I am, sometimes. At other times I'm completely numb toward the situation, numb to most of everything. I put the emotions to one side for a while because I get tired.

2018/02/19

This morning and yesterday I felt a tight tension in my body. I'm anxious now, sitting here on my bed. The sun has barely come out to visit through the clouds. Tim was depressed yesterday. I went to a business meeting with my partner to get a quote for our first contract finalised. We want to send it to the client today. I'm nervous about it. I'm concerned about my dwindling provident fund money; it wasn't supposed to take so long before I made some kind of progress. I know it's not helpful to focus on this. I'm writing my book and relishing it, I'm compelled to complete it. Tim is my person and I love him so; I pray that things will work out as I envisage it. I don't want to let him down. I can't allow this sense of hopelessness to break my speed now.

2018/04/09

I haven't written in my dairy for months. I was occupied with other things. Frankly, I wasted time watching

*YouTube videos and TV. I miss writing and creating.
About two months ago I completed my first oil painting.
It turned out beautifully. I was delighted to paint
something exquisite with a medium that intimidated
me initially. I've not worked on my book in a while. My
art has fallen by the wayside. The focus on my company's
success has been all-consuming and intense. I've also
been working at John and my mom's business again.
It's discouraged me in a way. I listen to Esther Hicks
every day now. My understanding of life and the way
the Universe works – as well as my place in it – has
increased exponentially. Over the weekend I went to a
family function and saw our big huge family. I felt such
a profound appreciation for my family. I woke up with
an abject sense of distress for my mother. I wanted to cry
for her. She looked forlorn and bewildered at a family
gathering last night. She lost her temper when my cousin
asked her to pose for a picture. She is worn out and
depressed. I wish I could help her. I hate feeling utterly
helpless.*

At the end of March in 2018 Tim and I decided to do something we had discussed often but had not taken the literal leap of faith towards doing. Soaring. We decided to tandem skydive with professionals. It was a challenging adventure we had postponed for too long.

That day will be imprinted in my mind for many years to come. There were many emotions, fear, excitement, joy, terror, and disbelief. It was a lovely, warm, sunny day. There was a light breeze when we arrived at the skydiving school. Three couples were there to jump, including us. Tim and I decided to jump first. The roller-coaster of emotions was a spinning, turbulent frenzy. We met our tandem instructors. They were professional and safety-conscious. They gave a quick course on what to expect and what we had to do with our bodies while we were in the air. As we dressed in the parachuting gear, my stomach clenched while I considered how perfectly bizarre this was. We had to wait for quite some time because the wind picked up. The time finally came when the weather conditions were perfect, and the clouds disappeared. We had to climb on the back of a trailer, and they dropped us off next to a tiny red aeroplane. We squashed ourselves in. It was a relief to know Tim and I would jump at almost the same time.

We settled in and they instructed us to get into position. I sat with my back to my tandem instructors' body, and Tim sat in the same position with his instructor. The plane lifted off. It slowly gained altitude. I was bloody scared and wondered how often this plane went up daily. It seemed unusually flimsy. We were in the Hartebeespoort area. The instructor showed me the dam below us. My heart was beating at a thousand times a minute. I deliberately practised deep breathing. When we finally reached altitude, they opened the side door and a young lone-jumper got ready for his jump. He checked his watch for altitude, shouted something to his friends, showed a thumbs up, and threw himself joyously out of the aeroplane door. I was dumbfounded. He flew out like a rag doll. The wind swept him away in a flurry. My eyes searched for his shape in the sky, and I realised after a second that he was the pinprick in the far away distance. Adrenaline flooded me. I was excited and terrified, but the lone-jumper's nonchalance reassured me a bit.

Tim and his tandem instructor got ready to jump. They positioned themselves on the edge of the exit. Before I knew it, they were gone. I could not escape it, it was my turn next. We moved to the edge of the door. I crossed my arms over my chest as directed. My instructor spoke to me the whole time. He asked if I was ready. I had no choice, I had to be. I took a deep breath, and we jumped out of the plane into the vast freedom of the air. We fell at a speed. The air rushed against my face. I screamed out loud to get a breath. I yelled because I felt effervescently alive. What an indescribable feeling of freedom! The freefall continued for what seemed to be a long, long time, and then – suddenly – the parachute shuddered open. We soared through the air, the fine vapour of the clouds making a myriad of rainbows

271

below us. The instructor said he would try to find my Guardian Angel through the clouds. There was a soft pillow of clouds just below us. Our shadows reflected upon it. The aura of our shadows reflected upon it too. He said those were our Guardian Angels. I did not want the soaring to end. But, as in life, we had to come back to the ground. We landed safely, and I felt more alive than I had in my whole life. This leap of faith was worth the effort and roller-coaster of emotions.

I was back working at my mom and John's business. I was completing a cycle. I worked feverishly with my business partner, but to no avail. We did not get anywhere with the business in the amount of time that I set out. At the same time, I did not hear back from the Pharma company. I experienced a combination of relief and disappointment. I applied for jobs I would have liked to do. I got no responses. I was adamant that I made this hard move for a reason. I wanted to find a job that I loved. I wanted all the pain I had been through to have purpose. There was also my belief on the line. I believe with my whole heart that we live in a Universe where we attract our experiences but if I'm a deliberate creator, well, I was doing a terrible job. One of my favourite sayings is 'what doesn't work on the outside of you, is what is not working on the inside of you'. I think Louise Hay said that, but I can't quite remember where it got stuck in my mind. This outcome wasn't the end of the world.

It was okay to work for my mom and John again. It was also okay to still work towards what I wanted. I was obviously still not entirely sure about what I wanted to do, and this gave me the time to reconcile my wants with my actions and what I was expending my energy on.

It was terrific to spend time with my mom at work, and she needed me there. After every smoke break, I would kiss her on the cheek before she walked upstairs to her office, while I went to my desk. We spent quality time together, even more so than before the December holidays. She leaned on me quite a bit. I did not mind. I was fretful about her. I saw her every day and I knew there was something terribly wrong. I could do nothing to help her, but I would talk to her every day while we sat and smoked outside. I would even – every now and then – get a smile out of her.

I always yearned for acceptance and affirmation from everyone around me. I was often the one on the edge of the family unit because I didn't quite understand how it worked. During the years before my growth I squashed my authentic being to get acceptance from the men I met or the people I cared for. Surely the people I loved the most should love me for *me*? Surely, they should see my worth? I tried everything to be acceptable, because all I wanted was love. My heart yearned for love. My inner child was screaming because, from day one, that love was never received.

I pushed them over the edge and pulled them back again. I drove them crazy, I became a victim, I became a nag, I became a nuisance. At the end none of it worked. The expectations I carried of those I loved to love me in the way I wanted them to, fell flat on its face. I wanted them to change, I wanted them to be who I wanted them to be. I released the expectation that my mother would leave John, because that is not my journey or life lessons, it is hers. I released my expectations that John would apologise to me, because it is his life's journey. I let go of the expectation that my father would see me more often or would somehow make it up to me for being missing for the first key years of my life. That's his journey. The only one who can love me in the way I want to be loved is me. I can love myself by allowing myself to see the potential within me. I'm a part of God/Universe/Source and I'm loved and uplifted. I have incredible purpose because of who I am.

2018/04/21

> On Thursday I had a terrifying, traumatic accident with a large truck. I drove down the N1 Southbound towards Bryanston just after a rain shower. There were still a few droplets falling from the sky. It was a normal day. I had a refreshing yoga session in the morning. I felt better

than usual. At the decline close to an offramp, I saw a truck in my peripheral vision. It drove in the left-hand lane. Suddenly it started turning sharply toward me, it was slightly ahead of me. I could see the man in the driver's seat. When the truck came towards me, his eyes grew larger. He was afraid, and I saw his soul in them. So was I. The truck came toward me at a tremendous speed. I put my foot on the breaks, I tried to move my car to the right, trying to get through the gap between the truck and the barrier. It was too late. The impact struck me. The airbags went off. I lost consciousness for a few seconds. I looked around at the smoke, dazed and confused. I opened my door, it wouldn't open, I then opened my window. I needed to get out of the car. I climbed out of the window and kneeled on the barrier of the highway. I touched my chest, my arms, my legs. I breathed in deeply several times. I saw a bloodied form climbing out of the truck. I shook uncontrollably. A man was stretched out on the other side of the highway. Why did he just lay there? Sirens shrieked. A woman walked towards me. She asked if I was okay and offered me some water. I drank it whilst frantically searching for my phone. I called my mom. No answer. Again. Again. She answered on the third attempt. I said I had been in an accident. Tearfully, she fired off a series of questions. Thinking back, I can't remember what she asked. I told her I was okay. I could walk and breathe. Nothing was broken. There wasn't any blood. I seemed to be okay. I heard a woman screaming, 'Don't drive over his arm!'. The truck driver was dead, lying on the other side of the highway. One of the medics explained this to me. The impact propelled the truck driver through the windscreen. At first, I thought it was just someone taking a nap.

When that truck came hurtling toward me, my only thought was 'I want to live, I want to live, I want to live'. Death tempted me at the helm of my misery, knocked on my door countless times with its sickle promising to silence the screaming torture that made my mind its home for decades. Yet in that split second when the truck driver's eyes locked with mine, I understood. I understood the progress that I have made, I understood that agony had purpose, I understood the magnificence of existence, I understood that it wasn't just about me, I understood that I still have so much more to do here.

I understood that I have purpose.

In that moment I knew what my life's purpose is. My life's purpose is to live.

AFTERWORD

The first person I called when I finally managed to find my cell phone in my car was my mother. I was taken to the hospital with the passenger of the truck and checked for dire physical injuries. I was unscathed bar two large bruises where my seatbelt pushed into my skin when the car jolted to a sudden stop. The passenger was bleeding; it seemed he was injured quite badly. I was exceptionally fortunate. Timothy came to the hospital to see if I was okay. He said the highway was still packed with traffic because of the accident. My car was written off. When the doctor let me go, all I wanted to do was to see my mom and my sister. Tim took me back to the office where my mom waited for me. Her eyes were bloodshot from crying. She told me I should never scare her like that again. She said she couldn't live without me.

Two months later my mother committed suicide. She used the .38 revolver. She shot herself in her temple. I knew she wasn't well. I knew something terrible was about to happen. Her mental health had deteriorated over the years, and I saw it. Despite this, she still exuded strength. I never thought she would do something so extreme. None of us did. It rocked us all to our core. I had sincerely hoped she could find the strength within herself to do what had to be done for her to find the happiness that she so thoroughly deserved. Our hearts were shattered. John did not expect her to do this either and it threw him off too.

In writing this book and being where I'm today after all that has happened, I've made a couple of conclusions.

I do not condone John's deeds. I do not accept it either. I have however learnt to accept him. He will never change. If it wasn't for him, I would not have learnt the life lessons I've learnt. I would not be as powerful as I am today.

Inadvertently, by subjecting me to his abuse, a formidable, intelligent, discerning, wise and compassionate woman grew within me. He was hurting. He still is. The best thing that ever happened to him was my mother and us. All he ever wanted was a family. When he got what he wanted he destroyed it, because he himself was broken. The saying that 'hurt people hurt people' is perfectly apt. Sadly, it's the people they love the most who are the ones they wound the deepest.

My mother did her best with what she had. She was an incredible woman. At her memorial service it was evident that countless people would miss her humanitarian heart. She was in tremendous pain. She drank too much. I believe the alcohol enhanced her depression. It was a vicious cycle. She was exhausted and depleted. I still don't have a full grasp on what she experienced at home or the difficulties she faced daily, living with John and Alex. Work-related aspects also contributed to her state of being. She relied too much on her work. I did not ever feel wholly loved by my mother, but she loved me in the best way that she could. I miss her terribly, especially when I experience a difficult or challenging situation. I wish she was here all the time, because I miss her all time. It's getting easier, but it's still hard.

And finally, life has a way of throwing curve balls. Life does not get straight-forward and uncomplicated when you decide to get into recovery or when you decide to actively change your perspective. It does however get easier to deal with the curve balls. The growth that you experience is exponential, and it's all completely worth it. The more open-minded, honest and willing one becomes the more teachable one becomes and the more benefits one reaps. Living life is easy. It's fear and over-analysis that gets in the way. I was constantly worried about trying to find my purpose in life and trying to control all the outcomes of the lives of the people I cared about, yet all the time it was staring me in the face. All I needed to do was to live it.

REFERENCE LIST

1. *"You Can Heal Your Life"* Louise Hay, Hay House Inc. 2004
2. *"The Artist's Way"* Julia Cameron, Pan Books, 1994
3. *"Come to the edge."* Christopher Logue, 1962
4. *"Love, Freedom, Aloness"* Osho, Osho International Foundation, 2001
5. *"Clarity"* Audio Visual clip, Hay House World Summit, 2015, Dr Wayne Dyer and Esther Hicks
6. *"The Secret"* Directed by Drew Heriot, Produced by Paul Harrington, Rhonda Byrne, Written by Rhonda Byrne, The movie, 2006

ABOUT THE AUTHOR

Isla has developed a unique view on her life experience. She has, over time become a passionate individual with a great deal of compassion and empathy for the world around her. Her life journey has moulded her into an outgoing, fun and free spirit. She is currently completing her Reiki Master's course and has patiently watched as her small Reiki business grows.

Printed in the United States
By Bookmasters